THE ILLUSTRATED ENCYCLOPEDIA OF

WILDLIFE

VOLUME 12

The Invertebrates

Part II

Wildlife Consultant

MARY CORLISS PEARL, Ph. D.

Distributed by Encyclopaedia Britannica
Educational Corporation

Grey Castle Press

Published by Grey Castle Press, 1991

Distributed by Encyclopaedia Britannica Educational Corporation, 1991

THE ILLUSTRATED ENCYCLOPEDIA OF WILDLIFE
Volume 12: THE INVERTEBRATES—Part II

Library of Congress Cataloging-in-Publication Data
The Illustrated encyclopedia of wildlife.
    p.   cm.
      Contents: v. 1–5. The mammals—v. 6–8. The birds —
v. 9. Reptiles and amphibians — v. 10. The fishes —
v. 11–14. The invertebrates — v. 15. The invertebrates
and index.
      ISBN 1–55905–052–7
      1. Zoology.
    QL45.2.I44 1991   90–3750
    591—dc20   CIP

ISBN 1–55905–052–7 (complete set)
     1–55905–048–9 (Volume 12)

Printed in Spain

Photo Credits
Photographs were supplied by: *Archivio IGDA*: (L. Andena) 2358, 2368; (C. Bevilacqua) 2475; (Bucciarelli) 2349, 2351l, 2354, 2358; (A. Calegari) 2374b; (F. Chirillo) 2948; (C. Cirillo) 2367; (M. Giovanoli) 2369t, 2440b, 2497, 2568; (G. Negri) 2352; (La Palude) 2351r, 2356, 2357, 2380, 2451b, 2487, 2476; (M. Pirrizani) 2396, 2492b; *C. Bevilacqua*; 2448b; *I. Bucciarelli*: 2470; *H. Chaumeton*: 2384; *Bruce Coleman*: (J.H. Brackenbury) 2360; (J. Burton) 2373b; (B. & C. Calhoun) 2485; (Bob Campbell) 2413; (Eric Crichton) 2437; (G. Cubitt) 2404, 2417; (A. Daniel) 2372; (M. Fox-Davies) 2373; (John Fennel) 2433; (J. Markham) 2387r; (Andy Purcell) 2440t, 2466, 2467; (G. Rether) 2386; (H. Rivarola) 2443; (F. Sauer) 2342, 2343, 2348, 2350, 2361, 2381, 2445, 2506; (J. Shaw) 2341; (J. Taylor) 2392, 2393; (K. Taylor) 2346t, 2432; (P. Ward) 2403, 2491t; *A. Davies*: 2340; *Jacana*: (Champroux) 2422, 2442b, 2456; (F. Danrigal) 2445; (Dulhoste) 2390t, 2450b; (Gerard) 2419; (J.P. Hervy) 2390b, 2401, 2411, 2418, 1420, 2436, 2453; (C. De Klemm) 2400b; (Konig) 2378; (P. Lorne) 2337, 2346b, 2387l, 2391, 2395, 2451t; (C. & M. Moiton) 2376, 2382, 2383, 2442t, 2446t, 2450t, 2455, 2458, 2459; (C. Nardin) 2429; (Pegomas) 2399, 2400t; (P. Pilloud) 2370r, 2371; (K. Ross) 2344, 2374t, 2379; (Rouxaime) 2394; (J. Sommer) 2389; (H. Veiller) 2382b, 2457; (Y. Vial) 2375; (R. Volot) 2370l, 2447; (F. Winner) 2449b; *A. Margiocco*: 2408, 2494, 2502; *Marka*: 2426; (P. Curto) 2425; *NHPA*: (A. Bannister) 2347, 2409, 2412, 2413, 1452, 2480r; (G.I. Bernard) 2460; (N. Callow) 2433; (S. Dalton) 2339, 2353, 2363, 2435, 2499; (J. Sauvenet) 2510; *Oxford Scientific Films*: (P. Parks) 2427; *Titus*: 2446b.

FRONT COVER: A 17-year cicada (Bruce Coleman/Leonard Lee Rue III)

CONTENTS

A FLEETING EXISTENCE

Mayflies and stone flies spend the few days of their adult life on the wing, largely occupied with reproduction. Male web spinners also have short lives and are often eaten by females after mating

Mayflies are medium-sized winged insects that grow to approximately 1.5 in. in length. They belong to the order Ephemeroptera and occur throughout the world, with the exception of a few groups of islands, such as Hawaii, and Antarctica. Most of the adult forms are similar in appearance, so in many cases the differences between individual species are reduced to minor anatomical features that can only be seen under high magnification using a microscope.

Evolutionary history

Fossil remains of insects called *Paleodictyoptera* that had wing veins similar to those of the modern mayflies have been found. These date from the Carboniferous and Permian periods (290-280 million years ago). Mayflies evolved in the following geological eras until the Jurassic and Eocene periods (181-58 million years ago), when species similar to those found today appeared. These can be classified with the current families and genera.

Mayflies are short-lived animals. The adults usually die within one day of their final molt, or even within a few hours. Their scientific name Ephemeroptera derives from the Greek words *ephemeros*, meaning "living for a day," and *pteron*, meaning "wings."

Adults for one day

At the adult, or imago, stage, the mayfly has a cylindrical and lightly sinuous body with two lateral filaments or tails, called cerci, and a central cercus, at the tip of its abdomen. The tails are delicate and very long, often exceeding the mayfly's body length. The exoskeleton, or cuticle, is not well strengthened. The forewings are noticeably larger than the hind wings. They are clearly marked with horizontal and vertical veins. In many species they are iridescent. The hind wings are usually very small and in some cases may even be absent. When the mayfly is resting, it holds its wings at right angles to its body.

Mayflies are not brightly colored, and are usually either green or brown. However, there are a few tropical species that have rare, ornamental, gaudily colored spots. Mayflies have long, slender legs. The forelegs are better developed than the rest, especially in the males, and when the insect is still, they are held stretched forward.

Mayflies have compound eyes that are usually round and highly developed. In some males, they

reach enormous proportions and appear to be divided into upper and lower parts. The upper part of the eye points upward and enables the male to spot females flying above him.

As adults, mayflies have only one purpose—to mate and produce offspring. They cannot feed as their mouthparts do not function, and their digestive systems are sealed and full of air, reducing the density of the animal.

Damp habitats

Adult mayflies often congregate in damp places, such as on the banks of fast-flowing freshwater streams, rivers, lakes and pools. During the hottest part of the day, they rest in branches on the banks, only becoming active toward dusk. In some temperate areas, males gather together in swarms and perform an extraordinary mating dance—flying upward and then drifting down again, aided by their cerci.

When a female enters the swarm, she is seized by one of the males. He clasps her around her thorax

RIGHT During their larval stage, mayflies of the family *Ephemeridae* are entirely aquatic. They molt 20 times during their development. When they are fully grown, they float to the surface and molt into a peculiar winged form (the subimago) that resembles the adult in appearance but cannot reproduce. The subimago mayfly flies to the side of the pond and transforms into a fully formed adult. The subimago form occurs in no other order of living insects. PAGE 2337 Adult mayflies are fragile insects with heavily veined wings, inconspicuous antennae and slim bodies that end in long cerci, or tail appendages. Their mouthparts are vestigial— they no longer function. Adult mayflies cannot feed and live for little more than one day—just long enough to reproduce. Most frequently, they live in damp conditions— hiding in moist grass during the day and flying about in the evening. Shown here is *Ephemera danica*, known by fishermen as the green drake. It is the largest of Britain's mayflies, with larvae that burrow in the muddy bottoms of lakes and rivers.**

with his long forelegs, and brings his genital opening into contact with hers. Fertilization takes place internally, as the two insects sink toward the ground.

Each female then releases hundreds or thousands of fertilized eggs into the water. Some species settle on a plant stalk or rock near the bank, and repeatedly dip their abdomens into the water, releasing their eggs in several small packets, while others fall to the surface of the water and release their eggs in a large mass.

Unusual egg-laying methods

Females of the genus *Baetis* have more unusual egg-laying methods. They slide along under the water surface looking for ideal sites in which to hide and protect their eggs. To be able to survive and breathe in such hostile conditions, the female mayflies flex their wings back over their bodies so as to store a supply of air, then fall to the bottom of the water as divers would in a pressure tank.

Each species has its own specific needs concerning the type of water in which its eggs are deposited. Some prefer the rushing waters of waterfalls and alpine or hill streams with rocky or pebbly bottoms. Others prefer the quiet waters of level rivers rich in vegetation and with a sandy or muddy bottom. Some mayflies favor the calmer waters of freshwater lakes, ponds and marshes.

Larval development

Once abandoned, the eggs fall to the bottom where they remain firmly fixed by their sticky coating. When the larvae hatch, they lack respiratory appendages and have only two cerci at their extreme tip. When they first molt, all species of mayflies closely resemble one another, making it impossible to tell them apart. However, after a few molts, the larvae begin to take on a different appearance depending on the species, and they develop gills on the sides of their abdomens. These are simply protrusions of various shapes, sometimes blade-like, heart-shaped, leaf-shaped, lance-shaped or feathery, which run the length of their

ABOVE Mayflies are the only insects to have a winged form that molts. Another distinguishing characteristic is that the front pair of a mayfly's wings are larger than the hind pair. In a resting position, the adult continues to extend its wings at right angles to its body. Within hours of maturing, the shiny, colorful insect mates and dies.

bodies. The gills allow air exchanges between the surrounding environment and the body, enabling the larvae to absorb the oxygen present in the water. The middle cercus gradually appears between the two side cerci. It varies in size depending on the species.

Mayfly larvae usually take between one and three years to develop and undergo 15-25 molts before reaching adulthood, depending on the species. When they are ready to metamorphose from the last aquatic stage of larval development, they rise to the surface of the water. Their outer covering, or cuticle, splits open and the young, but sexually immature, subadult mayfly emerges. The subadult molts again very quickly, and a sexually mature adult appears. Mayflies are unique among the insects as they are the only species to have a winged form that molts.

Unlike the close similarity that characterizes the adults, there are often noticeable differences in the older larval stages, even within members of the same genus, and these permit precise identification. The larvae can generally be grouped into four distinct categories, based essentially on their ecology and behavior.

Swimming species

The swimming species, typical of stagnant or slow-flowing waters rich in submerged vegetation, belong to the first category. Their cerci, which are covered in very thick bristles, function as propellers as a result of the rhythmical, snake-like movements of the body, enabling the animal to move by fits and starts with remarkable speed.

The second category contains species that crawl slowly over the muddy bottom of stagnant or almost stagnant waters. They are very poor swimmers. These larvae camouflage themselves convincingly by covering their backs with a thick layer of waste material.

The third category includes flat-shaped larvae that live among the rocks typically found at high altitudes on the beds of mountain streams. Larvae belonging to this group have adapted to their particular environment by developing extremely flat bodies that enable them to hide and move agilely in cracks, rocks or heaps of stones—the typical substrate of steep torrents. However, these organisms cannot swim, and if separated from the bottom they are swept away downstream. To prevent this, they have developed special anchoring organs that allow them to remain attached to the substrate and resist the current.

Diggers

The fourth category contains a few species called diggers. They live in water with a muddy or sandy substrate, where they dig deep tunnels in the bottom and between the roots of aquatic plants, using their long, shovel-like front legs.

Irrespective of their environment, mayfly larvae have a phytophagous (plant-eating) diet, eating algae and other submerged vegetation. Some species also eat waste matter from plants. The larvae, in turn, are eaten by freshwater fishes and are an important link in the food chain.

Mayfly larvae cannot tolerate any type of organic or chemical pollution. In recent years, the continuous deterioration of the quality of our water has brought a progressive and serious reduction in the populations of mayflies.

A FLEETING EXISTENCE

Reaching for the sky

Before a mayfly larvae (nymph) completes its development, it undergoes a final metamorphosis that transforms it from an aquatic to a terrestrial insect. The metamorphosis usually takes place out of water, and nymphs of different species take different routes to the open air, depending on their habitats. In species that develop in still or sluggishly moving water, mature larvae reach the surface by producing a bubble of gas under their body coverings of cuticle (exoskeletons). After it has surfaced, the mayfly larva floats safely on the water until a clearly defined split appears along the whole length of its back. A slightly underdeveloped adult mayfly (called a subimago) soon emerges from the split and flies up into the air, leaving its larval skin behind.

Some mayfly species undergo their aquatic phases of development in mountain torrents and fast-flowing streams. The nymphs crawl onto the bank and—after drying in the air—molt in the same way as their slow-water cousins. Mayfly larvae of certain other species metamorphose into adults underwater, anchoring themselves to objects just beneath the water's surface, such as weeds or fallen twigs. As soon as they emerge, the new adults swim rapidly to the surface—kept safe from drowning by their impermeable cuticles.

Precise timekeeping

One of the most extraordinary aspects of mayfly metamorphosis is its perfect synchronization: although developing mayflies of the same species spend up to a year in the larval stage—probably in different bodies of water—emergence takes place en masse. In any region inhabited by mayflies, a swarm of newly emerged adults appears on one particular day of the year—and sometimes within the space of only a few hours. Zoologists still do not understand the mechanism by which the larvae's inbuilt "alarm clocks" all go off at the same time. The most likely explanation is that factors such as light intensity, water temperature, atmospheric pressure and speed of the current combine to trigger the process of metamorphosis.

Different species of mayflies emerge at different times of the year. Some appear early in the first months of spring, allowing the next generation of larvae to enjoy rapid development during the hottest

ABOVE Dew rests on the discarded, molted skin of the subimago mayfly. Mayflies pass through 15-25 molts in three years before becoming sexually mature. The freed adults have fragile bodies with membranous wings, short antennae and long cerci at the end of their abdomens. They spend the few days of their short lives in an airborne quest for mates, often indulging in striking aerial dances, flying upward and slowly parachuting downward, to impress females.

summer months. Other species wait until late summer or early autumn, when predators are fewer and competition for food has diminished.

Two-stage development

The underdeveloped mayfly that emerges from metamorphosis is called a subimago—a young adult that betrays itself externally through obvious under-development of the legs, cerci (abdominal appendages) and eyes. As subimagos, most species are sexually immature, with nonfunctioning or incompletely formed reproductive systems. The subimago stage of development is unique to the order of mayflies.

Immediately after they emerge from the larval stage, the winged subimagos of most mayfly species fly to a suitable surface—such as a branch, rock or tree trunk—where they lodge, gripping firmly with special adhesive organs on their legs. After a time, which varies from hours to days depending on the species, they undergo a final molt and abandon their thin

ABOVE Adult mayflies are readily distinguishable from other insects with net-veined wings by the disparity in size between the large forewings and the small hind wings. Mayflies mate in midair, and smaller males are carried underneath their partners. The elongated forelegs of the male mayfly *Ephemera ignita* enable him to reach around the female and establish a firm grip on her lower abdomen.

cuticle body coverings at their resting places. Some species undergo their final molts during their maiden flights, shedding their subimago skins in midair.

As in the larva/subimago metamorphosis, the final transformation of a subimago into an adult mayfly is synchronized with that of others in its area. Members of some mayfly species form huge swarms of several million insects. In central Europe, this phenomenon is especially prevalent, and the mayfly swarms are exploited commercially—the masses of insects are collected and used as animal fodder or fertilizer.

Aerial acrobatics

During their brief adult lives, mayflies enter intense competition to find partners with which to mate. Almost all their energies are directed toward the vital task of regenerating the species.

At dusk, or on a damp, cloudy day, male mayflies group together in large swarms to perform spectacular mating flights. The males perform their frenzied mass dance in clearings near water, or above the surface of ponds, lakes and rivers. Although it appears to be entirely random, the dance is a precise mating ritual. Each male mayfly breaks off from the swarm to make long, vertical flights characterized by agitated and irregular wing movements. At the peak of its ascent (which may be remarkably high) it suddenly freezes in midair and, with unfolded wings, drops passively toward the ground. At the last possible moment before contact, the insect recovers control, only to repeat its dizzy ascent with renewed vigor.

The female mayflies, who have been lying in undergrowth, rise slowly and fly horizontally through the manic swarm of males. The males have specially adapted eyes for seeing females as they fly above them and, as a female enters the swarm, an exhausted male seizes her from below and holds on tightly with his forelegs. The mayfly couple then link their genitalia together and mate—drifting slowly toward the ground. After mating, which lasts only a few seconds, a male mayfly usually falls to the ground and dies. The females outlive the males long enough to lay their fertilized eggs in water—either in one large mass or in

packets deposited at intervals. In some stream-dwelling species, the females dive underwater to lay their eggs. A year passes before the next generation of mayflies develop into full adults.

Adapting to mountainous conditions

Species of mayflies belonging to the family Heptageniidae live above the tree line among alpine pastures, and some inhabit even higher altitudes. Mountain-dwelling mayflies are typically larger than average, with peculiar forewings and cerci and forelegs that are noticeably longer than those of most other species. Apart from the more highly developed eyes of the males, there are no visible differences between the sexes. Most adult mountain mayflies gather near fast-flowing water where they live for several days (an above average life span for adult mayflies). The females deposit their eggs by immersing their abdomens in the water—either by skimming low over the water's surface, or by holding onto the stream banks with their forelegs.

The larvae have flattened, streamlined bodies that enable them to slip between cracks and stones on the bottom and facilitate smoother passage through the water. Their heads are noticeably flattened in shape, with large eyes resting on the top. The larvae breathe through a series of gills that lie along the sides of their abdomens.

The larvae of mountainous mayfly species traverse the bottom of fast-running streams and raging torrents by anchoring themselves to the riverbed with strong hooks at the ends of their legs. During the evolutionary progress of the family Ecdyonuridae, their larvae developed their first pair of gills, resembling rubber suckers in shape, on the underside of their bodies. The gills have gradually lost their original function and now serve to anchor the larvae to the bottom. Other species, occurring in mountain streams, have specially adapted ribs along the sides of their gills, enabling them to wedge themselves firmly between rocks and pebbles. Other related species are less well adapted to strong currents. Although their bodies display the same flattened shape, their gills lack special modifications.

Short bursts of swimming

Other species of mayflies have evolved to survive in stagnant or still water. They are usually small to medium-sized, and have a characteristically delicate

ABOVE The aquatic larva of the mayfly *Heptogenia sulphurea* climbs out of the water to molt into the preadult subimago, a stage of development that is unique to these insects. The winged subimago flies for a short distance and **then molts again after a few hours to form a clear-winged, sexually mature adult. The hind wings of the adult are reduced in size, but the forewings are large and have a crisscross pattern of triple-branched veinlets.**

appearance and coloring (usually bluish green or gray). There are marked differences between the sexes in species that inhabit still water. The males, for example, have distinctive, rounded eyes with a vertical groove that divides the eyes into two parts.

The larvae of the still-water families Baetidae and Siphlonuridae are able to swim, and their bodies demonstrate perfect adaptation to life in still water (with plenty of submerged vegetation). They have cylindrical, sinuous bodies that terminate in three appendages on their abdomens (cerci). Each appendage has a coating of long hairs that provides a larger surface area in the water. The larvae beat their appendages up and down to propel themselves through the water.

Climbing aquatic plants

Larvae only sustain movement through the water in short bursts, and the insects do not spend much of their life swimming. They only swim to make short dashes from one hiding place to another or to escape from predators. Usually, the larvae use their well-developed legs and strong claws to walk along the bottom or climb the stems of aquatic plants.

Certain species of swimming mayflies occur in fast, freshwater habitats at high altitudes. During the larval

ABOVE Many mayfly nymphs are well adapted to their aquatic life-style. In some species, the appendages, or cerci, projecting from the rear of the insect are feathered with fine hairs. When the cerci are agitated, the nymph is propelled through the water. Although nymphs spend most of their time walking on the bottom, some are capable of short bursts of high speed underwater.

stage of their development, they do not possess the structural modifications typical of fast-water species. Despite retaining their cylindrical larval shape, they lack a middle appendage (cercus) and do not have a fringe of hairs along their other cerci. They have also lost their ability to swim and move along the bottom by attaching themselves to the substrate.

Crawling and burrowing

During the larval stage of some mayflies, the young live in sluggish or still water. They feed on decaying plant matter, moving with sinuous body movements between cracks in the substrate. Their dark brown or chestnut bodies are elongated with gills that are often forked in shape and resemble a snake's tongue. Some species prefer muddy bottoms, where they camouflage themselves with small particles of soil and decaying vegetation. These fragments become firmly lodged in the thick bristles that sprout from their bodies. Each time the larvae molt, they must renew their protective coating.

Other mayflies are burrowing insects during the preadult stages, preferring the clay or sandy bottoms of lowland streams. They employ all their legs while digging, but burrow mainly with their robust forelegs and long, tusk-like mandibles. Usually, the mayflies dig U-shaped tunnels, so that if a predator enters through one entrance they can escape through the other. They are active at night, when they emerge from their holes to search for food. They normally feed on plant waste, although fresh vegetation is sometimes taken.

Some of these burrowing species, especially *Ephemera danica* and *E. vulgata,* adapt well to the most diverse environments. It is not uncommon to find their larvae on the rocky and pebble-strewn beds of fast-flowing streams, where they live in gaps or pebbles on the bottom.

Stone flies

The 1500 species of the order Plecoptera are commonly known as the stone flies. Their classification name derives from the Latin *pleco* or "pleated," a reference to the fan-like folding at the end of their hind wings. They are secretive creatures that normally live near fast-moving streams throughout the world. Compared with most other insects, their anatomy is fairly primitive, and their larvae closely resemble the adults.

The life cycle of the stone flies is typical of the more primitive insects. There are two distinct stages of development that occur in two completely different habitats. The larvae live in water, whereas the adults are flying insects. Fossil traces of stone fly-like insects have been found in rocks from the Permian era (280 million years old). These fossils closely resemble modern stone flies, particularly in the structure of their wings.

Body shape

Stone flies vary in size from about 0.1in. to between 0.8 and 1.2 in. in length (the distance between extended wingtips can be as much as 2.7 in.). They are soft-bodied, weak-flying insects that range in color from brown to light green. They have two pairs of well-developed, membranous wings, biting mouthparts, long, slender antennae, and cerci on their abdomen.

Their wings have a clearly arranged pattern of veins along their length and width, forming a dense network, or reticulum. The stone flies' forewings are slightly longer and narrower than their hind wings, and are not used in flight. When the stone flies are at rest, they clasp their forewings closely to their bodies to protect their smaller hind wings, which they use for flight.

Heads

The stone fly's large head has thread-like antennae and two well-developed compound eyes. Stone flies also have three simple eyes, or ocelli, arranged in a triangular shape on their head. Their bodies are usually large and cylindrical in shape. The abdomen is slightly depressed and ends in two, multijointed cerci that are usually long and resemble antennae. The stone flies' legs increase in size from the first pair to the third pair and end in two sharp claws.

The most primitive stone flies are the family Eustheniidae from Australia and Chile, but the unusually large Pteronarcidae of North America retain similar primitive features. The families Leuctridae, Capniidae and Nemouridae are widely distributed in the Northern Hemisphere, while the Perlidae is the largest family represented in many parts of the world.

A poor flier

Despite their appearance, stone flies are very poor fliers, and their aerial movements are somewhat slow and clumsy. They are, however, skillful walkers and can often be found running quickly along tree trunks and rocks. In some species the wings of the males gradually diminish in size until they become short stumps.

In other respects, species of stone flies are remarkably uniform. Almost all species share the same body shape, drab coloration of the exoskeleton and habitat. Stone flies live in mountainous or hilly regions covered with rich vegetation, and they venture far from surface water. They are quiet and sedentary by nature. During the day, they are inactive and remain motionless on rocks or sometimes among the pebbles on a lakeshore. At rest, they are almost invisible because of their excellent camouflage. They generally become active at dusk, although they sometimes venture out at dawn to make short, searching flights or walk around on the ground and on branches.

Stone flies have a relatively short life span that varies in length among species—from a few days to a maximum of several weeks. The adults feed on plants, normally tender leaves or buds. Some adults are short-lived because their mouthparts have become reduced and they are unable to ingest food.

Because of their short-lived adult stage, the stone flies' main occupation is finding a mate. The courtship ritual takes place in sheltered places, such as

ABOVE Despite their large, well-developed wings, stone flies are not very good fliers and usually crawl or run when disturbed. Adult stone flies are often found resting on or under stones, bark or foliage. During the day, the winged adults usually remain motionless, and begin to move around only at dusk. At the back of their heads, between their large compound eyes, stone flies have three simple eyes, or ocelli, positioned like the points of a triangle.

under tree bark or beneath stones at the water's edge. Shortly after being fertilized, the female binds her small eggs into a gelatinous mass.

After a short rest, the female takes off with her egg mass and lays it on the surface of a stretch of fast-flowing water. Alternatively, the female may walk to the banks of a stream and delicately immerse her abdomen, so releasing the egg sac. On contact with the water the gelatinous capsule dissolves, freeing the eggs.

Giant predators

The larval stone flies resemble the adult stage in appearance and behavior, differing only in their habitat and the absence of wings. They are completely aquatic and generally spend their time on the beds of fast-flowing streams.

Stone fly larvae require clean water, usually in areas of strong turbulence—where there is a high level

of oxygen in the water. They breathe through special tracheal tubes—tuft-shaped gills that are arranged under the neck, at the leg joint, or between the cerci that form the forked tail. Unlike the gills of mayfly larvae, they are never located on the sides of the abdomen.

Vegetarians and predators

A stone fly larva's diet, although varied, is mostly vegetarian: some plant-eating species feed on aquatic moss or algae, while others feed exclusively on decaying plants and other waste matter. Most vegetarian stone flies (including the three families that are common in Europe) are small to medium-sized— but the giants of the stone fly world reach over 1.5 in. in length and are voracious predators toward the end of their larval stage. They usually feed on mayfly larvae and larvae of true flies; with their flattened bodies, they are able to follow their prey into the narrowest crevices in a stream or lake bed. Carnivorous stone fly larvae have highly developed mandibles that are covered with many sharp teeth for grinding down animal tissue.

Carnivorous stone fly larvae are the largest bottom-dwelling organisms living in mountain streams. As predators occupying the top of the food chain, they never collect in large numbers but congregate in small groups. These groups range over large hunting territories, chasing their prey on their unusually long legs. Carnivorous species are normally large, and some have body coverings that are delicately speckled in yellowish greens and browns.

Perfect harmony

Vegetarian stone fly larvae are sometimes found in large numbers in the same stream. They form underwater communities made up of hundreds of individuals, often of different species, living in harmony together. The larval stages of the most common cold-water species usually live among stones, while other species dwell among layers of decaying leaves on the streambed, or in the algae that covers the rocks on the bed.

Metamorphosis

The larval stages of stone flies last from one to three years, depending on the species. The period is usually relative to the size of the adult stage. When the larvae

TOP **Stone fly nymphs lack wings and have tufts of filamentous gills on each side of their bodies. They spend their whole lives underwater which must be clean and well oxygenated as they depend entirely on their gills for respiration.**

ABOVE **When a stone fly larva is ready to molt for the last time, it crawls several feet from the water onto a stone or tree, anchors itself with its hooked feet and splits down the back, releasing the winged adult form.**

are fully mature, they release hormones into their blood to make them leave the water. The larvae emerge from their streams and cling to tree trunks, rocks and stones, where they wait for the final molt that takes them into the adult stage. Adults normally appear at night, emerging through a long split that appears lengthways along the back of the larva. The newly emerged adults remain next to their discarded larval skins until their wings are perfectly dried and spread out.

Pollution indicators

The larvae of most stone fly species are accurate gauges of water purity, since they live in pure mountain streams, showing a marked preference for the icy waters of glacial outflows. Stone fly larvae are among the best bio-indicators, being extremely sensitive to physical and chemical variations in their environment. The slightest pollution of their habitat can reduce their numbers or even cause them to disappear totally.

Web spinners

Web spinners belong to the order Embioptera, a small order of insects containing over 800 species—all very similar in shape and size. Three-quarters of these species were discovered on a recent series of zoological expeditions.

ABOVE The wings of the male web spinner are long, membranous structures that stiffen during flight. Like the female, the newly hatched male web spinner spends the early part of its short life in silken tunnels that its parents spin in the soil, beneath stones and under the bark of trees. It then undertakes a short dispersal flight to discover a breeding partner. Although the male does not feed, it uses its jaws to grasp the female web spinner during mating.

Web spinners are small insects that measure 0.16 to 0.24 in. in length. They occur throughout the warmer parts of the world, particularly in the tropics, South America, and the Amazon Basin. Web spinners look rather like small earwigs but have soft, jointed cerci instead of pincers.

Virtually unknown by most people, web spinners have unusual characteristics of both behavior and structure. They normally live under stones and beneath bark, where they create networks of silk tunnels to hide in. The secretive nature of web spinners ensures that they remain one of the least studied groups of insects.

Ancient silk makers

Some 330 million years ago a chance mutation in an insect species produced a freak—an insect that could produce silk from its front legs. The ancestral

web spinner could probably spin only a small sheet web—just enough to cover itself and keep it hidden from predators. With this new advantage, the insect lived longer than other insects and was more successful in the evolutionary struggle. The silk-spinning skill was passed down from one generation to the next, until it was inherited by modern web spinners—enabling them to spin complex tunnel systems.

Shaped by life

Both male and female web spinners have evolved bodies adapted to a life of fast movement. Their streamlined bodies have short legs for running through tunnels that offer little room for maneuver.

Female web spinners are wingless—but the males have two pairs of membranous wings that enable them to fly to new colonies to find mates. Most other tunnel-dwelling insects lose their wings after their mating flight, but web spinners retain them. When a winged male web spinner reverses in a tunnel, he bends his wings forward over his head to protect them from friction from the tunnel ceiling. Normally, flexible wings would hinder an insect's flight, but evolution has compensated male web spinners by giving them a special type of wing vein: when they are at rest the vein is flat and flexible, but during flight it fills with blood, causing the wing to stiffen.

ABOVE The cylindrical bodies of the web spinners are specially adapted for life in tubular, silken tunnels. They spin the tunnels with their feet by secreting silk from glands in the swollen base segment of each front leg. The tunnels protect the insects from predators and the effects of desiccation. The web spinners make their homes in dark places and feed at night on dead and decaying plant life. Because of their secretive habits, few people have ever seen them.

Communal life

Web spinners are characterized by their large communities that sometimes grow to include several thousand members. Except for mothers and their young, web spinners do not display the kind of social interactions found in the communities of ants, termites and bees—rather, their communities are more similar to the congregations of greenflies and scale insects on plants. When the first ancestral brood hatched under a small silk sheet 330 million years ago, it is possible that they remained safe beneath its cover, which they slowly extended.

Web spinners usually eat vegetable matter, although adult males do not feed—even though they have fully formed jaws. A male only uses his jaws to hold onto a female during mating, and he dies soon after he has fertilized the female. The female survives to rear her young, which number 200 or more.

ON WINGS OF GAUZE

Although their wings have a transparent delicacy, dragonflies are swift and powerful fliers; the slender damselflies have a weak, fluttery flight and keep their wings elegantly erect over their backs when at rest

LEFT The downy emerald dragonfly *Cordulai aenea* selects a territory, or "beat," wherever there are trees and bushes on which it can rest. The beat may be an area that is suitable for hunting prey or, especially if it is over water, it may be the territory chosen by the male for breeding. The male defends his territory strenuously against other males, often receiving torn wings in battle.

aquatic. They have internal or external gills and mouthparts designed for grasping and chewing.

Ancestors of the dragonflies first appeared about 300 million years ago in the Carboniferous period. They lived in damp forests and closely resembled modern species in both body design and behavior.

Dragonflies and damselflies fall into three suborders. One suborder is that of dragonflies, or Anisoptera—robust and powerful insects with strong, nonidentical wings. By contrast, the suborder of damselflies, or Zygoptera, consists of delicate and feeble insects with weak, almost identical wings. The third suborder, called the Anisozygoptera, contains primitive and transitional species. It is less clearly defined than the other two suborders and displays some characteristics of each of them.

The shapes of the nymphs also fall into categories. Dragonfly nymphs have rounded bodies, large eyes and no readily visible gills. Damselfly nymphs are thinner and have characteristic three-pronged gills that project from their rears.

The best of both worlds

Most animals occupy a single habitat—either on land, in water or in the air. Dragonflies, however, live in two distinct types of environments, one for each stage of their lives. Nymphs inhabit water, and adults spend most of their time in the air. A major advantage of having different habitats for each stage in the animal's life cycle is that there is less competition for food and space. Members of a species can thus exploit all their habitats to the full.

Almost all species of dragonfly and damselfly spend the nymphal stage underwater. The period of time that nymphs remain in the aquatic stage varies from as little as 40 days to as long as 6 years, depending on the species and on conditions within their particular habitat. Species that live in warm waters where food is plentiful develop more quickly than those that inhabit water that is cold or lacking in nutrients. Temperate

There are more than 5000 species of dragonfly and damselfly in the order Odonata. They range throughout the world and are particularly abundant in the tropics and the Far East. Dragonflies and damselflies are medium to large-sized predators, and, like many of the most ancient insect orders, they mature in nymphal stages.

Adult dragonflies usually have long, narrow abdomens, two pairs of almost identical, powerful wings, and three pairs of strong legs. Their eyes are large and well developed, and their mouthparts are specially adapted for biting and chewing. Since adult dragonflies cannot fold their wings, they spend most of their time in flight and are generally inactive when on the ground. Dragonfly larvae—also known as nymphs—are usually

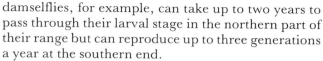

damselflies, for example, can take up to two years to pass through their larval stage in the northern part of their range but can reproduce up to three generations a year at the southern end.

During the aquatic phase, nymphs molt from 9 to 15 times before reaching maturity and grow to a length of 2-2.4 in. Most species that live in the temperate parts of the world use the last stage of their nymphal development to overwinter, emerging as adults in late spring. A few species overwinter at an earlier stage and emerge as adults in the summer.

Different species of dragonfly and damselfly nymphs live in a variety of habitats, ranging from ponds, streams, rivers and lakes to waterfalls, marshes, bogs and tree holes. Since different habitats require different physical adaptations, the nymphs vary greatly in anatomy. Adults, by contrast, vary far less in both habitat and appearance.

The deadly mask

Like most animals, a newly hatched nymph feeds on the yolk sac that it has retained in the middle of its gut. Once it has used up the yolk, it must actively hunt for its food. On the whole, dragonfly and damselfly nymphs are opportunist feeders. They often go for long periods without eating, and take any prey as long as it is roughly their own size.

Some nymphs rely on their sight to detect prey. Others feel the vibrations of moving prey with their antennae. Those that use eyesight are daytime feeders. They are usually drab green or brown in color, so they blend in with the vegetation on which they wait, alert and immobile, for their prey.

When a nymph senses the direction from which a potential meal is approaching, it moves its body in

ABOVE LEFT A resting, robust-bodied dragonfly holds its wings straight out at its sides. Dragonflies are swift, agile fliers, and are among the fastest of all the insects.
ABOVE Streamlined and fragile in appearance, a damselfly holds its wings together above its body while resting. Damselflies are weak fliers and generally live near to the water where they breed.
PAGE 2349 A dragonfly is unable to fold its wings along its back and holds them open in the typical cross shape.

INSECTS CLASSIFICATION: 3

Dragonflies and damselflies

The order Odonata contains a total of 5000 species of dragonflies and damselflies, and is divided into three suborders. Dragonflies belong to the suborder Anisoptera, which contains three superfamilies: the Aeshnoidea (hawker dragonflies); the Cordulegasteroidea (golden dragonflies); and the Libelluloidea (broad-bodied dragonflies). Damselflies belong to the suborder Zygoptera, which contains 21 families within four superfamilies: Coenagrionoidea (damselflies); Lestioidea (emerald damselflies); Hemiphleboidea (Australian reedy pool damselflies); and Calopterygoidea (demoiselles). Both dragonflies and damselflies occur throughout the world, and are especially abundant in the tropics. They often live close to water—ponds, streams, ditches, canals or reedbeds—where they breed. The third suborder, Anisozygoptera, contains just one family, the Epiophlebia, from the Himalayas and Japan.

of land insects—called spiracles—on the sides of their thorax. Another indication relates to the breathing method used by present-day dragonfly nymphs.

A nymph's abdomen pulsates almost imperceptibly as the insect draws water into its rectum, extracts the oxygen, and then expels the water. Such a method of breathing would work on land, too, if it were used in conjunction with the normal breathing processes. To work in water, the area of the rectal passage needs to be larger.

Dragonflies can breathe in water because their rectum has become greatly folded and richly supplied with breathing tubes. The damselflies have developed external supplementary gills called lamellae. Although nymphs can survive the loss of these gills in well-oxygenated water, they sometimes perish if the water is warm and stagnant.

The ability of some nymphs to survive out of water in moist air is further evidence of their terrestrial ancestry. One Hawaiian species is completely terrestrial in all its nymphal stages.

From water to air

As nymph dragonflies mature, they prepare for the transition from water to air. To complete their development, they must undergo several internal and external changes. In some species, this can take several months.

Nymphs that have eyes stretching around to the backs of their heads when they become adults show the first signs of physical change. As they approach the adult stage, their compound eyes develop, rapidly becoming larger and expanding round their heads. In the British emperor dragonfly, the change in eye shape can be detected 45 days before the nymph emerges as an adult.

The next stage in the change from nymph to adult dragonfly involves an increase in the insect's rate of breathing. It occurs suddenly, in some species about 13 days before the adult emerges. Although it is not completely clear why the nymph's breathing rate increases, it is thought that a mature nymph needs extra oxygen in order to complete its transformation.

Among the nymph's subsequent physical changes, its mask changes into the mouthparts of an adult. The wing buds on its back develop, starting to overlap and become erect. Its abdomen becomes swollen, and its gills cease to function.

ABOVE Bright and vivid colors are typical of male dragonflies and damselflies. Some, like this damselfly, have scales that diffract the light so that the wings appear to be pure in color, often green, red or blue. Bright colors are important in mating rituals. They serve to signal the male's readiness to mate. Faded colors often mean that the insect is past its prime.
PAGE 2353 The female hawker dragonfly, *Aeshna grandis*, possesses an egg-laying tube (ovipositor) that can pierce and then insert eggs into plant tissue. Although this is a relatively slow process, it affords the eggs considerable protection.

order to face it. Slowly, and with small rocking movements, it closes in on its victim. When the prey is within striking range, the nymph lunges forward and shoots out its grasping lower lip. The lip is called a "mask" because it covers the lower portion of the nymph's head when not in use. There are two sharp hooks or fangs on the mask, and the nymph uses them to grasp its prey and drag it away to eat. A nymph can strike its victim in less than three-hundredths of a second.

Many millions of years ago, dragonfly and damselfly nymphs may have lived on land. One indication that this may have been the case is that all species have the closed remains of the breathing holes

LEFT Most dragonflies are large insects, with some species measuring as much as 6.7 in. from wingtip to wingtip. However, they pale into insignificance when compared with one prehistoric species that had a wingspan of approximately 30 in.
BELOW Dragonflies and damselflies mature in stages, a process known as incomplete metamorphosis. When the adult dragonfly emerges from its final molt, it first hangs upside-down by its abdomen. When fully emerged, it remains on the discarded nymphal skin until its wings and body are completely dry.
PAGES 2356-2357 The male damselfly transfers his sperm sac to the female by means of a secondary sexual organ. Here, the male is in front of the female, and they are in the typical "wheel" shape.

As well as changing physically, dragonfly nymphs also change in behavior. They cease to feed and begin to search for a suitable place to emerge—by waterside plants, on rocks or on the shore. Nymphs that live in the mud at the bottom of pools congregate in the warmer shallows; nymphs of weed-living species move nearer the surface. Both types of nymph move by night. Then, still at night, they manage to select an area that will remain shaded after the sun rises. How they can do this is not understood.

As with many insects, environmental conditions trigger the nymphs' developmental changes. Consequently, all nymphs of the same species tend to emerge on the same morning. As a result, they may fiercely compete for surfaces on which to molt. Some nymphs may have to crawl as far as 50 ft. in order to find a suitable site for emergence.

Shedding the final skin

Every species has its own unique method of emergence and completes the process in a different amount of time. In the case of hawker dragonflies, the nymph hauls itself clear of the water at a given time, usually going up the stem of a reed. Then it prepares to molt its old skin, a process call ecdysis. Once in position, it digs its claws into the surface and remains motionless for about 10 minutes. A small split then appears along the nymph's back. Slowly, the split enlarges, and after about 20 minutes the insect's head, thorax and limbs are free of the shed skin, or exuvium.

Among dragonflies, the half-emerged adult hangs upside-down, attached only by its unemerged abdomen. After a while, the adult dragonfly drags its abdomen free and rests in the position that the nymph originally

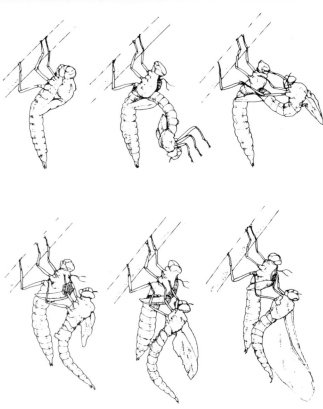

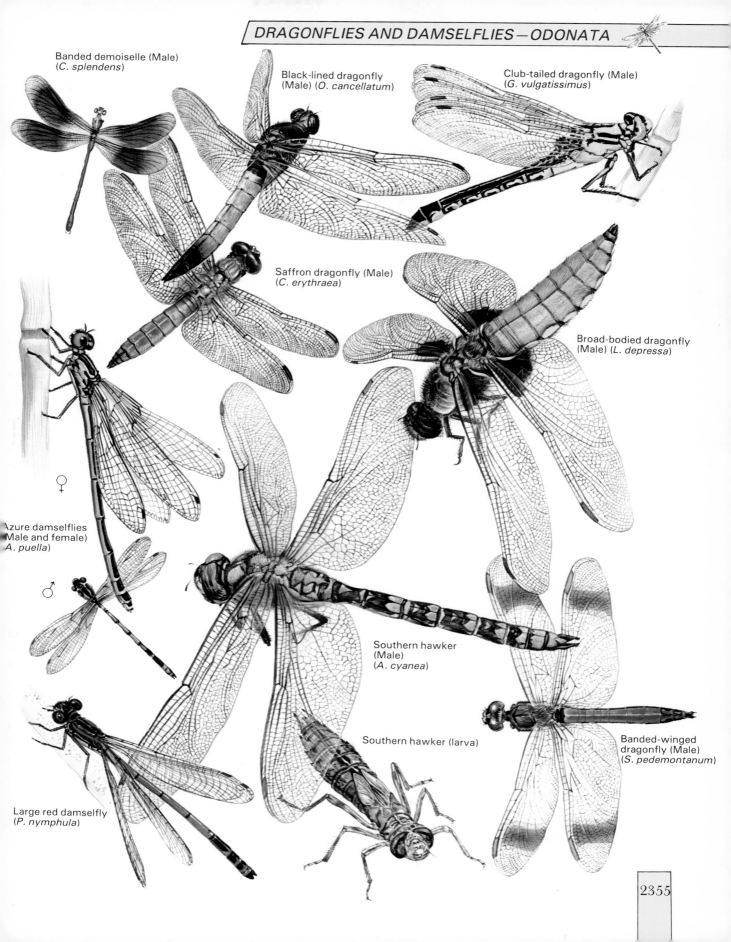

Banded demoiselle (Male)
(*C. splendens*)

Black-lined dragonfly
(Male) (*O. cancellatum*)

Club-tailed dragonfly (Male)
(*G. vulgatissimus*)

Saffron dragonfly (Male)
(*C. erythraea*)

Broad-bodied dragonfly
(Male) (*L. depressa*)

Azure damselflies
(Male and female)
(*A. puella*)

Southern hawker
(Male)
(*A. cyanea*)

Southern hawker (larva)

Banded-winged
dragonfly (Male)
(*S. pedemontanum*)

Large red damselfly
(*P. nymphula*)

2355

ABOVE The male saffron dragonfly has a bright red coloration extending even to the large compound eyes, which are the same shade as the body. Saffron dragonflies are usually found in Ethiopia and India, but also occur in the Mediterranean region. They take their name from the females, which are yellow in color.

held. Its wings slowly inflate using blood pressure. The process takes about an hour, although in some species it can take three times as long.

Lunch on the wing

Like nymphs, adult dragonflies and damselflies are voracious eaters. They require a lot of food because they are highly active insects. Some species start feeding within hours of emerging from their nymphal skins. Like nymphs, they eat virtually anything that comes their way, as long as it is not too large or too tough to tackle. They catch and eat nearly all their food on the wing, using their long legs rather like a sweep net and then scooping their prey toward their jaws.

Dragonflies, like most insects, have compound eyes made up of thousands of individual cells called ommatidia. However, a dragonfly's eyes are special in two ways. First, they consist of an enormous number of cells—up to 30,000; second, the cells are not all identical. The cells are usually large on the upper surface of the dragonfly's compound eye, and they become progressively smaller as they descend the curve of the eye. In some broad-bodied dragonflies, the transition from large to small cells appears as a distinct band. It is thought that a dragonfly uses its upper eye surface to detect objects that are flying toward it and its lower eye surface to spot resting or stationary objects.

Adult, but not mature

Soon after its wings have hardened, the adult dragonfly starts beating its wings. Like all cold-blooded animals, its body must be at a certain temperature in order to work efficiently. By beating its wings, the dragonfly both exercises them and raises its body temperature in preparation for its maiden flight.

A dragonfly does not mature sexually as soon as it becomes an adult. Initially, its sexual organs are inactive and it lacks its full adult colors. One of the most important purposes of the maiden flight is to keep the dragonfly out of the way of sexually mature adults while it completes its development.

Dragonfly "puberty" can last from two or three days up to three weeks. In one group of dragonflies, sexual development takes from the time of emergence to the following spring. During this period, the male attains his true colors and develops a characteristic sheen. Males usually take less time to develop than the females.

Since male dragonflies reach sexual maturity before the females, they have an opportunity to set up the mating and breeding territories. Each day, the male dragonfly leaves his roosting perch and heads off to his chosen site. Once there, he keeps his eyes open for intruders into the airspace above.

If an intruder is a female of the same species of dragonfly, the male tries to mate with her. If it is not, the male attempts to knock it out of the air. He gets underneath the intruder and then rapidly gains height in order to strike with his back. Territorial fights are often audible, and they can cause wing damage to both defender and intruder.

Territorial limits

The size of a dragonfly's territory depends on the size of the adult insect. A large dragonfly can fly further, faster and with more power than a small one. Also, larger dragonflies tend to have better eyesight and can react more quickly and precisely. However, territories are rarely the same size all year round. At the beginning of the mating season when males are not so abundant, the size of each territory is larger. As the season progresses, the number of males increases and individual territories get smaller until a saturation point is reached.

If all dragonflies and damselflies fought for exclusive control of all territories, they would have no time for anything else. Fortunately, certain families can

RIGHT Dragonflies have compound eyes that are made up of thousands of individual cells, or ommatidia, that vary in size. The large, upward and forward-facing ommatidia on the upper surface of the eye enable the insect to spot moving objects up to 115 ft. away. The smaller, downward-facing ommatidia are used to detect stationary objects from above.

BELOW Some species of damselfly lay their eggs on plants underwater, often immediately after mating, and sometimes before the male has released the female (A). Dragonfly nymphs have an extensible "mask" (B), which they shoot out to grab prey (C). The nymphs hold their prey tightly by two pointed "fangs" (D). When not in use the "mask" folds back against the nymph's head.

live together, sharing the same zones. The hawker dragonflies, for example, prefer open stretches of water, as do the emerald dragonflies. However, the hawkers patrol at a height of about 6 ft. 6 in., whereas the emeralds tend to keep much closer to the water. The broad-bodied dragonflies keep close to reedbeds, while club-tailed dragonflies usually congregate around less well-vegetated areas.

Male dragonflies and damselflies rely on their eyesight to recognize females, so their excellent vision plays an important role in their mating and reproductive cycles. Some males react to the amount of light that passes through the female's wings. If the female has dark-colored wings, a characteristic pattern of light will pass through and alert the male. The female's body colors, size, and flight movements such as zigzagging also stimulate the male.

Love in flight

Dragonflies and damselflies usually mate on the wing, but the males of some species, such as the broad-bodied dragonflies, like to mate with females that are laying eggs. By contrast, male hawker dragonflies find the down-curved abdomens of the egg-laying females unattractive. Female hawker dragonflies sometimes adopt an egg-laying attitude in flight in order to deter the males.

Few species of dragonfly or damselfly have courtship displays. Since both sexes recognize and respond to each other visually, ritualized courtship is unnecessary. In those species where it does occur, the male usually flies toward the female and then hovers in front of her. While in this position, he displays colorful patches on his legs or abdomen. The

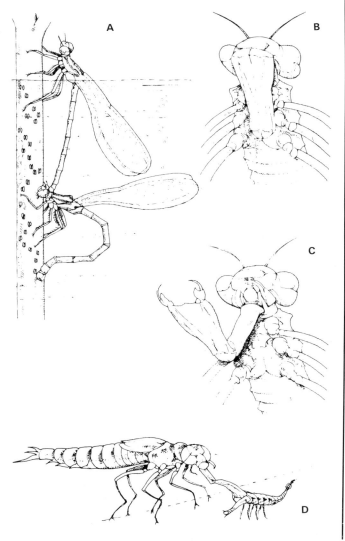

patches indicate the male's stage of development. If the colors are faded, then the male is past his prime and the female rejects him.

Advanced mating method

Dragonflies and damselflies provide an important clue to the evolution of insects. Most primitive insects reproduce using sperm parcels called spermatophores. The male usually produces a single spermatophore and either leaves it on the ground for the female to find or drags the female over it. Dragonflies and damselflies take the process a step further by engaging in bodily contact. The male transfers sperm to the female using a secondary sex organ on his abdomen.

After passing the recognition stage, the male dragonfly grabs the female by her thorax and loops his abdomen up until he has positioned it near or on her head. Then he uses special appendages at the end of his abdomen to grasp the female firmly. Sometimes the male has such a strong grip that he dents the female's eyes. Both his appendages and the parts of the female that he grasps are often specifically designed so that members of different species cannot interbreed.

Once the male has a firm grip on the female, he lets go with his legs and transfers the sperm from his genital opening to the secondary sex organ on the

ABOVE Damselflies elegantly erect their wings over their backs when at rest. The wings are richly veined, transparent and narrow toward the base. Because their wings are weakly muscled, the damselflies are poor fliers.

FAR RIGHT Damselflies often clean their eyes and antennae with their front legs, much as a cat cleans its face. They not only clean the sense organs on their heads, but use their rear legs to clean and groom their abdomens.

underside of his abdomen. Mating occurs when the female draws her abdomen forward and at the same time grabs the male's abdomen with her legs. The female then brings her genital opening into contact with the male's secondary sex organ and the sperm is transferred again. The position they are now in is often called the "wheel." Dragonflies and damselflies can mate either in the air or perched on a suitable surface.

After mating, most dragonflies let go of one another. By contrast, damselflies remain together until the female has laid her eggs. In some species that lay their eggs inside underwater plants, the male has to perch on the tip of his abdomen so as not to release the female. In other species, the male has to relinquish his grip completely when the female submerges herself.

Egg distribution

After mating, dragonflies and damselflies fly off— either alone or in tandem—in search of somewhere to

LEFT Although dragonflies generally live by water, which is where they breed, their powerful flight often carries them far away from their breeding places, and they occur wherever there are trees and bushes on which they can rest.
BELOW The map shows the distribution of some species of dragonfly and damselfly.

Cutting edge

Dragonflies always lay their eggs in the type of environment that they themselves inhabit. For example, pond dwellers only lay in ponds, never in lakes. Bog-dwelling species—among the most primitive of the dragonflies—always search out a suitable piece of bog. They force their abdomens down into the damp moss, and lay a cluster of sticky eggs. However, by laying their eggs directly into the nymphal habitat, they often damage their wings so badly that they cannot fly any more and starve to death.

Some dragonflies and damselflies lay their eggs directly into plants to hide them from predators and parasites, and protect them from the extremes of temperature and aridity. The females of most species that place their eggs inside plants have serrated edges on their egg-laying appendages or ovipositors. They use the sharp edge to cut into the plants and then lay their eggs in the stem.

lay their eggs. They have many methods of laying and distributing their eggs. Some take great care to find the most suitable locations; others scatter them at random. As in all aspects of their lives, dragonflies rely on their sight to locate egg-laying grounds.

Female dragonflies have been observed trying to lay their eggs on shiny cement, car roofs, and even pools of crude oil, mistaking them for water. One of the ways in which dragonflies minimize such mistakes is by water touching. When a dragonfly discovers what appears to be water, it flies very low over it and touches its abdomen against the surface. Some dragonflies skim along roads for the same reason.

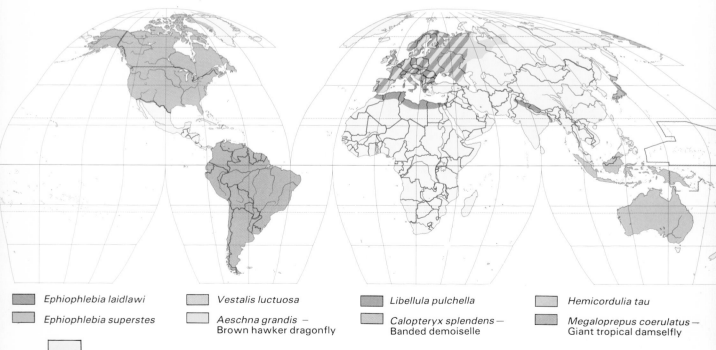

Ephiophlebia laidlawi	*Libellula pulchella*
Ephiophlebia superstes	*Calopteryx splendens* — Banded demoiselle
Vestalis luctuosa	*Hemicordulia tau*
Aeschna grandis — Brown hawker dragonfly	*Megaloprepus coerulatus* — Giant tropical damselfly

JUMPING SONGSTERS

The chirping choruses of grasshoppers and crickets are common in country fields and hedgerows. In both groups of insects, their songs are usually courtship invitations to prospective partners

Crickets and grasshoppers have evolved powerful hind legs and sophisticated communication systems to cope with life in dense vegetation Their cheeps and chirps are a familiar sound on warm nights all over the world.

The crickets, grasshoppers, katydids and locusts all belong to the order Orthoptera. There are more than 20,000 species spread throughout the temperate and tropical regions of the world, although katydids occur mainly in America and locusts live primarily in tropical areas. Orthopterans vary considerably in size, some species measure less than 0.4 in., while others reach nearly 8 in. in length. The females lay eggs that hatch into nymphs and develop in stages (they undergo incomplete metamorphosis).

Crickets and grasshoppers first appeared about 220 million years ago and have adapted to most land environments—from deserts to jungles and from high mountain peaks to the depths of caves. Despite the diversity in their size and habitat, most species of crickets and grasshoppers have the same general appearance.

Locomotion—legs and wings

Grasshoppers and crickets have distinctive hind legs that are usually larger than their other two pairs. Their hind legs have sharp spines that are highly effective in defense, and well-developed muscles enable the grasshoppers or crickets to leap high in the air to escape would-be predators. In some species, notably the grasshoppers and locusts, their wings take over at the peak of the jump and carry them even further away.

Not all crickets and grasshoppers have wings. However, those that do have them, have two pairs. Their forewings, situated above their abdomens, have a leathery appearance and serve to protect their membranous hind wings. When not in use, they fold their hind wings beneath their forewings. When unfolded, their hind wings often reveal bright patches of color. Grasshoppers in particular, use this as a tactic to startle enemies.

Crickets and grasshoppers are not usually good fliers, and most just flutter a little to increase the distance of a jump. However, grasshoppers do have a rudimentary flight-control mechanism; by twisting their abdomens in mid-flight, they alter the pitch of their wings and correct any instabilities. For all but a few species, however, flight remains primarily a means of escape. Their normal method of locomotion is a series of leaps and bounds.

Obvious differences

The order Orthoptera is large and consists of two suborders: the suborder Ensifera, which contains the crickets, the katydids and the long-horned grasshoppers; and the suborder Caelifera, which contains the true or short-horned grasshoppers and the locusts. The species that belong to these two groups have major visible differences. Crickets and other members of the suborder Ensifera usually have long, jointed thread-like antennae that are often longer than their bodies. They have biting mouthparts that are more or less symmetrical, and in some species the males have

BELOW **Crickets and grasshoppers are the insect long-jump champions, occupying the first three places in the league table. Adult grasshoppers hold first place with a maximum jump of 29.5 in., and crickets land close behind with 23.6 in. Taking the size of the insects into consideration, however, the tiny flea, leaping 11.8** in., would emerge the clear winner.
PAGE 2363 **A swarm of desert locusts,** Schistocerca gregaria, **can number over 300 million insects per square yard. Within the swarm, the locusts fly as a small group and the group feeds together when it reaches crops or grass.**

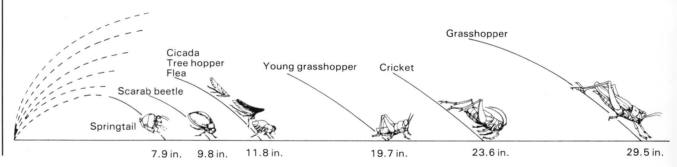

Springtail   Scarab beetle   Cicada / Tree hopper / Flea   Young grasshopper   Cricket   Grasshopper

7.9 in.   9.8 in.   11.8 in.   19.7 in.   23.6 in.   29.5 in.

German grasshopper
(*O. germanica*)

Ugandan lubber locust (*P. brunneri*)

Thorny leaf cricket
(*A. hewaniana*)

Cone-headed grasshopper
(*A. mediterranea*)

Desert locust (*S. gregaria*)

Migratory locust
(*L. migratoria*)

Giant leaf katydid (*P. grandis*)

European short-winged
grasshopper (*A. fusca*)

Solitary phase of the
migratory locust (*L. migratoria*)

Field cricket (*G. campestris*)

2365

ABOVE Italian tree crickets are always pale in color, and are among the most tuneful singers in the insect world. Their high-pitched trills provide a frequent accompaniment to a hot summer's evening. Most of the sounds generated by crickets are too high in frequency for human ears to detect.

produce their sound. They also possess an organ known as a "drum" that amplifies the resulting sound. Grasshoppers produce sound in much the same way except that their toothed "files" are located on the inside edges of their hind legs. These methods of producing sounds are called stridulation.

The sounds vary greatly in frequency, ranging from 2000 hertz (unit of frequency per second) at the low end of the scale, up to 100,000 hertz at the other end. Most of the sound produced is far above the range of human hearing because the rubbing movements made by the insects are so rapid.

A good ear

Crickets and grasshoppers possess hearing organs that are situated on their first abdominal segment. Sound reaches them via specially adapted breathing holes in the sides of their thoraxes. These expanded breathing tubes open out into sacs that are covered with a drum-like skin, called a tympanal membrane. Although separated by internal air spaces, these tubes are not completely insulated. Sound vibrations from the air enter the breathing tubes and are amplified by the tympanal membrane.

Signature tunes

Every species of cricket and grasshopper has its own particular type of song. Because each call is made up of several significant factors, the variations are almost limitless. Some crickets listen for the length of time between the pulses of sound produced in each chirp. In one species the song consists of a series of chirps at intervals of one-third of a second. Each chirp consists of two to six pulses of high-frequency sound, the message being contained in the intervals between the pulses. In other species it is the repetition of the chirp that carries the message, and not the duration of the pulses. Others are attuned to pulse repetition, and still others listen out for a combination of some or all of these factors. For many years it was thought that only the pulses contained within a chirp were important in getting a response from another cricket. In recent experiments, however, bursts of pure tone with no rhythm, played to several different species, produced positive responses—demonstrating that their communications system is even more complex than previously thought.

The ability of crickets and grasshoppers to make sounds is most important during the mating season,

enlarged jaws. Most females in this group have a long, curved egg-laying tube, called an ovipositor. The true or short-horned grasshoppers and the locusts of the suborder Caelifera have shorter, more robust antennae. The females' ovipositors are much smaller and not readily visible.

File and drum

Leaping away from danger is a characteristic shared with many other insects. The ability to send and receive sounds, however, is characteristic of only a few orders. Grasshoppers and crickets have evolved this adaptation in response to their life-style and habitats. Most orthopterans live in thick foliage, completely concealed from other members of their species as well as from predators. In order to communicate with each other, especially males to females, they have developed sound-producing techniques and "ears" to listen for any response. Crickets have a toothed "file" on one forewing and a hard ridge on the other, which they rub together to

and it is almost always the males who do the calling. The males find a suitable place to call from; discarded cans and bottles are ideal places because the sound waves are amplified by these containers and therefore travel further. In areas free of litter, they usually sit on a stem or leaf to prevent ground clutter from muffling their calls.

Each species of cricket and grasshopper begins calling at a specific time of day. Some call in the morning or at midday, but the vast majority begin at dusk. Because it is dark they have a certain amount of protection from predators. However, if a cricket senses danger nearby it plays a clever trick with its call. By altering the pitch of its wings, it "throws its voice" and changes its apparent location.

A temporary deafness

After mating has taken place, the females of some species are prevented from mating again because they have large egg masses inside them. These egg masses constrict their hearing ability, leaving them deaf to the calls of other males until they have laid their eggs. In one species, the male attracts the female with his song. When she is close enough, he offers her a secretion from a gland on the back of his thorax. While the female is busy eating the liquid, the male mates with her. During mating the male transfers a number of small sperm packets, called spermatophores, to the female's genital opening. The female lays her eggs in holes in the ground or inside plants. The species that deposit their eggs inside plants have saw-like appendages on the base of their abdomens, which they use to cut into the plant to make room for the eggs.

Cricket thermometers

The mating calls of male crickets and grasshoppers lead females of the same species to them. But not all the calls the females hear come from males that

ABOVE **Life in thick vegetation means that grasshoppers are generally out of sight of their fellows. The males use their calls to attract and guide females to them. Each species has its own particular mating song. If accepted by the female, the smaller male climbs onto his mate, and with the rear of their abdomens together, they mate. The male passes his sperm, in a sac, into the female's sperm receptacle where they are stored until she lays her eggs.**

BELOW **Crickets and grasshoppers produce their song by a method known as stridulation. Crickets produce their sound by rubbing their wings together very quickly. One forewing has a toothed file vein on the underside, the other has a hardened ridge (A). Grasshoppers have toothed "files" on their hind legs (B), formed from one of their veins, that they rub against the edges of their forewings. The resulting sound is amplified by an organ called a "drum."**

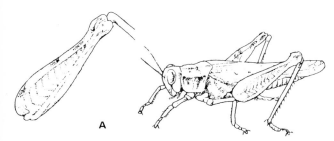

A

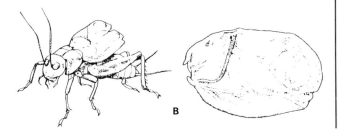

B

ABOVE Large insects often have legends and stories attached to them, and the great green bush cricket is no exception. In Italy, it is thought that if a mother catches one in her child's bedroom and then ties it by some thread to the bed it will bring the child fame and fortune. In Britain, the same insect is mistakenly named the great green grasshopper. Crickets and grasshoppers are often confused, but the true grasshoppers have short, sturdy antennae.

are ready to mate. For those species of cricket and grasshopper where the message is carried by the rate of pulses, the air temperature could have crucial significance. Fluctuations in temperature have an important effect on their communication system. As the air temperature increases, so does the speed of the male song. The metabolism of cold-blooded insects is very sensitive to temperature (also, sound waves travel faster through warm air because it is less dense). If there were no compensating factor, mating could only occur at one particular temperature.

Fortunately for the crickets, an evolutionary countermeasure does exist. Both sexes are equally affected. In laboratory conditions females at a given temperature only reacted to males at the same temperature. An offshoot of this research has revealed that some crickets and grasshoppers can be used as living thermometers. In one species 100 chirps per minute means that the temperature is exactly 63°F.

Fighting talk

Apart from mating, crickets and grasshoppers also use their songs for a variety of other purposes. When two males have a dispute over territory or a female, they emit a different pattern of chirps and pulses. Both males face each other and raise their hind wings slightly. They challenge each other with aggressive chirps, and if neither gives way a ritualized fight takes place. These fights are only partly ritual, and in the more aggressive species they sometimes lead to the death of one of the rivals. The victor often eats the loser.

Some grasshoppers and crickets give a short chirp when moving from one source of food to another—a call that warns others that the sudden movement is not in reaction to a possible danger.

The order to which the crickets and grasshoppers belong is very diverse in form and behavior, and a description of a "typical" species is impossible. Some are solitary, some mass in great swarms, and others do both. Some species are great fliers, while others are entirely wingless. Some are fragile, twig-like creatures, and others are much more robust.

Giant wetas and cooloola monsters

Giant wetas and cooloola monsters belong to the superfamily Stenopelmatidae. They occur mainly in Australasia and America. Cooloola monsters are large, wingless crickets, that have only recently been discovered in northern Australia. Measuring almost 2 in. in length, they have large mandibles and powerful, spiny hind legs. Like their relatives, they are predominantly vegetarian, but sometimes they feed on other insects and invertebrates.

The wetas are restricted to New Zealand and its coastal islands. The word "weta" derives from the Maori language and applies to local cave crickets as well as to the true wetas that live on the ground or in trees.

Alarming sounds

The giant wetas are among the heaviest known insects and can reach a weight of 2.5 oz. They are wingless, and have heavily armored exoskeletons with stout spines along their legs. Their hind legs are much longer and more powerful than their other two pairs. Despite their fearsome appearance, giant wetas are slow-moving, unaggressive insects that tend to frighten predators rather than fight with them. When alarmed, they raise their hind legs vertically above their

RIGHT Generally, crickets and grasshoppers have only the spines of their powerful hind legs to use in defense, although grasshoppers sometimes open their wings to reveal patches of color that may startle an enemy. A few species have more elaborate defense mechanisms, particularly some members of the family *Bradyporidae*. When held by their abdomens, they squirt a jet of blood from their leg joints. The jet is quite powerful and can travel over 1.5 ft.

INSECTS CLASSIFICATION: 4

Crickets and grasshoppers

The crickets and grasshoppers make up the order Orthoptera, which contains over 20,000 different species in 61 families. The order is divided into two suborders: the Ensifera and the Caelifera, each of which is further subdivided into several superfamilies.

The suborder Ensifera contains four superfamilies: the Stenopelmatidea includes the giant weta, *Deinacrida heteracantha*, of New Zealand and the cooloola monster, *Cooloola propator*, of northern Australia; the Tettigoniidea contains the bush crickets (such as the great green bush cricket, *Tettigonia viridissima*, of southern Europe, North Africa and Asia), the koringkrieks of southern Africa, the katydids, the giant leaf crickets and giant katydids of the family Pseudophyllidae, and the long-legged bush cricket, *Sago pedo*, of southern Europe; the Schizodactyloidea, which includes the splay-footed crickets; and the Grylloidea, which contains the true, field, house, and cave-dwelling crickets as well as the mole crickets of the genus *Gryllotalpa*.

The suborder Caelifera has six superfamilies. One of the largest—with some 7000 species—is the superfamily Acridoidea. It includes the desert locust, *Schistocerca gregaria*, of Africa and Asia; the Egyptian locust, *Anacridium aegyptium;* and the ground locusts (family Tetrigidae). Other superfamilies include the Trigonopterygoidea (containing leaf bush hoppers); the Tridacttyloidea (with the pygmy mole crickets); and the Cylindrachetoidea, which includes the false mole crickets.

heads, then pull them down rapidly, producing a sharp, crackling sound as their legs rub against their abdomens. Giant wetas also produce a hissing sound by telescoping the plates of their abdomens together.

Threatened species

New Zealand broke away from the super continent Gondwanaland nearly 90 million years ago. As a result, the islands contain very few indigenous mammals, enabling the giant wetas to evolve in an environment that lacked the principal insect predators. In their natural environment, the only predators of these crickets are lizards and various birds such as the kiwi and the kingfisher. The introduction of rats by European settlers during the 19th and 20th centuries is thought to be the major cause of the decline in numbers of the giant wetas, which now occur only on small islands and in the high mountain regions.

During the day, giant wetas rest among palm leaf litter and other plant debris, only emerging at night to feed. Giant wetas are vegetarian and search actively for food, even climbing trees.

The tettigoniids

The superfamily Tettigoniidea contains about 6000 closely related species that live in the warmer parts of the world. The group includes the bush crickets, the katydids, the long-horned grasshoppers and the leaf crickets. Although there is a wide variety of shapes and colors within this group, most species display a series of characteristics that make them instantly recognizable. Most species are green or brown in color; their antennae are usually longer than their bodies (from where the long-horned grasshoppers derive their name). Their legs are covered in spines

ABOVE The large wart biter bush cricket derives its name from its supposed ability to get rid of warts. It is believed that if the cricket bites off a wart with its powerful jaws, then the wart will not return.

ABOVE RIGHT One of Europe's most impressive insects is the long-legged bush cricket, which can reach 4.7 in. in length. It is strictly carnivorous and captures its prey using its powerful, spined forelegs.

and their hind legs, although often enlarged, are rarely used for jumping, as most species live high up in trees or other foliage. Some species lack a hearing organ, and many lack fully formed wings. The species that possess wings hold them tent-like over their backs.

Also included in this group are four species of ambidextrous crickets, so called because they lack a clearly defined file and ridge arrangement on their forewings. Unlike nearly all other crickets, they can call to a mate by rubbing either their left wing over their right wing, or vice versa.

Not all tettigoniids are green or brown in color. One species that lives in the Sudan is black with white markings on the sides of its thorax and abdomen. These crickets grow to about 0.3 in. in length and do not have wings. They occur only in areas where ants live in abundance. Their markings provide protection because they resemble ants, which are distasteful to predators because they produce formic acid.

The wings of some species of tettigoniids resemble the leaves of plants, others look like grasses, and some have decorated and toned wings that take on the appearance of bark or lichen. Male tettigoniids use their forewings to produce sounds. Even species with small vestigial wings still retain their noise-making organs.

Long-legged bush crickets

Among Europe's most striking insects are a group of related species that are not typical of the tettigoniids because they live on the ground. One of the largest in this group is quite common in southern Europe, especially in Italy. Female long-legged bush crickets grow to a length of 4.7 in. (including their ovipositor). They live in hot, dry areas that have low-lying bushes, and they walk slowly along the ground during daylight. Long-legged bush crickets are wingless but have well-developed legs. Each of their front legs bears a row of sharp spines—giving a clue to their dietary requirements. Long-legged bush crickets are strictly carnivorous. They are powerful hunters and use the same method as the mantids to capture their prey. When a long-legged bush cricket has closed in on its prey, it throws out its forelegs and hugs the victim tightly to its thorax. It then embeds its spines into its prey's body, making escape unlikely. With a swift movement it bites its victim behind the head and kills it.

The long-legged bush cricket is able to reproduce without fertilization by a male—a process known as parthenogenesis. There are no male long-legged bush crickets in existence, and the females reproduce without mating.

The great green bush cricket

Britain's largest tettigoniid, the great green bush cricket, also called the great green grasshopper, belongs to the same family as the long-legged bush cricket.

The great green bush cricket occurs in southern Europe, northern Africa and Asia. It is a large insect, measuring up to 2.8 in. in length (including the female's ovipositor) and is bright green in color, enabling it to blend in with its surroundings. These

crickets are omnivorous and eat leaves and buds as well as other insects. Sometimes they occur in very large numbers and cause extensive damage to crops.

Burying their eggs

During the summer, great green bush crickets sing during the afternoon and continue into the night, but only when the nighttime temperature is above 53.6°F. Once the temperature falls below this point, they become sluggish and stop singing. They mate on the ground, and afterward, using their long, hard ovipositors, the females dig into the soil and lay their eggs. The eggs remain in the ground throughout the winter, and the soil provides a degree of insulation against the extreme cold that would otherwise kill them. The hatchling nymphs emerge in the spring. They usually eat only vegetation and remain close to the ground. After reaching adulthood, the great green bush crickets become more omnivorous and spend most of their time high up in the foliage of bushes and trees.

The wart biter

The wart biter occurs throughout temperate Europe and Asia. It is rare in Britain, where it is confined to a few localities in the south. The wart biter is related to the great green bush cricket, but is slightly smaller and has a darker green coloring. The insect has powerful jaws with sharp mandibles. When biting, it exudes a fluid from its mouth that is supposed to cure warts. The wart biter has an omnivorous diet, and is a voracious hunter. It will kill an adult grasshopper when it can catch one.

Koringkrieks—armor-plated insects

The koringkrieks of southern Africa have stalked eyes, long legs and spines covering their backs. These armor-plated insects are formidable creatures and are greatly feared by the local people, who believe them to be deadly poisonous. However, there is no evidence to suggest that they are any more distasteful than many other crickets.

The thick, spiny plating on the koringkrieks' back covers the males' noise-producing (stridulating) organs. Their song is a loud, rasping noise that does not help their unpleasant reputation. Like most species of crickets, female koringkrieks are unable to produce any sound. Koringkrieks are predominantly

ABOVE Female crickets have an egg-laying tube, or ovipositor, projecting from the rear of their abdomens. The ovipositor is generally long and curved, nearly doubling the insect's overall length, and it is usually pushed into the ground so that the eggs are laid well below the surface, safe from frost.

nocturnal insects, but occasionally sit motionless on bushes during the daytime. They are omnivores and will eat anything, living or dead, including the dead of their own species.

Katydids and flatfoots

The katydid lives mainly in tropical America, and its name derives from its call. On hot summer nights the males sing to the females with their distinctive three-part song that sounds like "ka-ty-did, ka-ty-did." However, they sometimes miss out one of the parts of the song and repeat just two different sounds.

A family closely related to the katydids contains some of the largest insects on earth. The giant leaf crickets and giant katydids have wingspans measuring 10 in. Most of these large species occur in and around India and Australasia. Like the true katydids, they resemble leaves in appearance.

The superfamily Schizodactyloidea consists of mainly desert-dwelling crickets, including the splay-

THE RUFOUS GRASSHOPPER
— A SUMMER SONGSTER —

The production of sound (stridulation) is a notable feature of crickets and grasshoppers. Stridulation plays an important part in the courtship behavior of males. The courtship songs of male crickets and grasshoppers differ among species, ensuring that only the females of the same species respond to their call.

Accomplished caller

The rufous grasshopper is Britain's most accomplished insect songster, and may be heard throughout the late summer. Sometimes, its courtship songs continue until November and, exceptionally, into December. The rufous grasshopper lives in southern England and southern Wales, particularly in areas with chalky and limestone soils, which support its favorite plants—marjoram and thyme.

The adult rufous grasshopper measures 0.6-0.9 in. in length. It is usually brown in color with an orange tip on the end of its abdomen, which is darker in the males. The female has a purple-red head and thorax, a feature that gives the species its common name.

Wide repertoire

As with all grasshoppers and crickets, only the male rufous grasshopper has a wide repertoire of sound. The most conspicuous song that it produces is its "calling" or courtship song during the breeding season in summer. Males call singly or in groups when no females are present. The mating call of the rufous grasshopper resembles the noise of a clockwork toy winding down, and lasts for about five seconds. Usually, one male starts to call, then another joins in, until all the males in a hedgerow are singing in chorus to attract potential breeding partners.

A receptive female responds to the mating call of the males with a short chirp and moves in the direction of the call until she encounters the group of males (the calls of the male and female enable them to locate each other among the tall grasses and plants of their preferred habitat). Both sexes continue calling until visual contact is made.

Courtship rituals

When a female comes into view, the male begins his courtship ritual, altering his call to court and serenade her. During his elaborate courtship dance, the male waves his white-tipped antennae to gain the female's full attention. His song declines in volume to a faint chirp (his mouthparts waggle from side to side about twice a second)

and he nods his head up and down in rhythm with the song for a period of about five seconds.

The male's movements increase in tempo, and the watching female is attracted by the male's antennae. During the final phase of the courtship ritual, the male produces a short burst of weak chirping and raises his rear legs high in the air. The dance culminates in a convulsive jerk of the male's body that causes his rear legs to make a loud click.

The whole performance lasts 10-20 seconds and may take place several times before the female accepts her suitor. Unreceptive females usually deter overzealous males with a swift kick from their rear legs. The male also has a short "warning" or territorial song that it sings in the presence of other males.

The mottled grasshopper, a more common species, can be heard in most parts of Britain from June onward. Its song consists of a series of short buzzes that increase in volume and last for about 10-15 seconds. The premating display is simpler than that of the rufous grasshopper, but contains the same basic head and leg movements.

ABOVE The mottled grasshopper, *Myrmeleotettix maculatus*, is a common species throughout Britain. Its mating call consists of a series of short buzzes that last for a period of 10-15 seconds and is accompanied by an elaborate courtship dance.
RIGHT When the rufous grasshopper is engaged in stridulation, his long hind legs rise and fall rhythmically in time with his song. If he moves his legs slowly, the note is low. It becomes progressively higher in pitch as the movement speeds up.
FAR LEFT The mating song of the male rufous grasshopper, *Gomphocerippus rufus*, plays an important part in its courtship ritual. It produces a song that is peculiar to its species by rubbing together specialized veins on the bases of its front wings, so that only the females of the same species are attracted for mating.

footed crickets. They have developed special spines and pads on their feet that spread their weight evenly and provide extra traction, enabling the splay-footed crickets to move quickly and safely on soft, shifting sand. The splay-footed crickets have long wings that curl back into a tight curl when they are at rest—reducing the surface area exposed to the fierce desert sunlight.

The true crickets

The superfamily Grylloidea contains nearly 2300 species, including the true, the field, the house, the mole and the cave-dwelling crickets. Members of this superfamily have long, thin antennae, robust thoraxes, and a pair of highly developed hind limbs that are suitable for jumping. True crickets are small insects, and most do not exceed 0.8 in. in length. Their noise-producing organs consist of a row of teeth on one wing cover and a scraper on the other. The crickets pull the scraper across the row of teeth, causing their wings to vibrate. The sound is amplified by a flat area called a mirror.

Nearly all crickets need high temperatures and a humid environment to survive. They often live under cover, in caves or cracks in the ground, and even share houses with human beings. The group does, however, contain some species that have adapted to living in arid conditions. Crickets are principally vegetarian, but some species are omnivorous, feeding on the larvae and adults of other insects.

ABOVE Field crickets cannot fly and live in pastures and meadows. They mate and hibernate in burrows that they dig with their large, powerful jaws. They are fiercely territorial, often injuring or killing an intruder.

BELOW The leaf crickets live off the ground in trees or bushes. They are nearly all nocturnal. The adults are often colored to match the surrounding vegetation, where they rest during the day, concealed from predators.

The field cricket

The common field crickets are among the best known of the European crickets. They are about an inch long when adult and have shiny black exoskeletons. Their eyes are small, and they have long, thin antennae. Field crickets, like the true crickets, have powerful hind legs that enable them to jump well. In Europe they usually live in meadows and forest clearings, although some species occur in more mountainous regions.

Field crickets usually live above ground during their preadult stages and dig burrows. Their nests consist of a crooked tunnel that descends into a round chamber. The adult crickets spend all day resting in their nests, only venturing out at dusk to feed. Field crickets eat leaves, but they will also take seeds, roots, fruit, and even animal matter. They are voracious

feeders, but do not cause any real damage to crops because they occur in relatively small numbers.

Summer song

At the beginning of the summer, the field crickets start to sing. Their song consists of a single, repeated note. While calling for a mate, male field crickets remain alert to what is happening in the immediate vicinity. If they sense a disturbance nearby, they quickly return to their burrows and hide until the danger has passed. If a rival male field cricket is causing the disturbance, the original male substitutes the repetitious mating call for a special warning call. If the intruder persists, the two males fight. These fights are surprisingly fierce, and often one of the combatants is seriously injured or killed.

Once the male has successfully attracted a female, he leads her down into his burrow, where he allows her to crawl onto his back and then mates with her. The female then seeks out a suitable site on which to lay her eggs. Using her needle-like ovipositor, she forces the eggs into the ground. A female field cricket can lay up to 200 eggs, which hatch after about a month into nymphs that look like miniature, wingless adults.

Initially field cricket nymphs live among the leaves on which they feed (they also provide concealment from predators). The nymphs molt seven or eight times, and when the cold season begins they dig a small burrow where they shelter from the cold through the winter. The following year they reappear and complete their development. At the end of the summer, after they have mated, the adult field crickets die.

Prize fighters

The aggressiveness that male crickets show to each other made them highly regarded in the Orient as fighting insects. The Chinese people selected several varieties and bred them to encourage their fighting qualities, and cricket fighting became the sport of kings. The Chinese designed special diets, such as flower soup, mosquitoes and human blood, for the most successful fighters. However, before a fight the field crickets were starved to increase their aggressiveness. The fight took place amid great ritual and festivity. The brief fight took place in a highly decorated bowl and usually ended in the death of one of the combatants.

ABOVE The house cricket has fully developed wings and long, angled hind legs. It hides by day and comes out at night to look for food. It has become a regular and unwelcome lodger in houses throughout the warmer parts of the world. They are indiscriminate feeders and will nibble almost anything, including clothing and paper.

An uninvited guest

Although house crickets live in houses—as their name suggests—they also live in shops, warehouses and farm buildings throughout the world. They are small in size, only reaching about 0.59-0.67 in. in length, and are pale yellow in color with brown markings. The house cricket originates in the subdesert regions of northern Africa and western Asia. Their present worldwide distribution can be directly attributed to human activity. Inadvertently packed in with cargo, these insects have settled in many countries, and they are now found in virtually all the warmer regions of the world.

The house cricket thrives in dark, warm places where it remains hidden during the day. At night it emerges to scavenge for food. In human dwellings, the house cricket often causes considerable damage because it eats a wide variety of foodstuffs. When large numbers of these crickets infest a house, foodstuffs, cloth, wool, paper and other organic materials rarely escape their attention for long.

The one redeeming feature of the house cricket is its melodious song. As usual only the male sings. In their natural habitats, the eggs of house crickets take up to 12 weeks to hatch, but because they now live predominantly in warm human habitations, house crickets are able to produce over five generations in a year.

LEFT Cave crickets have adapted to life spent in almost total darkness. Their antennae are extremely long, and their eyesight has become of secondary importance. All their limbs, especially the hind legs, are elongated, giving them great agility when scuttling over irregular rocky surfaces. Cave crickets are found in all regions.

They have lost most of their coloration and have evolved extremely long antennae and legs. Some species have also taken to living with humans, but they do not pose as big a problem as the house crickets because they are more fastidious feeders.

The males of some Oriental species are greatly prized and kept as caged pets because of their song. In Japan the crickets were kept in small bamboo cages. The manufacture of these cages became such an important industry that the cage makers had their own special trade guild.

Public enemy number one

Many people are familiar with the short-horned grasshoppers of meadows and plains, but few immediately associate them with the infamous locusts of biblical plagues, which even today cause crop damage of disastrous proportions. Locusts and grasshoppers belong to the superfamily of Acridoidea—one of the largest divisions in the order Orthoptera—with nearly 7000 species spread throughout the world. Although they are plentiful in warmer regions, acridids also inhabit most temperate countries. Of the 7000 species of locusts and grasshoppers, only about 20 are capable of causing large-scale damage. While most tropical areas suffer from at least one form of plague locust, Africa has six of the most damaging species, including the most destructive of them all—the desert locust.

The biblical locust plague is thought to have been caused by the desert locust, and with good reason: recent times have seen swarms containing roughly 40,000 million locusts—measuring nearly 400 square miles across. A swarm of this size is a great threat to humans since it requires nearly 89,000 tons of food per day—enough to keep 400,000 people alive for a whole year.

Since desert locusts inhabit desert and subdesert regions where rainfall is erratic, they travel en masse to increase their chances of survival as they search for food. They earn their worldwide reputation as public enemy number one, by ranging over 11,584,000

The wood cricket

The wood cricket occurs throughout southern Europe, ranging into western Asia and North Africa. In Britain it is restricted to parts of Devon and Hampshire. Adult wood crickets reach 0.27-0.4 in. in length and have a dark brown coloration with lighter markings. Neither male nor female wood crickets have wings. They live among the deep leaf litter of deciduous woodland, especially under oaks, holly and bracken around sunny clearings. They do not wander far from the dense cover provided by the undergrowth, and do not appear in exposed locations. They feed exclusively on dead leaves and associated fungi.

The life cycle of some wood crickets lasts two years, while all other crickets have only one generation per year. The wood cricket's eggs hatch in midsummer and by autumn the nymphs have reached their fifth or sixth molt. They overwinter at this stage and complete their development the following spring, emerging as full adults by July. The adults generally live until November, although some overwinter again, only to die early in the next spring.

Cave-dwelling crickets

Some species of cricket have become specially adapted to life in caves, especially in North America.

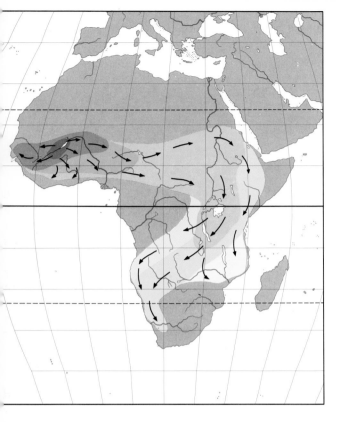

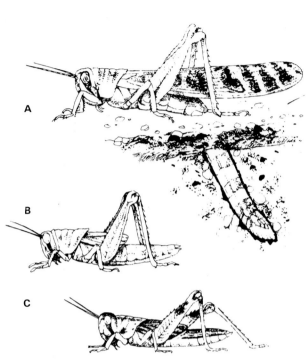

ABOVE **A recent swarm of African migratory locusts traveled across half the continent. The dark red area shows where the swarm started, and the lighter colors plot its spread over a 12-year period. Swarms of this size devastate crops and threaten thousands of people with starvation.**

ABOVE RIGHT **Female locusts have an extendible abdomen that they force into the earth in order to lay their eggs (A). Locusts change their coloration as well as their behavior, when they swarm. They are paler in their solitary phase (B) and grow darker (C) when they become gregarious.**

square miles of the Earth's surface and affecting more than 60 countries.

Protecting the eggs

All swarming locusts and grasshoppers experience the same basic life cycle. Female locusts are able to lay three egg pods during their lifetimes. They usually lay their eggs in holes in the ground—in groups, or pods, of between 20 and 100. After laying, a female locust secretes a foam that covers her eggs and plugs the hole—protecting the eggs from dehydration. The foam may also contain chemicals to repel parasitic microorganisms. When there have been repeated egg-layings in a small area, the density of egg pods on

the ground is as high as 1000 per square yard; egg fields are areas of ground that are packed with locust egg pods. The usual incubation period of the egg pods is 14-70 days, depending on the temperature, although some species lay eggs that remain dormant for up to three years.

Hoppers

Young locusts, known as hoppers, lack wings and reproductive organs, but otherwise resemble adults—except that their heads are large in comparison to their other body parts. A newly hatched hopper is pale green in color but gradually turns a darker shade as it grows. During its development it molts its chitinous body covering (exoskeleton) five times, emerging each time a little larger and a little more mature in appearance. During the hopper stage, locusts group together in "bands," which can contain as many as 20,000 hoppers on a single square yard. Hoppers feed voraciously on vast amounts of low-lying vegetation and constantly need to seek out fresh sources of food for growth.

As in other phases of a locust's life cycle, temperature plays an important part in the hoppers' feeding patterns. At night, bands of hoppers climb into

ABOVE The African migratory locust always starts swarming in the same region. All the swarms originate from the floodplains of the Middle Niger valley in Mali. Once it was realized that the locusts always swarmed from this area it was possible to control them to a certain extent. The dense laying pattern found in locust egg fields makes them very vulnerable to spraying from the air. The non-flying hoppers can also be doused with insecticide in this way.

tall trees and bushes to roost, and in the morning they all move around to the side of the bush that faces the rising sun. After they have warmed up, they leave their tree or bush·and resume their search for food—traveling or "marching" as a band. Hoppers rarely feed while they are on a march, but if they do it is appropriately called "snack-bar" feeding. The hoppers start feeding in earnest only when the day draws to a close.

Fledgling flight

After a young locust has completed its hopper stage, it passes through an intermediate or fledgling stage before it achieves full adulthood. Although fledgling locusts have wings and sexual organs, they are unable to breed for a further 40 days. The ovaries of the female locusts, though present, are underdeveloped to conserve energy, which they need for migration.

Swarms of fledgling locusts migrate vast distances—some have traveled as far as 3000 miles: one recent swarm flew across the Atlantic Ocean, from Africa to South America. Locusts are strong fliers, capable of traveling at speeds of over 11 miles per hour and remaining airborne for up to 17 hours. Despite their remarkable powers of flight, they rely heavily on favorable winds to aid their migration.

Although they are used to large numbers of fellow insects during their hopper phases, adult locusts are not usually social insects. But to prevent their swarms from breaking up, they temporarily set aside their natural preference for solitude and behave as social insects—stimulating other locusts to move with them.

Changing color

Locusts often undergo a color change as they develop from immature fledglings into sexually mature adults, usually reaching sexual maturity at the beginning of the rainy season. Sometimes, the change happens rapidly—an entire swarm may change color within a few days. Most hoppers blend in with their backgrounds, but as they reach adulthood their bodies take on striking colors; desert locusts, for example, change from pink to bright yellow.

Covering the world

With the capacity to lay over 200 eggs in her lifetime, a female desert locust can, theoretically, increase the number of locusts 100 times per generation. Assuming that there are equal numbers of males and females in a swarm, a swarm of 2 square miles could produce, in four generations, enough locusts to infest all 34 million square miles of the Earth's land surface.

At the weather's mercy

Despite their colossal breeding rate, most locusts of a new generation do not reach adulthood. They are at the weather's mercy, and have many enemies in the animal kingdom.

Female locusts devote much energy to finding the right egg-laying site (hence the phenomenon of repeated layings on the same egg fields) since they can carry their eggs for only three days before having to release them; if locusts have to leave their eggs on sun-baked or stony ground, they dry out before they can hatch. Although the eggs are laid in a foam case and have a thick leathery skin, they need moist conditions if they are to hatch; thus, scarcity of rain keeps the numbers of locusts in check.

A host of predators

Locust populations are kept under natural control by a host of predators, both large and microscopically small. Probably the most important is the locust fly—an ordinary-looking fly that resembles a common housefly. Female locust flies often hover above a group of egg-laying locusts, waiting for their chance to fly down and lay their own eggs on top of the locusts' egg pods. When the locust fly's eggs hatch, the maggots burrow down and feed on the unhatched locusts. Even if they do not actually eat all the eggs, the larvae's intrusion is usually sufficient to prevent any from hatching—as many as 20 percent of the eggs in a field can be destroyed by locust fly larvae. Blister beetles, a group of African beetles, have been responsible for the destruction of egg fields. Like locust flies, their larvae feed on locust eggs.

If locust eggs survive long enough to hatch, the young hoppers run the new risk of falling prey to marauding ants—and to each other: hoppers practice cannibalism even when there is an abundance of food. Fungi, viruses and bacteria present yet another threat,

ABOVE Migratory locusts make use of strong winds to assist their long, swarming journeys. Although they have well-developed wings, they could not sustain flight over 600-mile distances without considerable wind assistance.

BELOW After its fifth and final molt, a winged adult locust gradually emerges, and when it has secured itself to a branch it discards the old cuticle. Its new exoskeleton is soft, and the young locust is vulnerable to attack.

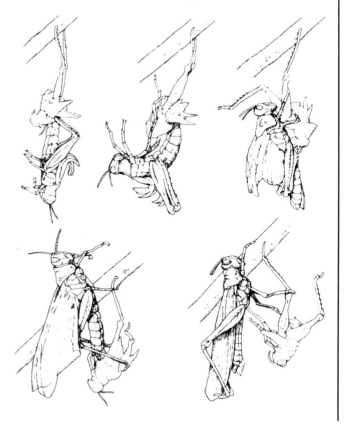

THE MOLE CRICKET
— A FORMIDABLE DIGGER —

The family Gryllotalpidae, or mole crickets, are large, burrowing insects that lead a subterranean existence. They are a cosmopolitan family, with various species in different parts of their range. Like the true moles, the mole crickets' limbs are highly specialized to meet the demands of their underground life-style. They have powerful, spade-like front legs, equipped with sharp, flattened spines that they use to "shovel" earth as they burrow. They also use their front legs to pull themselves along existing tunnels.

Protective covering

Mole crickets protect their thoraxes from the erosive action of the soil as they burrow with a tough carapace that is adapted from their cuticle. They have shorter antennae than other families of crickets, and their eyes are also reduced in size. To compensate for the lack of sense organs on their heads, the mole crickets' bodies have a covering of short, brown hairs that are sensitive to outside stimuli. These hairs give the mole crickets their dull-brown coloring and help to camouflage them.

Mole crickets are omnivorous, voracious feeders. They eat large numbers of insect larvae, other invertebrates, and also attack growing plants. Sometimes, mole crickets damage food crops, such as potatoes, sugar beets and strawberries; they also spoil garden lawns because of their burrowing nature.

Nocturnal creatures

Mole crickets are almost totally nocturnal and rarely appear during daylight. Certain species are capable of flight, and in warmer countries they are often attracted to the lights of houses. In parts of Africa, mole crickets occur in such large numbers that they constitute a "plague." But these occasions are rare, and the plagues never last very long.

Mating usually occurs in spring. Once the male mole cricket succeeds in attracting a female to his burrow with his mating call, he crawls out into the open and fertilizes her. After mating occurs, the fertilized female does not return to her own burrow but digs a new tunnel that ends in an egg

chamber up to 2 in. in diameter. The
male sometimes helps to construct the
new burrow and chamber. There is
only one wide entrance to the new
burrow. The female strengthens the
walls of the underground burrow by
mixing the soil with saliva before she
compacts it with her powerful forelegs.

Parental care

   When the female has completed the
egg chamber, she lays between 200 and
300 eggs. Mole crickets show strong
parental care, and the female carefully
tends and guards the eggs until they
hatch 20-30 days later. The larvae take
two years to complete their development.
They are small, dark creatures that
resemble their parents (except for the
absence of wings).

   After four weeks, the larvae leave the
egg chamber by digging tunnels for
themselves. The young disperse rapidly
in search of food and begin an
independent life. They spend the whole
winter feeding and only reach the
winged adult stage of their development
in the following year. Despite having
the external appearance of adults, their
reproductive organs are not fully
mature, and it will be another year
before they are able to breed.

TOP Mole crickets are nocturnal
creatures. They spend most of their
time in burrows. Their streamlined
shape enables them to travel more
easily down narrow tunnels.
ABOVE The forelegs of a mole cricket
resemble those of the mammalian
mole. They are powerful digging
implements, that are well adapted to
underground life.
RIGHT The mole cricket's egg chamber
is carefully constructed. The walls are
covered with a cement mixture that
the female produces by mixing her
saliva with soil.
LEFT The male mole cricket uses his
wings to call for a mate, but he does
not have a "mirror" to enable the
sounds to resonate. Instead his
burrow serves as the amplifier.

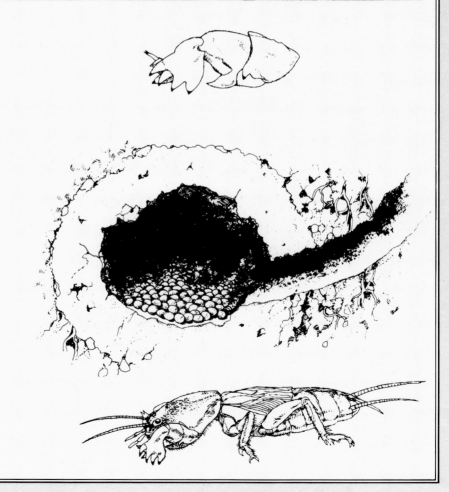

TOP The Egyptian grasshopper can reach 3 in. in length, and is often mistaken for a swarming locust. However, the Egyptian grasshopper rarely gathers in swarms, and only a few have ever been recorded.

ABOVE Short-horned grasshoppers, so called because of their short antennae, are common insects and they abound in meadows and fields. They never occur in large numbers and are not considered a serious agricultural pest.

destroying huge numbers of eggs, hoppers and adult locusts each year.

Birds eat thousands of locusts, both in the hopper stage and in the winged adult form. European storks, for example, consume huge amounts: 1448 hoppers were removed from the stomach of one captured stork. But humans are possibly the locusts' worst enemy. In many countries, humans compete with locusts for scarce food supplies, using technological methods such as fire, insecticides, aerial spraying, and even poison gas to control their numbers.

The winds that locusts use in their migrations often fail to carry them to suitable breeding sites. A swarm once ended up on the south coast of England, a most unsuitable location for a species used to desert heat. Entire swarms have been blown out to sea and drowned, but some are luckier—in one instance, a swarm landed on a boat in the mid-Atlantic, over 1000 miles from Africa. Sometimes up to 99.6 percent of a swarm die before reaching sexual maturity.

Nonswarming grasshoppers

The vast majority of locusts and grasshoppers are nonswarming, inconspicuous insects (strictly speaking, only swarming acridids are locusts). The Egyptian locust, a nonswarming species, is one of the largest European insects, measuring 2-3 in. in length. It usually inhabits hot, dry areas with little vegetation. Despite its large size, the Egyptian locust rarely causes damage to crops, since it does not associate with swarms of other Egyptian locusts at any stage of its life.

Cone-headed grasshoppers

With heads that are greatly elongated and pulled forward, cone-headed grasshoppers are among the strangest looking of all nonswarming grasshopper species. They are commonly found in damp fields.

Ground locusts are small insects—rarely more than an inch long—that live in all regions, in damp conditions and especially under leaves around the edges of ponds. Their heaviest concentration is in the tropics, where many species have humped backs with spines or high crests. Unlike true grasshoppers, ground locusts have forewings that are absent or reduced to mere pads; elongated projections from the thorax protect their hind wings. Both their sound-making and hearing apparatuses are missing.

MIMICS AND DECEIVERS

Stick insects and praying mantids are masters of deception.
The stick insects camouflage themselves by mimicking the
twigs on which they live, while the motionless, praying posture
of the mantis disguises a deadly hunter

All true stick and leaf insects belong to the order Phasmida and are collectively known as the phasmids. As their name suggests, stick and leaf insects resemble plants. Stick insects, also called walking sticks, tend to be angular and elongated. Some species grow to a length of 14 in., making them the longest but by no means the heaviest known insects. Leaf insects also have elongated bodies; flat abdomens, extended at the sides; and flattened and expanded legs. Most stick and leaf insects occur throughout the tropical or subtropical areas of the world, and most species live in Southeast Asia. All stick and leaf insects have two compound eyes, three ocelli, and thin, short antennae. The young, or nymphs, grow by stages.

Camouflaged for survival

The phasmids spend most of their lives on grasses, trees and shrubs. Because most species of stick and leaf insects lack effective weapons against predators, and do not have the agility to run or jump away, they have become specialists in "cryptic camouflage." In appearance, many species imitate twigs, branches, stems or leaves—an effective form of mimicry that renders the insects almost invisible until they move. Some species can change color to match their surroundings, and others gradually become darker in color as night closes in.

Detailed deception

Leaf insects have extremely flattened thoraxes, abdomens and leg segments although their feet remain undistorted. Their body outlines are interrupted by irregular indentations along all the edges of their bodies and limbs. Most adult leaf insects possess wings. Although not used for flying, they have evolved into instruments of pure deception. Unlike most other insects (that have the thickest vein along the leading edge of their forewings) the wings of leaf insects have the thickest vein running along the hind edge. When leaf insects fold their wings, the veins lie together giving the appearance of the central vein of a leaf. The illusion is enhanced by smaller veins radiating to the edges of the wings.

Most stick and leaf insects are nocturnal and move around only under cover of darkness. During the day they hang motionless by their hind limbs, with their forelegs stretched out in front of their heads. I

ABOVE The leaf insect is the true master of cryptic camouflage. Its body and legs have the exact appearance of real leaves. The small nibbled areas along its body imitate the effects of other insects feeding on a leaf.
BELOW Only discovered in 1914, the grylloblattids form a separate order of very primitive insects. They are about an inch long, and are usually pale brown or pale yellow in color.
PAGE 2383 Stick insects demonstrate extreme adaptation to life in the tropical forests. Protective coloration in some species has turned into realistic imitation of the foliage.

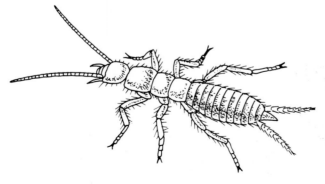

disturbed, they often just fall to the ground. At night, in order to remain as undetectable as possible, they move with small rocking motions, giving the impression of twigs or leaves swaying in the breeze.

Cannibals when crowded

Stick and leaf insects are too slow-moving to be effective predators, and they have not developed any specialized weapons to capture prey like their relatives, the mantids. Under normal conditions the phasmids are entirely vegetarian, but when kept in overcrowded conditions they become highly cannibalistic. Leaf insects feed exclusively on leaves. But because of their perfect camouflage, they occasionally take a bite out of another leaf insect.

Spiny stick insects—giant pincushions

Some of the largest insects in the world are stick insects. Among these are a few that break the "unarmed" rule. One American species produces a powerful irritant that it sprays over a distance of 12 in., to temporarily blind and choke any would-be attacker.

The Papuan spiny stick insects, found in Southeast Asia and Australasia, grow up to 10 in. long and measure over 1.5 in. across at their thickest part. Covered in spines and with powerful leg muscles, they are the porcupines of the insect world and have few natural enemies. Another large stick insect, called the Malaysian wood nymph, inhabits the forests of the Malaysian Peninsula. Also covered in spines, its body is bright green on top and dull green underneath. With an average body length of 8 in., a Malaysian wood nymph resembles a giant green pincushion. Like all stick and leaf insects, both of these monster species eat plants in all stages of their life.

Eggs glued to leaves

Most stick and leaf insects reproduce without fertilization by males (known as parthenogenesis) and in some species males do not exist. To complete their plant-like impersonation, the eggs of many species closely resemble seeds. Most female stick insects show no maternal instincts toward their eggs, and usually just flick them away with a sharp movement of the abdomen. Some ground-dwelling species use a spade-like appendage to insert the eggs into the soil or into a crack on a tree trunk. Others glue their eggs to suitable food plants.

INSECTS CLASSIFICATION: 5

Stick and leaf insects

The order Phasmida contains approximately 2500 stick and leaf insects. They are divided into 11 families grouped into two suborders: Timematodea and Phasmatodea. The suborder Timematodea contains only one family—nine species of small, wingless animals (possibly related to the earwigs) that live in California, Arizona and Nevada.

The suborder Phasmatodea has the order's remaining 10 families, of which the largest is the family Phasmatidae with over 500 species. The suborder contains such species as the Papuan spiny stick insect, *Eurycantha calcarata*; the Malaysian wood nymph, *Heteropteryx dilatata*; and the Macleays specter, *Extatasoma tiaratum*, of Australia. Leaf insects belong to the family Phylliidae; most of them belong to the genus *Phyllium*—for example, the giant leaf katydid, *P. grandis*.

Grylloblattids

The 15 species of grylloblattids form the small insect order Grylloblattodea. Measuring 0.8 to 1.2 in. in length, they occur only in the cool zone above the tree line in North America, Japan and Siberia. The species *Grylloblatta campodeiformis* is found in the Canadian Rockies.

Incomplete metamorphosis

The eggs take between six months and three years to hatch, depending on the species and on weather conditions. The young stick insects hatch via small trap-door structures in the egg's shell. Emergence is often a strenuous task for the hatchling. Although the trap-door opens easily, the hind legs of the nymph often get caught on the egg skin. If the nymph is unable to free itself from the egg capsule, it dies of dehydration or starvation. Most species rely on their small size and twig-like appearance to avoid detection. However, the newly hatched Macleays specter imitates a ferocious bull ant, discouraging any half-hearted forest predator. Stick insects grow by incomplete

metamorphosis: they develop in stages, slowly becoming more like the adults.

The grylloblattids

The order Grylloblattodea, as its name suggests, bears a similarity to two other groups of insects: the crickets (order Gryllidae) and the cockroaches (order Blattodea). Sometimes called "living fossils," they are thought to be the only members of the ancient order Protorthoptera.

The first of these insects, *Grylloblatta campodeiformis* (discovered in 1914 in the Canadian Rockies at an altitude of about 6500 ft.), derives part of its name from its resemblance to a cricket and a cockroach. It takes the final part of its name from a blind, wingless and pale-bodied insect called a campodeid. Since the discovery of this first insect a further 15 species, belonging to three genera, have been found in western North America, Japan and Siberia.

The grylloblattids are a recently discovered order of small, primitive insects no more than 0.8-1.2 in. long. They have flattened bodies—enabling them to squeeze under stones or into cracks in the ground— that are pale yellow in color. Unlike most species of insects, they only live above the tree line and they range right up to the permanent snow line. The harsh environments that grylloblattids inhabit are relatively poor in food resources. For this reason these insects must conserve as much energy as possible.

Grylloblattids are fully active at night, when they search for food, which includes both plant and animal matter. They are sensitive to external factors and require a constantly damp environment. They avoid strong light and even moderately high temperatures. Their optimum temperature, of about 37.4°F, is unusually low for an

ABOVE An earwig's most distinctive feature is its forceps, formed by the two unjointed cerci at the tip of its abdomen. The forceps are important in defense and in capturing prey. Earwigs have chewing mouthparts, and most are omnivorous.
ABOVE The European earwig is an omnivorous, nocturnal insect that has been introduced into South Africa and Australia. It molts four times before becoming adult. In temperate climates, its life cycle lasts for about one year.
FAR LEFT Stick insects use pigment cells beneath their cuticles to change color according to the temperature, humidity and light intensity.

insect. Grylloblattids are most active between the temperatures of 35.6° and 60.8°F. If the temperature rises above 82.4°F, grylloblattids often die. Because they live in the cold, they develop slowly. The females lay their eggs a year after mating, and the eggs hatch the following year. The nymphs take five years to complete their development, and molt eight times. The adult insect usually lives for another two years, although some individuals have lived for nearly nine years.

Earwigs

The order Dermaptera contains the inaccurately named earwigs. Although they have a tendency to crawl into dark crevices, earwigs have no particular preference for human ears (only a few such cases are known). Their name probably derives from "ear-wings," which describes the shape of their infrequently seen hind wings. The earwigs' favorite habitat is undeveloped flower buds, and a more likely explanation for their name is that it derived from the early Saxon word earedwic (*eared* meaning "bud" of any cultivated plant—especially corn—and *wic* meaning "dwelling place").

Practical pincers

The most characteristic feature of earwigs is the pair of large pincers, or forceps, positioned at the rear of their abdomens. Male earwigs have curved pincers, whereas those of the female are straight. Earwigs use these pincers for a multitude of purposes. During nocturnal hunting forays, earwigs use their pincers to hold and pin down their prey. They lift the prey toward their mouthparts by curling their abdomens over their thoraxes, in a similar way to scorpions. Earwigs also adopt this posture as a defensive stance when they feel threatened. The pincers are capable of delivering a sharp nip and are a useful defense weapon. The species of earwigs that have wings use their pincers to fold their hind wings underneath their shorter wing covers. These wing covers, called elytra or tegmina, are tough and leathery. Their hind wings are large and delicate, and it is from these that the earwigs derive their scientific name—Dermaptera (from the Greek *derma,* meaning "skin," and *pteron,* meaning "wing").

Flat, shiny bodies

There are about 1500 species of earwig and nearly all have elongated, robust, flattened bodies that may vary in length from about 0.1 in. to over 3 in. They are generally brown in color, and some species have a metallic luster. Earwigs have two compound eyes, but no ocelli. They hunt and move around by touch. Their antennae are constantly feeling out their surroundings, and they remain on the ground even when the earwigs are at rest.

Habitat

Earwigs live in all warm and temperate regions, but they are essentially warmth-loving insects and are at their most abundant in tropical and subtropical regions. However, they have adapted well and occur in most areas throughout the world. Some species live on mountains, even at snow level, while others have successfully colonized the seashore. Predominantly nocturnal, earwigs spend their days hidden in damp, sheltered cracks, under tree bark, in leaves, and below rocks and fallen trees. They often live in groups of up to 100 individuals. Some earwigs are poor fliers or even wingless, but have compensated for this by developing strong running legs that, together with their agile bodies, enable them to achieve fairly high speeds.

INSECTS CLASSIFICATION: 6

Earwigs

The order Dermaptera contains some 1500 species of earwigs, which are grouped into 11 families and three suborders. The first suborder, Forficulina, contains nine families, one of which—the family Labiduridae—included the giant earwig of St. Helena (an island in the South Atlantic Ocean) that is now probably extinct. The family Forficulidae contains the common earwig, *Forficula auricularia.* The second suborder, Hemimerina, contains the single family Hemimeridae, whose 11 species live as parasites on African giant rats. The third suborder, Arixeniina, also contains a single family—the Arixeniidae, which contains five species from Malaysia, Indonesia and the Philippines where they are parasitic on bats. Most earwigs live wherever it is warm—from temperate to tropical regions—though some species occur on high mountains near the snow line or along the seashore.

Living on rats and bats

One species of earwig shares the habitat of a Southeast Asian bat. Unlike most earwigs, its body is hairy and tubular. It feeds on dead skin, excreta and other waste products associated with the bats, and only lives in places where the bats roost. Another species is even more parasitic in its behavior. These earwigs live on the skin of South African giant hamster rats, where they feed on dead skin and bodily secretions. In this group, the young earwigs develop inside their mother's body where they feed through a type of placental connection that closely resembles the situation of mammals.

Maternal instincts

Earwigs use their multifunctional pincers during mating to hold the females as they perform their ritualized courtship dances. The females usually greatly outnumber the males in a given population, and have the ability to store the male's sperm inside their bodies for up to a month. They do this because they might only mate once, and that could happen before their eggs are ready to be fertilized. The females of most species lay between 20 and 50 eggs in a shallow burrow. Unlike most insects, female earwigs remain with their eggs, covering them with their heads and forelegs. Earwigs' eggs have thin shells and are highly susceptible to fungal infections and dehydration. The females constantly lick and touch their eggs to increase their chances of hatching.

Tasty offspring

Female earwigs are protective toward their eggs and will attack any intruder. The hatchling nymphs are also well-cared-for by the female, who covers them with her body for a few days or even weeks, licking them and keeping them clean. As the nymphs become more active, they move further away from the female until they become totally independent. At about this stage, the mother loses her maternal instincts and develops a distinctly cannibalistic approach to her brood, and the young earwigs scatter.

The nymphs are usually a small, pale version of the adults, although in some more primitive species the nymphs' pincers are long and segmented. The nymphs usually molt four or five times before they reach adulthood.

An extinct giant?

Most earwigs are small animals no more than one inch long. One earwig species, however, like other isolated island species, had evolved into a giant in the absence of local competition. On the remote South Atlantic island of St. Helena, the giant earwig, at 3 in. long, had few natural enemies. However, since humans have destroyed most of the animal's natural habitat and introduced several species of predatory vertebrates, it has probably become extinct. Recent expeditions have failed to discover any evidence of its continued existence. Another contributing factor toward the disappearance of the St. Helena giant earwig could be a result of overcollection by too many scientific expeditions eager to capture this giant curiosity. Attempts are being made to halt the destruction of what little natural habitat is left on the island, but it is probably already too late for the St. Helena giant earwig. Other unusually large earwigs do still exist in Australia, notably the aptly named *Titanolabis collossea,* which grows to approximately 2.8 in. in length.

ABOVE Whenever cockroaches are mentioned, people immediately think of dirty kitchen pests. In fact only a very few of the 3684 known species occur as pests in human habitations, and most are found in the forests of warmer regions. **Cockroaches are quite fastidious about their own cleanliness, and are constantly licking and wiping their antennae. Cockroaches excrete as they feed, causing health problems when they raid human food supplies.**

Cockroaches—the successful competitors

Cockroaches belong to the order Blattodea and are one of the most successful insect groups on earth. Highly adaptive, cockroaches have learned to exploit most environments. They occur from sea level to the tops of mountains as high as 6500 ft. Deserts, swamps, jungles, tundra, cities and isolated houses all provide a comfortable home for cockroaches. Some of the 3684 described species live entirely in caves, while some Asian cockroaches are completely amphibious. Only about one percent of species live in close contact with human beings, but that has been enough to gain them a bad reputation as food spoilers and disease carriers.

Age-old structure

Cockroaches first appeared some 340 million years ago during the Carboniferous period, and they have changed little since then. Although each species has adapted to its habitat, all cockroaches have basically the same shape. They have flattened bodies and enlarged thoraxes that act as protective hoods for their heads. Their heads are triangular, and they have flat faces with their mouthparts angled downward. They have two large compound eyes, and most species also

LEFT The large domestic American cockroach may have originated in Africa and spread to Europe in the holds of ships. It is found in warm, humid environments. Today this usually means sharing the homes of human beings.

BELOW LEFT The German cockroach is the smallest of the domestic cockroaches, no more than 0.4 in. in length. In this species, the female carries the egg sac, or ootheca, around with her until the nymphs hatch.

have two ocelli. If they have wings, the first pair has become leathery and forms a cover for their membranous hind wings. Only the large tropical species fly consistently well, and most cockroaches only use their wings as a kind of parachute when they jump.

Many shapes, sizes and colors

The heads and jaws of cockroaches resemble those of the related mantids, and, although the young of both insects develop in stages, undergoing incomplete metamorphosis, the similarities end there. The total length of cockroaches varies between 0.4 and 6 in. depending on the species and the requirements of its particular habitat. Burrowing cockroaches tend to be stocky and wingless, with strong spade-like limbs; tree-dwelling insects are slim, with long, slender legs enabling them to run fast; and species living under bark have flattened bodies. The majority of cockroaches have a brown coloration; the rest are pale green, brightly striped or spotted with black, yellow, or even red. Often, the backs of their elongated hoods have a decorative design, sometimes in strong metallic colors.

Strong digestion

Cockroaches are true omnivores and will eat anything—from other cockroaches to the plastic covering of electric cables. Some species, such as the wood-eating cockroach from Asia and North America, have a more specialized diet. Wood is a nutritious food if the tough cellulose can be broken down, but most animals cannot do this. The wood-eating cockroach has overcome the problem by employing a type of single-celled protozoan, which lives in the insect's intestines. These protozoa are small enough to break down the thick walls of the cellulose cells, releasing the nutrients that the cockroach absorbs.

Community living

Cockroach nymphs do not possess the intestinal protozoa at hatching, and acquire them only after eating the droppings of their parents. In order to survive, the young must remain near their parents, and a form of society develops. Only one other group of insects has made use of a similar relationship with microorganisms—the termites. It is thought that termites evolved from cockroaches, and that this is how the highly social behavior of the termites first started.

A taste for love

Many cockroaches perform an odd courtship ritual before they mate. The male taps the female with his antennae and suddenly turns around. The female then licks a glandular secretion on the male's back, while he bends his antennae backward and strokes her.

A protective coating

Most species of cockroaches lay eggs. The eggs pass out of the insect's reproductive system coated in a

INSECTS CLASSIFICATION: 7

Cockroaches and mantids

Cockroaches and mantids both belong to the order Dictyoptera, but each occupy their own suborder within it. More than 3600 species of cockroaches belong to the suborder Blattodea and are grouped in five families. They include the Cryptocercidae (wood-eating cockroaches) of North America and Asia; the Blattellidae, which contains the two domestic pest species—the oriental cockroach, *Blatta orientalis*, and the German cockroach *Blattella germanica*; two woodland species of the dusky cockroach, *Ectobius lapponicus* and *E. sylvestris*; and the Mediterranean marginated cockroach, *Hololampra marginata*; the family Blaberidae with the hissing cockroach, *Gromphadorhina portentosa*, from Madagascar that reaches 6 in. long; and the Blattidae that contains the American cockroach, *Periplaneta americana*, of tropical and subtropical America.

The mantids make up the suborder Mantodea which contains about 1800 species in eight families. Mantids occur in most warm regions (the majority are tropical), and include such species as the European praying mantis, *Mantis religiosa*, in the family Mantidae; the tiny *Perlamantis alliberti* of southern Europe and North Africa; and the dwarf tree mantis, *Ameles abjecta*, of North Africa and southwest Asia.

ABOVE The small furniture cockroach originated in the tropics, but is gradually becoming established as a pest in Europe. Advances in modern communications have meant that some cockroach species have been able to spread to even the most inaccessible corners of the globe, traveling on boats and even aircraft. Because of its highly adaptable nature, the cockroach is one of the few animals likely to survive any catastrophe.
PAGES 2392-2393 The head of the *Anamesia* cockroach points downward, protected by an outer carapace that extends from its thorax.

secretion that hardens to form a protective shell, creating an egg sac called an ootheca. The ootheca is usually deposited shortly after it is fully formed, although in some species the females carry it with them. Several species of cockroaches carry their eggs internally in a uterus or brood sac for the full gestation period. In one species, *Diploptera punctata,* the eggs are not only retained inside the body but actually derive nutrition from the mother while in the brood sac (the eggs themselves have insufficient yolk for complete embryonic development).

Female cockroaches display a certain amount of maternal care for their young. Even when not carried, the ootheca is often cared for until it hatches. The cockroach nymph goes through 6-12 molts before it reaches the adult stage. Each nymphal stage is clearly identifiable by the size of the developing wing pads. During their subadult stages, vast numbers of cockroaches are eaten by predators.

Family life

The female cockroach encourages her offspring to follow her in search of food before they have complete control of their limbs. The newly hatched young walk behind their mother on their tiny, fragile legs. At the first sign of danger, they quickly seek refuge behind her legs or underneath her wings. The young cockroaches mature slowly, molting 6 to 12 times before metamorphosing into adults. As the young grow, the amount of parental care that the females exercise gradually decreases.

Before they reach full adulthood, the young cockroaches become completely self-sufficient in defense and in feeding themselves. Cockroaches occur in small colonies of about 10 individuals. The members of the colony are all of the same age and, presumably, are members of a family group. They continue to demonstrate the gregarious behavior patterns that they learned as youngsters throughout their lives.

2391

ABOVE **The woodland cockroaches, including the dusky cockroach and the tawny cockroach, live among dead leaves in the forest undergrowth. These are the least-known species of cockroach because they are not found in human habitations. They feed on dead insects and have an important role in the recycling of decaying matter. Some woodland species have adapted very well to cold climates, and flourish in sub-Arctic regions.**

Transportation

In species of domestic cockroaches, limitations on the space in which they live forces different families to congregate into colonies that number hundreds or thousands of individuals. Because of their small environment, the adults and young of different families are forced to live in close proximity with each other, but there is generally no territorial or mating rivalry between individuals of the same species, nor any other type of observable specialization. Each individual cockroach lives in harmony with its neighbors.

The domestic cockroach

The term "domestic cockroach" refers to fewer than 10 species of cockroaches that have become successful at living in close association with humans (they thrive in the warm, humid conditions that humans prefer). Originating in the tropics, the domestic cockroaches occur almost everywhere. Because of their flattened bodies, they are able to climb into narrow crevices, behind cupboards, under floorboards and into drains and sewers. They are transported over long distances by humans in trains, buses, trucks and aircraft.

The domestic cockroaches have overcome their inability to survive outside warm habitats by adapting to living in buildings. Consequently, they have been able to colonize temperate and cold zones where they would otherwise have perished. Their artificial life inside houses, buildings and transport enables them to feed on the roam around in search of food. Because of their wide diet, they eat all accessible household foods, as well as papers, shoe polish, the bindings of books and ink. They will even devour the small rims of white skin at the roots of human fingernails.

A black name

The oriental cockroach is a notorious domestic pest. Often incorrectly called the "black beetle," it occurs worldwide except for the extreme polar regions. Growing to an average length of 0.8 in., the oriental cockroach has strong limbs with sharp bristles along their edges. The color of its outer cuticle ranges from dark brown to black (females are almost completely black in color) giving the oriental cockroach its popular name of "black beetle."

The oriental cockroach cannot fly; the male has small wings that do not reach the tip of its body, and the female has vestigial wings. Its wings are attractive in appearance, with rust-colored veins and an iridescent sheen. It has a pair of long, thread-like antennae on its head that carry sensitive receptors. As the oriental cockroach moves, it waves its antennae backward and forward in the air, detecting the slightest change in its surroundings. Despite its reputation, the oriental cockroach is clean in its habits. It constantly pulls back its antennae toward its mouth to lick them clean.

The oriental cockroach can be considered a useful domestic scavenger because it gets rid of decaying material. Unfortunately, it fouls the surfaces and exposed food that it touches with its own excrement and the filth that gathers on its feet. Cockroaches that wander over exposed foodstuffs transmit diseases, with serious implications for human health. The oriental cockroach is considered a significant carrier of many dangerous illnesses, including polio and several forms of salmonella food poisoning.

A case of unfair competition

One species often gains a decisive advantage over another by developing characteristics to suit a particular environment. The German cockroach does not exceed 0.4 in. in length. It has a yellow-brown body, distinctive, yellow-ocher rear wings and two large, dark oval shapes on the first segment of its thorax.

The German cockroach often shares the same habitat as the oriental cockroach, and has generally been overwhelmed by its larger and more robust cousin. But beginning in the 1980s, it has almost completely ousted the oriental cockroach from many regions, partly because of an adaptation that was previously considered to be of little importance.

The inner parts of the German cockroach's limbs act as suction pads by secreting an adhesive substance. Consequently, it is able to move rapidly over hard, glossy surfaces, such as tiled walls, polished furniture and glass. The modern home is increasingly full of such materials, giving the German cockroach a built-in advantage over other species in the competition for food, and its population has increased rapidly.

A heavy breather

The inch-long American cockroach, another common domestic pest, probably originated in Africa. Its body is uniformly light-brown in color, with well-developed antennae that grow to twice the length of its body. It has been carried by ships (where it is commonly found in holds) and established itself in several European ports. The minute furniture cockroach has reddish forewings, decorated with white spots, during its adult stage. It proliferates in tropical countries and has recently been introduced into temperate regions, where it is gradually becoming acclimatized.

The Malagasy hissing cockroach, a giant tropical species, has not spread from its primary habitat. When agitated or threatened, this 4.7-6-in.-long monster makes a threatening hissing sound, an unusual characteristic among cockroaches. The hissing cockroach produces sound by constricting the aperture of the breathing tubes, or spiracles, on the sides of its body. By "clenching" muscles in the abdomen, the insect forces air out of the narrow holes and hisses at its enemies.

The woodland cockroach

The least known of the domestic cockroaches is the woodland cockroach, commonly found in the thick carpet of leaves that covers forest floors. It leads an almost exclusively nocturnal existence, feeding mainly on the carrion of other insect species, which it locates through a well-developed sense of smell. In this way, it contributes to the rapid recycling of organic substances.

ABOVE Crested mantids are characterized by irregular, spiny projections on their lower body segments, as well as by their distinctive crest. Their long forelegs are held against their bodies in a "praying" position when the mantid is waiting for prey. The eyes of the mantid are large and because they are located on the side of the head, give excellent all-around vision. The mantid is able to pinpoint its prey without moving its head and betraying its position.

The dusky cockroach has a yellowish brown body color that provides particularly effective camouflage. It occurs in woodland habitats throughout Europe, from Lapland to the Mediterranean shores. The species *Ectobius sylvestris* is similar to the dusky cockroach. It thrives in warm, humid conditions and only occurs in the warm humid woodlands of central and southern Europe. *Hololampra marginata* is a small cockroach that grows to less than 0.4 in. in length. It ranges along the coastal regions of many Mediterranean countries. It has shiny, black forewings, the sides and veins of which are picked out in brilliant white, making it unmistakable.

The praying mantids

Mantids comprise 1800 or so species in the suborder Mantodea. They inhabit all the tropical

ABOVE The common praying mantis blends in superbly with the surrounding vegetation. All the nymphs are the same pale green color when they hatch, and later become darker, or take on a brown coloration, to match their particular habitat.

BELOW All mantids are very aggressive insects. The females sometimes attack the males during mating. Even though the males may be decapitated, nerve cells inside their bodies enable them to continue mating.

regions of the world, but few species have adapted to life in temperate regions. Mantids prefer the tropics, since their food supply—other insects—is less likely to be affected by changes in the weather. Although different mantid species have different decorative body colors, they generally resemble each other in structure. Sexual differences are marked in most species: males are more fragile in appearance and are usually smaller than the females.

The rather small, almost triangular, mantid's head has a pair of thread-like antennae of medium length and two large, usually protuberant, compound eyes; the size of the eyes indicates the role that good eyesight plays in a mantid's predatory life-style. Mantids' bodies are slender, with three thoracic segments, each of which shows a different development. The first is greatly elongated and tapering, in many instances making up more than half the insect's total length, while the other segments are small in comparison. Their mouths have particularly strong jaws that resemble those of cockroaches—superbly evolved for chewing; mantids are related to the cockroaches and share other similarities in development.

Evolutionary changes

Most mantids possess two pairs of well-developed wings, but it is not unusual to find species whose wings are either partly formed or entirely absent. Both pairs of wings usually contain different patches of color.

Through evolutionary development, mantids' forewings lost their function of flight and acquired instead a purely protective function—taking on the consistency of parchment. The membranous hind wings are usually folded like fans across large, pronounced veins that run lengthways along the wings. The mantids' long, mobile forelegs enable them to be identified at a glance, being their most prominent physical features. Their component parts and joints have undergone radical evolutionary changes: the femur—the large limb segment nearest to the body—is triangular in shape, frequently deeply furrowed and often dotted with strong spines; the next leg segment, the tibia, has more strong spines. The structure of the two leg segments and their intervening joints makes them one of the most efficient instruments of prey capture in the whole animal kingdom.

The different mantis species vary considerably in total body size. The tiny *Perlamantis*, for example, is no more than 0.6 in. long—possibly because it lives in the temperate regions of the Northern Hemisphere (which are generally too cold for mantids). At the other end of the scale is the gigantic *Idolamantis*, of the tropical rain forests of Africa, with a length of over 6 in. However, despite their varying sizes, the majority of mantid species exhibit remarkable similarities of behavior.

Common European praying mantis

The most interesting aspects of mantis life-styles are exemplified in the behavior of the most famous mantid species, the common European praying mantis. The species usually lives among leafy branches and on blades of grass throughout southern Europe; it prefers to rest in strong light and often remains motionless for hours, as if sunbathing. When the mantis rests, it holds its forelegs side by side in an extended position—it is this attitude of prayer, rather than its behavior, that gives the species its name.

Ferocious predators

Praying mantids are highly effective predators, some of the most ferocious in the animal kingdom: with their perfect natural camouflage they blend into their backgrounds, where they wait, motionless, for their prey. Thus a mantid's "sunbathing" routine is merely a device to trick an unwary victim into a false sense of security. While it holds its body still, a praying mantid constantly watches its victim with its large, compound eyes. Mantids' eyes are keen, and their location on the side of the head provides excellent all-around vision—they can keep track of their prey without having to move their heads.

All mantids are carnivores. They feed mainly on other insects—even large ones such as butterflies, grasshoppers and beetles. When an unsuspecting victim approaches, a mantid launches itself toward it at a great speed, with its forelegs extended forward. It throws its forelegs around its prey's body and sinks a row of long spines into its victim, preventing any possibility of flight. Once its prey is immobilized, the mantid drags it slowly into dense foliage and eats it. Powerful jaws make short work of the toughest exoskeletons, although mantids are sometimes choosy feeders that leave prey half eaten.

Predator as prey

In spite of its aggressive behavior and natural camouflage, a common mantid is not entirely safe from predators. Its most dangerous enemies are species of the digger wasp family that paralyze prey with their stings and feed their helpless victims to their larvae. When a wasp threatens it, a common praying mantis often assumes a defensive posture and confronts its attacker. Rising up to its fullest height, it holds itself erect on its slender back legs, spreading out its brilliantly colored hind wings and extending its forelegs. More often than not, a mantid's posturing is ineffective, and it falls victim to an equally deadly foe.

Natural camouflage

At its simplest, mantid camouflage takes the form of protective coloring. Common praying mantids share this characteristic with many other species, including *Iris oratoria*, an inhabitant of several Mediterranean countries. The species is characterized by its long forelimbs and by two brilliant violet spots—one on each hind wing. The mantid usually hides its spots beneath camouflaged forewings, but if it is threatened it reveals the spots, which resemble two large eyes, and intimidate its attacker. The species shows a remarkable variation in average mantid coloring, faithfully imitating not only the basic colors of its habitat but all the subtle hues of the vegetation.

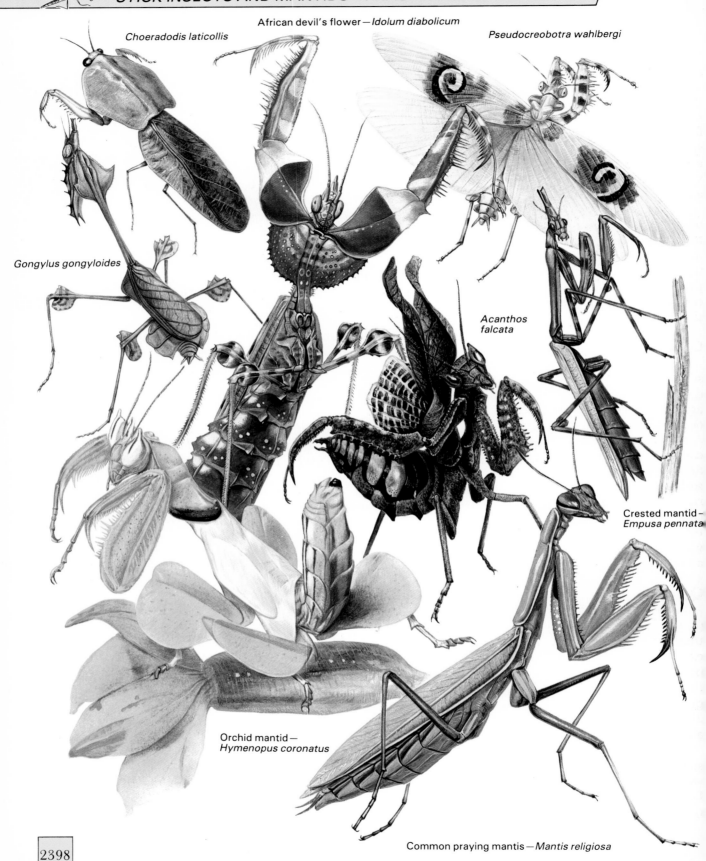

African devil's flower—*Idolum diabolicum*

Choeradodis laticollis

Pseudocreobotra wahlbergi

Gongylus gongyloides

Acanthos falcata

Crested mantid—*Empusa pennata*

Orchid mantid—*Hymenopus coronatus*

Common praying mantis—*Mantis religiosa*

An early evolutionary adaptation among mantids that has made them a successful order of insects can be seen in species living in the heart of luxuriant tropical forests. Besides their usual color camouflage, these species possess a number of useful strategic accessories. They imitate their surrounding vegetation with large leaf-shaped prothoraxes or extra-long, thorn-like femurs.

The species *Idolum diabolicum* are common inhabitants of tropical rain forests. Their remarkable swollen femurs, shaded in tones of pink and violet, are easily mistaken for the flowers of their host plants. However, the evolutionary adaptation of *Idolum diabolicum* could prove to be its downfall: a small change in the environment may cause the species to become extinct, since it would be unable to adapt to its modified habitat.

Courtship: a hazardous affair

Male mantids find courtship a hazardous affair since they risk being eaten by their partners before, during or after mating. A female that is hungry or agitated may attack and eat her suitor—although this occurs less frequently than is commonly believed.

A male mantid approaches a female quietly and cautiously from behind and, when he is close enough, he jumps onto her back. He is smaller than his mate, so he is usually able to find a position beyond her reach. During mating, the female mantid enters a calm, trance-like state, but as soon as the male has released his sperm, she becomes violent. Without wasting time, the male thrusts himself off his partner and runs to safety.

Quick-exit eggs

Praying mantids deposit their eggs in a tough egg sac (or ootheca) that is unusually large—larger sometimes than the insect itself. Soon after fertilization, a female excretes a thick, sticky substance from special glands in her abdomen; the substance solidifies on contact with the air, forming a type of cylindrical capsule that is greenish gray in color. The female mantid lays her 200-400 eggs in the center of the capsule before abandoning it among branches or in undergrowth.

Mantid eggs are formed from tiny plates that lie in such a way as to provide easy exit for the nymphs when they hatch at the end of the following spring. Usually all the eggs hatch at the same time and the nymphs disperse quickly into surrounding vegetation

ABOVE The female mantid lays 200-400 eggs in a toughened egg capsule, or ootheca, which is then abandoned in the foliage or undergrowth. The young nymphs are born with fully developed forelegs, and begin hunting soon after hatching. Like many mantids, this species, *Iris oratoria*, has two bright spots on its hindwings. When the mantid is threatened, it unfolds its hind wings, revealing these two large "eyes." Sometimes an enemy is intimidated and leaves the mantid alone, but this defense mechanism is usually ineffective.

—before falling victim to their brothers and sisters. Despite their small size (0.1 to 0.2 in. in length), they resemble adults in their general appearance, the only differences being an underdeveloped thorax and an absence of wings. The wings and thorax develop gradually in the course of following molts.

The natural ferocity of mantids is apparent even at birth. During their first phase of development, the tiny mantid nymphs feed mainly on aphids, and in some regions they play an important role in limiting the populations of the pests.

At the beginning of its life, a mantid nymph is pale green in color. During the course of successive molts it turns either a darker green, or develops a brown coloring—whichever provides the more effective camouflage.

Tree mantids

Most of the 1800 species of true mantids inhabit their primary environments, in hot regions amid thick vegetation (a species' primary environment is the one in which it has experienced various evolutionary changes before achieving its modern form).

Tree mantids are admirably adapted to tropical forests, woodlands and dense undergrowth. In such an environment, danger is ever-present.

The greatest differences between male and female mantids of the same species occur in one of the largest tree mantids—the species *Ameles abjecta*, common to the dry woodlands of North Africa and southwest Asia. The males have slim bodies and well-developed wings, whereas the females are very fat, with swollen abdomens, and their wings are reduced to mere stumps.

Rock mantids

Rock mantids are terrestrial insects that live in desert or semidesert environments. Zoologists believe that these creatures represent the highest form of mantis evolution, since they display unusual predatory behavior and peculiar body structures. Rock mantids have small wings, and, unlike tree mantids, they move with remarkable speed. They have highly developed hind legs, as well as strong predatory limbs—adapted for seizing prey after a fast chase. Female rock mantids cover their egg capsules with sand and gravel and take care of them, instead of abandoning them like other species.

Primitive mantids

A species of Australian mantid has many primitive anatomical characteristics and is considered to be a living example of the probable ancestors of the suborder Mantodea.

The small and primitive *Perlamantis alliberti* inhabits the warm and semiarid areas of southern Europe and North Africa. It is classified as a primitive species because its wings and forelegs are underdeveloped.

TOP The cryptic camouflage of mantids is sometimes very specific, and does not always mimic green plants. At rest, the species *Geomantis larvoides* could easily be mistaken for a seed pod or a piece of dead wood.

LEFT The characteristic triangular head means that mantids have very powerful jaws and are able to bite through the toughest exoskeleton. Although they are very aggressive predators, mantids quite often leave prey only half consumed.

THE FORTRESS BUILDERS

The towering mud nests that termites build are among the most impressive structures created by any insects. Each one is a fortress at whose heart lies entombed the colony's only egg producer—the giant queen termite

The 2300 species of the order Isoptera are land-dwelling insects that generally lack eyes and wings. Commonly known as termites, they derive their popular name from the Latin *termes*, a word that was applied in ancient times to any small creature, such as termites, woodworm beetles and the larvae of small butterflies.

Termites range throughout the world, but they mainly occur in the tropical zones of Africa, Southeast Asia, Australia and the Americas (except for Canada). Despite their preference for warmer climates, the termites have penetrated into cold, mountain regions. For example, some North American species have been discovered on the Rocky Mountains at an altitude of 6500 ft.

Resemblance to ants

Termites share a number of common features with ants. Both ants and termites behave as social insects. They pack themselves together into enormous colonies, in which each individual has a strictly regulated social position in the nest. Each termite has a basic task that ensures the smooth running of the colony. The colonies inhabit nests that consist of extensive systems of galleries in the soil or wood; termites also build large nests above ground that tower upward in elaborate structures.

Ants and termites live in a strict hierarchical order and divide into four biologically and socially distinct castes—the king and queen (reproductives), the supplementary reproductives (these develop in colonies that have lost a king or queen), the soldiers and the workers. Each caste has a definite social function in the running of the colony—whether providing food, building or repairing nests.

In both ants and termites, the colonies rely on the queen to produce the eggs. However, where queen ants mate only once, queen termites continue to mate throughout their lives with their partners, the king termites. Periodically, sexually mature, winged termites swarm out from their established colonies and mate, each pair helping to establish a new colony.

Sterile caste

Although most members of the ant and termite nests have reproductive organs, they are sterile because their drastically reduced gonads make them incapable of mating. Normally, the termite colony contains almost three million sterile termites, each contributing to the general management of the community by providing food, building and repairing the nests and caring for the offspring; members of the soldier caste are the defenders of the community.

Despite the external similarities in their social behavior, it is generally recognized that the termites are very remote from the order Hymenoptera (which includes the ants). The fossil evidence of the termites dates from the Miocene, Oligocene, and Eocene epochs almost 55-27 million years ago. In the course of their evolutionary history, termites have evolved an organizational structure and behavior pattern very similar to that of ants, although the two groups have developed independently of each other. The likely reason for their development of similar but separate behavior and characteristics (called their convergent evolution) is that ants and termites were confronted with the same environment and adopted similar solutions for identical problems.

Mole-like

Termites share similar external features and behavior patterns with the insectivorous, underground orthopterans known as the mole cricket. Both have developed similarly shaped front limbs to help their burrowing activity.

Close examination of the termites' outward appearance demonstrates they are easily distinguishable from ants. For example, termites' bodies are colorless and almost transparent, making them appear white or yellow in color. They also lack compound eyes, which are present and well developed in ants. As in most families of the order Hymenoptera, the ant's thorax is clearly divided from the abdomen by a narrow feature known as the petiole.

Gradual change

Ants belong to the "higher" insects, and their bodies undergo a complete metamorphosis or holometabolism during their development into adulthood. They experience many larval and pupal stages during their growth, each of which differs greatly from the previous stage. Termites undergo a less dramatic series of changes during their metamorphosis into the adult stage. The earliest stage of their metamorphosis is the larval stage. Despite their small size, the larvae already possess many adult characteristics.

Termites are close relatives of the cockroaches, but differ from the cockroaches in having two pairs of membranous wings and no ovipositor or external genitals. Because of their similarity to cockroaches, termites have been mistakenly described as "social cockroaches." The flying apparatus of the termites and cockroaches is primitive in structure, their veined wings rest in the same position, and the shape of their abdominal segments is identical. In addition, the complicated digestive system of the termites resembles primitive wood-eating cockroaches.

Higher termites

Termites subdivide into higher and lower termites, depending on the complexity of construction and management of their nests, the size of the nests and specialization of individuals. The 1639 species of higher termites belong to the family Termitidae. They are the most advanced termites in evolutionary terms; members of the family Termitidae comprise more than 70 percent of known species living in the warm regions of Asia, Africa, America and the Pacific Islands. They nest in trees, surface mounds or underground chambers, feeding on dead wood, grass, leaves, humus and other organic matter.

Intermediate levels of termites include the sawtooth termites of South America, the damp-wood termites and the harvester termites, which range through Africa, Asia and the Middle East. The 350 species of the family Kalotermitidae, commonly known as the dry-wood termites, are at the lower end of the evolutionary scale. They infest plantations and building timbers, and build their nests in dead branches.

Darwin's termite

The family Mastotermitidae, or Darwin's termite, has only one living representative—*Mastotermes darwiniensis*. Indigenous to the southern regions of the Australian continent, it has primitive body characteristics and feeding habits, mainly consuming wood and the pests of many materials.

Termites differ greatly in size according to their family. They generally range from 0.16 or 0.2 in. in length to a maximum of 0.8 in., but the mature queen termite reaches 5.5 in. in length. There is remarkable variation in shape between individuals of the same species. For example, the different castes of reproductives, soldiers and workers all vary in

ABOVE Soldiers of the fungus-growing termites guard columns of workers as they travel outside the nest in search of food for the colony. They are larger in size than the workers and have formidable, asymmetrically overlapping jaws.
PAGE 2401 The termite nest of the large African species *Bellicositermes natalensis* towers over 16 ft. above the surrounding savannah. The outer wall of the nest may be nearly 16 in. thick. Termite hills are completely enclosed, with no direct entrance to the outside world. A series of underground galleries leads from the inside to the various sources of food, usually processed from roots or dead logs.

appearance and development. The reproductives are fully winged; the supplementary breeders have small, pale bodies with reduced eyes and fleshy, non-functional wings; the workers and soldiers are small, wingless creatures (the workers have large heads with powerful mandibles).

The worker class

Apart from the immature insects, the rest of the nest is made up of the sterile castes. The workers are the least specialized members of the colony, living exclusively underground in darkness. Because of their shadowy environment, worker termites have a pale, yellowish white exoskeleton. They have large, toughened heads and lack compound eyes; usually, they have small

both the reproductives and the soldiers is their most important and demanding task, as the survival of the community depends on the workers' ability to find wood, the basic food of almost all the termites.

There is also subdivision of labor within the worker caste. Many species of termites have two classes of workers, large workers and small workers. They are distinguished from each other by their size and by their limbs and mouthparts.

The soldiers

When a termite nest reaches a certain population level, the queen produces a third type of termite. Commonly known as soldier termites, they protect the nest, the food supplies and the king, queen and workers. Unlike the other termites, soldiers have greatly enlarged, armor-plated heads. Sometimes, they have special head glands from which they can squirt a defensive secretion at their enemies.

The soldiers are usually larger than the workers. Like the workers, they have colorless abdomens, but their heads are darker in color than the rest of their bodies because they have a thicker, tougher layer of exoskeleton. Unlike the other termites, soldiers have large, powerful biting or snapping jaws, providing formidable weapons and representing their sole means of defense.

In the more primitive species of termites, soldier termites can appear at any stage of the colony's development. In the higher species, they appear at a precise point in the expansion of the new nest. However, all termite soldiers have to go through two stages of growth before they mature. The first is called the white-soldier stage, when the termites are usually pale, colorless and lacking the typical hard, external skeleton of the adult. The white-soldier stage is usually brief—in most species lasting only about two weeks and in some as little as a week. During this time, the termites eat little or nothing at all.

White-soldier termites

White-soldier termites frequently develop from ordinary workers, but among some species they arise from larvae. Both types of development can occur in a single nest, but do not always do so. In some species the larvae take on special characteristics after the first molt. Soldiers can be of either sex, but usually the soldiers of one species are all the same sex.

ABOVE Columns of workers of the snouted termite genus *Hospitalitermes* forage for lichens and other vegetation on the forest floor and around tree trunks. Both sides of the column are guarded by "nasuti" soldiers, which, although blind, can accurately fire sticky, poisonous secretions through their snouts at any predator that approaches. Their discharges quickly immobilize the enemy, allowing them to assault the predator with their strong mouthparts.

ocelli or simple eyespots whose precise significance is still unknown.

Unlike the worker ants and bees of the order Hymenoptera, the worker termites are sterile males or females. The termites only reproduce through fertilization. In the order Hymenoptera, the eggs that hatch female ants (either a worker or queen) have to be fertilized, while those that produce male ants are unfertilized, parthenogenetic eggs (the queen produces them without having to be fertilized by a male).

Diverse duties

The workers carry out a wide range of duties; they look after the eggs, care for the young larvae until they become independent, build, repair and clean the nest and provide food. The mouth-to-mouth feeding of

Once the white soldiers have become adults, their entire lives are devoted to protecting the nest. Their bodies become so specialized that the insects are unable to feed themselves. They can only eat regurgitated food, and rely on the worker termites to feed them.

The soldiers' tasks include the defense of the royal reproductives, stored foodstuffs, the nest itself and the internal galleries leading to the entrance. They also guard the columns of worker termites as they proceed to and from the nest in search of food.

Asymmetrical jaws

In some species of termites, the soldiers' jaws asymmetrically overlap. Their left jaw is longer than the right jaw, bends in the middle and straightens up again at its tip. During combat, the soldiers of the termite groups Capritermes and Pericapritermes snap their overlapping jaws open and shut rhythmically with great vigor, producing a loud noise audible from a distance of some yards away.

As the soldiers attack, their jaws lunge sideways to snap shut around the intruder's body, chopping it in half. Termites of the genus Macrotermes, such as the *M. bellicosus* (a common species in equatorial Africa), have enormous heads with wide jaws that are elongated, sickle-shaped or sword-shaped; they are always pointed and sharp as razors.

Blind valor

Like other members of the sterile castes, the soldiers are blind. Whenever intruders enter their nest, the soldiers immediately sense their presence with powerful, sensory receptors that cover their antennae. The sensory organs of the soldiers direct them to the site where the intrusion is taking place. The main enemies of the termites are aardvarks and pangolins, as well as reptiles and amphibians.

But the termites' most formidable foes are other social insects, particularly army ants and chirping ants. The army ants move in family units of over one million individuals and at a speed of about 66 ft. per hour, devastating everything in their tracks. Usually, ants attack the upper part of the termites' nest, where the building material has not dried completely.

Erecting barriers

During an attack, the worker termites at the center of the nest erect barriers to protect the royal chamber

INSECTS CLASSIFICATION: 8

Termites

The order Isoptera contains about 2300 species of termites in seven families. The most important is the family Termitidae (higher termites) which has over 70 percent of termite species and includes the fungus-growing termite, *Macrotermes bellicosus*, of Africa. The other families are the Serritermitidae (sawtooth termites) containing only one species, the *Serritermes serrifer* of South America; the Rhinotermitidae (damp-wood termites); the Hodotermitidae (harvester termites); the Termopsidae (rotten-stump termites); the Kalotermitidae (dry-wood termites); and the Mastotermitidae, which has just one species, the Darwin's termite, *Mastotermes darwiniensis*, of southern Australia.

and some of the cells where the larvae rest. The main body of soldiers flanks itself across the outer tunnels and attempts to stem the invading tide. Because they are specialized, the blind soldiers' instinct for survival means that many soldiers mistakenly attack each other during battle instead of the invading ants.

Despite having well-developed eyes and greater agility, it is unusual for an invading army of ants to completely destroy a termite colony. The soldier termites of the genus Cryptotermes lack jaws altogether, but compensate for their deficiency with enormous, strong, cylindrical heads that they together use to block up the outer entrance and prevent the enemy from entering the tunnels inside the nest. Once the danger is over, the surviving workers repair the damage to the nest. The queen continues to lay eggs, and the nest prospers as it did before.

Chemical warfare

Certain species of termites defend themselves with complex and deadly chemical weapons. The soldiers of the primitive Darwin's termite in Australia have two specialized types of glands inside their mouths. These produce a mixture that forms a gummy substance on contact with the air; the termites use this sticky weapon to trap the enemy before snapping them with their

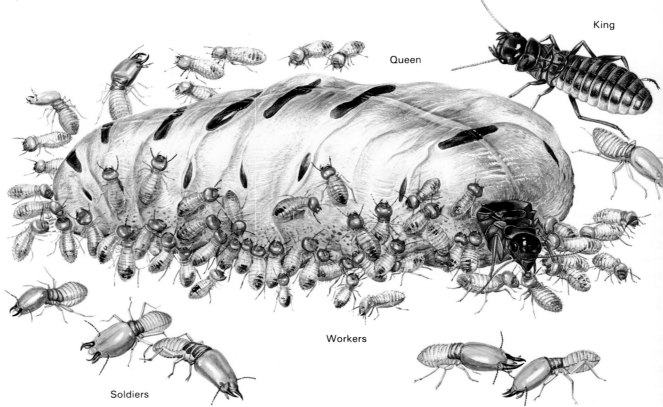

King

Queen

Workers

Soldiers

jaws. Many large species of termites shoot sticky secretions at their enemies, which they manufacture in highly developed glandular systems that occupy the greater part of their abdomens.

The termites' use of secretions as a weapon sometimes proves inconvenient because both the attacker and the defender can become hopelessly stuck in the sticky mass with no possibility of escape. The sacrifice of soldier termites does not unduly harm the economy of the termite nest, as the fallen are replaced quickly, re-establishing the original equilibrium among the castes.

Some termites, especially the members of the family Rhinotermitidae, have an enormous, external gland (fontanelle) in a cleft at the front of their large heads, from which they secrete gum. During an attack, they shoot the gum outward at their enemies, using strong muscles adapted for the purpose. Termites that squirt defensive secretions usually have drastically reduced jaws, although these do not completely lose their original biting function and the termites still use them to finish off any victim that survives the gum.

Pointed weapons

The most unusual members of the military caste are the large-nosed soldiers, or "nasuti," which give their

ABOVE During the incubation of her eggs, the workers of the termite group *Bellicositermes* support the enormously swollen abdomen of the queen by standing underneath her. The queen becomes so fat after laying her first eggs that she has to remain immobile for the rest of her life, and her sole function is to produce millions of eggs. A nucleus of worker termites feed and clean the queen, frequently moving her and carrying away the eggs that she produces. They are watched over by several soldier termites. The king, the only fertile male in the colony, always lives beside the queen.

name to the subfamily Nasutitermitinae. Although they are small and practically jawless, they have large, pear-shaped heads that elongate at the front and downward to form a long, conical protuberance.

The pointed snout or nose of the nasuti is hollow inside, connecting directly to a special, frontal gland in the head. The frontal gland is well developed in the nasuti, and secretes a special, sticky substance that they squirt out of the tip, like a water cannon. They can fire the glue-like substance over a distance of many inches at any unsuspecting attacker that they come across. As the projectile is launched, a volatile substance spurts out at great speed into the colony and acts as a chemical signal to the other soldiers to rush to the spot where the attack by predatory ants is taking place.

Nasuti cannot discharge their secretions in quick succession but only in a few bursts. When their round of ammunition is exhausted, the soldiers beat a rapid retreat. The soldiers of all species of termites display a common characteristic—they are incapable of finding their own food but must be fed mouth-to-mouth by the workers (in a system that is known as trophallaxis). The soldiers have the capacity to feed themselves, but, even though their mouths are theoretically capable of taking food independently, they do not know how to do so.

Digestion

Worker termites feed on the wood of living trees, dead tree stumps, logs or wooden buildings. Some species prefer wood that is either wet or dry; other species feed only on dry or fresh leaves and a sugary liquid that oozes from tree trunks, flowers and grass. Darwin's termite supplements its diet of wood with the fruits of special fungus gardens in its nest. But it has ceased to be strictly vegetarian and eats a wide variety of substances, seizing and chewing with its strong jaws any material that it finds.

Naturally, Australian farmers regard Darwin's termites as pests, but they are extremely difficult to combat. During raids, a single colony, consisting of more than a million individuals, tirelessly devour lumber, fences, rafters, hides, wool, food of every kind, paper, excrement, sacks, bones and, if there is nothing else to hand, the plastic insulation on electric cables and telephone wires.

Processing wood

Dead wood is the main part of the termites' diet. Worker termites have the sole task of searching for food and feeding the colony. The simplest way to transfer food is without processing it, but worker termites often swallow wood, which they then digest partially and transform into a milky-white liquid containing minute fragments of vegetable matter. The workers use the liquid to feed the other members of the community by the process of oral regurgitation (more accurately "stomodeal regurgitation," since the first segment of the termite's digestive tract is known as the "stomodeum").

Although the vast majority of termites are wood eaters, their digestive enzymes are incapable of breaking down the main component of their food, cellulose—a hard substance found in plant matter. Like the wood-eating cockroaches, the termites have overcome this difficulty by adopting an extraordinary system to digest cellulose.

The termites first break down cellulose into smaller molecules, or sugars, with the help of micro-organisms, or protozoa, that live in the termite alimentary canal. The breakdown of cellulose produces an enzyme called cellulase, which the termites can digest almost completely.

BELOW The first-born worker termites that the queen produces are unable to break down cellulose in wood, the main component of the termites' diet. During their early stage of growth, the young feed on a liquid (A) that oozes continually from the end of the queen's digestive canal (B). The workers become increasingly self-sufficient in seeking food and begin to collect it to regurgitate for the helpless royal couple.

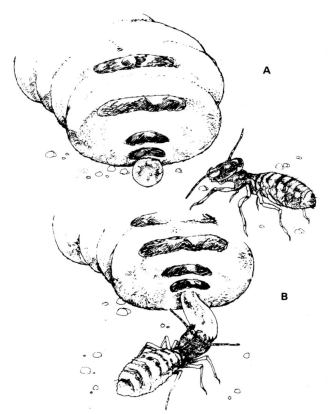

ABOVE **Trophallaxis, or food exchange, is the usual method of feeding the royal couple and the soldiers. The workers regurgitate a liquid, with a high protein content, directly into the mouths of the other members of the colony. Direct oral regurgitation enables the termites to circulate "pheremones" throughout the community. Pheremones act as social hormones within the** bodies of the termites, passing genetic information that regulates their activities.

FAR RIGHT **The tunnels and interconnecting chambers of their nest insulate the harvester termites from the outside world. The tunnels link the central, royal chamber with underground sources of food, forming a closed environment where the air is stagnant and light never penetrates.**

Permanent lodgers

The protozoa live in a state of mutual dependence with their termite hosts. These unicellular organisms belong to the flagellate group Hypermastiginae; they are easily recognizable by a thick profusion of long, whip-like appendages on the sides of their bodies. The degree of cooperation between these very different organisms is great. The termite provides the protozoa with an environment of uniform temperature and humidity as well as endless supplies of food. For their part, the protozoa and bacteria enable the termites to digest a food that would otherwise prove indigestible.

The system of mutual interdependence and mutual benefit is called symbiosis. The termite groups that adopt the system of symbiosis invariably have the protozoa in their gut, the organisms being transmitted from one generation to another through the secretions from the alimentary canal that feed younger workers. At birth, the larvae lack these intestinal protozoa and are fed by the workers with a liquid food that they secrete from their abdomen in a process known as proctodeal feeding.

A diet of decay

Some smaller termites have an exclusive diet of leaves and other decaying vegetation. They do not need protozoa in their gut because they rely on the action of bacteria, fungi and molds to break down the plant material they feed on. Termites, particularly the Macrotermitinae of the family Termitidae, live in underground chambers that prove suitable for the growth of a special fungus.

The fungus grows on the feces of the termites, breaking down the remaining cellulose in the feces that has remained undigested. The termites then eat the processed feces and digest the nutrients broken down from the cellulose. The fungus is unique to these termites.

Life in a termite hill

A new colony begins when a large number of sexually active, winged adults swarm from their original nest. In the species *Macrotermes bellicosus*, which is among the most common species of termites in Central Africa, the breeding behavior corresponds exactly with that of the higher termites. After swarming has occurred, the males and females—who at this point in their lives are identical in shape and outward appearance—pair off to mate.

There is a distinctly marked season of the year during which the larvae belonging to a nest reach their final stage of development and transform into winged adults. The larvae gather together and move to the outskirts of their overcrowded nest. They take no food and empty the final parts of their alimentary canals before metamorphosing into winged, adult reproductives. These adults spend a certain amount of time within the nest before swarming. During this

time, they stretch their flying apparatus by forcing air into the trachea that run along their wings.

Royal couple

The pairing of winged reproductives will form the future royal couple and create new nests. When swarming about in their old nest, the male and female reproductives are almost indistinguishable in shape. They have squat, bulky bodies supported on strong bristly legs with two pairs of delicate, slightly iridescent wings. Their wings are unequal in size and measure over two or three times the length of their bodies.

Despite the size of their wings, the termites are poor fliers because their wing muscles are underdeveloped. Their inability to undertake long air journeys means that they tumble to the ground after flying for only about 650 feet, their wings splitting along the base as they crash violently against hard rocks and obstacles. These potential new kings and queens have large, weak heads, enormous compound eyes, under-developed antennae and strong, serrated jaws.

House hunting

After landing, the male attempts to arouse his prospective breeding partner by touching her with his antennae and palps. But it is the female that chooses the male. If she accepts the male, the female turns in a half circle and immediately walks off, followed by the male. As the female moves away, the male ensures that he does not lose sight of her for a second. In other species, pairing occurs in flight. Having successfully courted the female, the suitor flies up and grasps her round the abdomen. The male then holds fast and amputates his wings. The female lands with the male on her back and tears off her own wings.

The termites' amputation of their wings is an essential part of their swarming behavior. They employ a number of methods to amputate their wings, but the commonest and most efficient maneuver is to fold the wings and twist the body in all directions until the edge of the wing meets an obstacle on the ground. The termite then pushes its wing against the obstacle until the wing breaks.

Traveling partners

The paired termites then immediately begin their nuptial walk, during which they travel considerable distances until they find a suitable site for building their royal chamber. Eventually, the female halts at a place that she considers suitable for nest building, generally choosing a humid place, sheltered by a rock or in a small depression in the ground. Once the female has chosen a site, the pair immediately begin to dig a royal chamber.

The male and the female, leaning back to back against each other, put their heads down and use their heads, jaws and legs to dig a small, vertical gallery at the end of which is a modest, elliptical underground chamber. The royal chamber is barely large enough to accommodate the couple. After preparing their underground cavity, the two founding members—who on reaching this point in the development raise themselves to the rank of a royal couple—isolate themselves from the outside world.

Mating ceremony

Gradually, the royal couple begin to exhibit their distinct characteristics. The fertilized female, her abdomen swollen with eggs, relies upon her stored food reserves to grow, reaching a gigantic size. In highly evolved species of termites, the queen swells to more than 5.5 in. in length and 1.6 in. in diameter, making her incapable of moving and feeding by herself.

The queen increases in size because her abdomen expands—a soft exoskeleton separates each armored segment of her abdomen. As the queen becomes pregnant, the soft and flexible exoskeleton expands until the hardened segments resemble thin strips on the surface of her bloated abdomen. The queen's large abdomen accommodates the millions of eggs she will produce during her life; she can lay over 30,000 eggs per day. The shape of the king does not alter radically. The king remains the only male capable of feeding her, and his life cycle of 10-15 years is spent in regularly fertilizing her.

Closed entrance

Throughout their lives, the king and queen reproductives remain entombed within their royal chamber because their tunnel entrance is closed with a bung or stopper (molded from a solid mixture of earth particles and saliva). The construction of the royal chamber is a laborious task that lasts for hours or days on end, depending on the compactness and solidity of the earth.

Finally, within the royal apartment, there follows a complex preparatory ceremony before copulation takes place for the first time. Sometime after breeding occurs, the fertilized queen begins to lay her first eggs, which are few in number. These develop into the first generation of inhabitants of the new nest.

Royal diet

The diet of the royal couple during the early phase of their lives within the royal chamber remains a mystery, particularly among the family Termitidae (higher termites) that build their nests above ground. Termites that build their royal chamber in wood draw their initial food supply for the larvae from the wood itself, while those termites that nest in the ground feed themselves and their larvae by digesting their now useless wing muscles and the large reserves contained in the abdominal cavity.

The newly hatched larvae are minute creatures that measure about 0.08 in. in length. They have soft bodies because of their subterranean life, and their coats appear colorless and fragile. They also lack compound eyes. In order to compensate for their blindness, the other sensory organs of the termite larvae become highly specialized, in particular the small, sensitive receptors that are situated all over

ABOVE After an attack, worker termites frantically rebuild their nests, cementing the earth with salivary secretions. Many soldiers also run to the place where the disaster occurred to defend their habitat from any intruders that might enter.

PAGES 2412-2413 Although the queen termite shows great parental care for her first generation of offspring, she then delegates the task to the workers. They carefully remove the eggs, carrying them to a special incubation chamber.

their heads. But their main sensory input comes from their antennae.

Parental care

Termites show great parental care from the moment that the larvae hatch. The parents clean and feed the newborn larvae, mainly on two types of food. At first, the queen offers them stomodeal food, a sugary and transparent liquid that oozes from her abdomen. The parents provide the food on demand by regurgitating it from their mouths.

Later, the larvae feed on the second type of food, which oozes uninterruptedly from the end of the female's digestive canal. When the larvae become completely self-sufficient in seeking food, they themselves begin to provide sustenance for their royal parents, who can then concentrate on breeding.

TOP After the queen lays her eggs, the workers carefully gather them together to transport them immediately to a suitable incubation chamber. The workers turn and clean the eggs regularly, with great care, until they hatch.

ABOVE During an attack on the termites' nest, soldier termites hurry to protect the entrances to the larval incubation chambers. When a breach occurs in the chamber, the soldiers carry the larvae to safety on their backs.

Several royals

Not all termites restrict themselves to having one royal couple. Certain species regularly have several couples or, at least, several queens in a nest. In other species, there are supplementary reproductives on the outskirts of the nests to ensure that there will always be a breeding couple in the new nest. Eventually, the workers isolate the secondary reproductives by closing the communicating passageways, forcing them to leave and form a separate colony.

When the colony lacks a royal couple, the workers rear new individuals that take over the function of the king and queen. These individuals, known as substitute reproductives, grow from immature insects that can rapidly bring their reproductive organs to maturity (although they continue to appear physically immature). If the nest is deprived of a single member of the royal

family, then either a replacement of the same sex is reared or, more usually, a new couple appear. The existence of secondary and substitute reproductives demonstrates the high degree of social regulation that exists in the termite colonies.

Hatching workers

The first brood of eggs consists of workers: very few members are of the soldier caste. The workers participate in the construction of foundations for the termite hill, built around the royal chamber. After rearing their first brood, the parents abandon their parental care and concentrate on breeding. The first generation of worker termites does not exhibit any particular specialization in the subdivision of labor and only carry out duties that are necessary for a comfortable life in the nest.

In a role reversal, they care for their parents, eagerly feeding them with regurgitated food and, with great patience, cleaning their bodies and the inside of the royal cell. A sense of personal hygiene appears as deeply rooted in the workers as in the royal couple who, isolated in the termite hill, mutually inspect the whole surface of each other's bodies carefully and intently. In the course of this strange activity, with each individual lying on its side, they rid themselves fastidiously of external parasites and minute particles of dust on their backs.

New workers

The new workers care for the royal couple and also take part in building the colony and searching for food. In the early stages of the colony's development, the nest consists of a system of underground galleries that the worker termites dig in the earth. Every gallery leads back to the royal cell, linking it directly with underground sources of food.

The termites' diet consists largely of dead wood, and, at this early stage of the community, the network of galleries can extend inside tree trunks and roots. The first worker termites greatly enlarge the royal chamber. They also smooth the walls of the royal chamber by coating them with layers of digested wood mixed with soil and saliva.

Second mating

Almost a month after laying the first batch of eggs, the royal couple mate a second time, causing the bloated abdomen of the queen to expand even further. After the birth of the second generation of the new colony, the king and queen show no parental care for their offspring. The workers seize the eggs in their jaws as soon as they are laid and carry them with great care to a suitably humid and well-aired incubation cell, where they are stacked alongside each other. The larvae that hatch from the second generation of eggs will develop into either soldiers or workers, depending on the needs of the colony.

Chemical control

Coordination and control throughout the colony occurs through the transmission of genetic information in the form of chemicals that are passed among the members of the colony. The king and queen are able to maintain their status by passing chemicals that inhibit larvae developing into new breeders until there is a time when they are needed.

As soon as the queen termite lays her eggs, the worker termites remove them from under her and take care of them throughout their incubation period. The workers turn over the eggs periodically and carry them from one part of their underground nest to another for safekeeping. They also continually check the egg surfaces for signs of parasite attack, especially by molds and bacteria. It is the job of the workers to destroy any parasites as quickly as possible so that they do not contaminate other eggs in the nest. The tiny larvae hatch after an incubation period of about 10 days, and the workers continue to feed and care for them until the larvae have shed their skins for the first time.

The queen

Deep in the termite nest, protected by her soldiers and cared for by her workers, the queen starts to grow. Although her head and thorax do not change size, her abdomen expands enormously as her ovaries grow larger and more fat accumulates on her body. The soft, flexible skin between the plates of hard exoskeleton on her abdomen stretches them further and further apart. After several years, the queens of some species can reach a length of almost 5.5 in. with abdomens 200 or 300 times their original size.

Burdened by an enormous abdomen, the queen is unable to move and relies completely on her workers to feed, clean and defend her. As compensation for

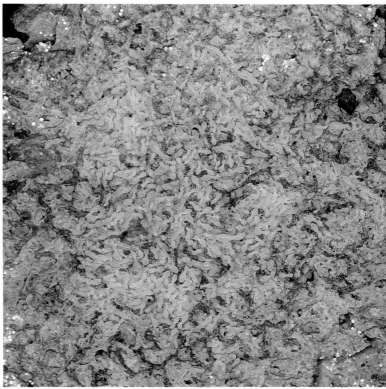

ABOVE Shortly before swarming takes place, the nest becomes a hub of activity. Worker termites vigorously attack the hardened walls of the nest to cut openings so that the winged termites can swarm out. Among some species of termites, the workers make exits a long way from the nests by excavating long tunnels toward the outer wall, often tunneling through rock-hard material.

their efforts, the queen allows her royal attendants to take small amounts of a nutritional secretion from her genital opening. They eat this with great relish. The same secretion also covers her eggs, and the workers rush to lick it off before taking the eggs to the incubation chamber.

The walls of the queen's abdomen contract slowly and rhythmically in continuous waves that are similar to the movements in the human intestine. The undulations, called peristaltic waves, assist in moving blood through the abdomen, thus helping the heart in its work. The assistance is vital for the queen's survival, since her abdomen cannot function adequately on its own when it is so swollen.

Although queens of different species of termite mature at different rates, most reach their full size by the end of the third year when their rate of egg production has also increased dramatically. Initially, the number of eggs that the queen produces varies from one egg every day and a half in some species to 100-130 eggs every six to nine days in other species.

At the height of production, queens lay over 30,000 eggs a day. Queens of the species *Odontotermes obesus* can produce a staggering 86,400 eggs a day or one egg per second—which amounts to over 31 million eggs a year. However, most queen termites can reduce their rate of production to avoid overcrowding in the nest. A wide range of predators and parasites also keep down the numbers of surviving eggs.

Insect architects

All termites need an enclosed environment to protect them from predators and from changes in humidity, temperature and atmosphere. They have evolved in a completely insulated environment over which they have some degree of control, and they venture outside their homes only in extreme situations—either to repair their nests or when the winged offspring swarm.

Termite nests vary considerably in shape, size and degree of complexity. Most species of termite hide their nests underground or inside dead wood, but a few build complex mounds and tree nests. Wood-boring species make the simplest nests. They consist of a series of connected galleries, dug out of the wood and under its surface so that there is no external sign of the termites' presence. The pair of termites that establish the colony choose a piece of wood suitable for a nest and dig out a chamber. The wood provides them with both their shelter and their source of food, but its size limits the size of the nest.

The more primitive species of termite also build the simplest nests. They put little effort into constructing specialized chambers and intricate tunnel systems. Primitive species also cause the most damage. Dry-wood termites eat wooden posts, furniture and buildings. Other species attack crops such as tea plants. However, in their natural habitat, termites play an important role in breaking down wood and other plant materials.

Slightly more advanced species of termite construct a network of connecting tunnels—either underground or on the surface—joining two or more separate food sources. Termites often build surface tunnels out of excrement that they mix with their saliva to form a cement-like substance. Some species that live in buried wood make underground tunnels connecting

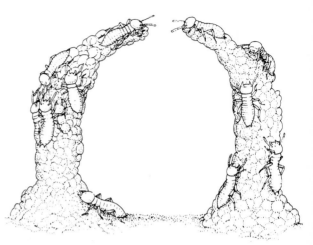

ABOVE Termites, such as the African species *Macrotermes natalensis* shown here, are the architects of the insect world. Using only saliva, earth, and their excrement, they can build structures almost 23 ft. high and able to withstand the baking heat and pounding rain of the African and Australian plains. The true building skills of the termites, however, are hidden beneath the nest's concrete-like external walls, where delicate arches and chambers are connected by myriad tunnel that fill the interior.
FAR RIGHT During swarming, equal numbers of winged male and female termites of the species *Odontoermes* emerge from their nest to fly away and establish new colonies elsewhere. The winged termites then embark on a nuptial flight, but rarely cover more than 50 ft. in distance before tumbling back down to the ground. After landing, they amputate their wings, and the male attempts to attract a breeding partner by caressing her with his antennae.

their nests to other pieces of wood. The original colony splits into several separate nests, each with its own offspring.

Underground nests

There are two main types of underground termite nests. The first is simply a series of small chambers and tunnels that the termites dig in the earth and line with a cement made out of saliva and earth, or excrement. The second type is more complex. The termites excavate a large chamber and then build partitions and smaller chambers within it. Both types have a hard outer wall that protects the inhabitants from predators and from the external climate.

Termite skyscrapers

The most complex termite nests start underground and grow to form a mound above ground. The mounds can be spectacular in size, and one recently discovered in northern Australia measured nearly 20 ft. in height and 98 ft. in circumference. In human terms, a building of comparable proportions would be over 3900 ft. tall, with a basement extending to a depth of 1640 ft. Termite mounds are familiar sights on African plains and in the Australian outback. However, like the icebergs they resemble, the most important part of their structure is below the surface. Often the mound contains only a chimney-like structure in which no termites live.

There are two main types of termite mound. One, built by primitive species, consists of a large number of similar chambers. The other is more complex. It has a central area made of horizontal layers and the surrounding walls consist of a thick, hard material with many small channels in them. The queen's cell is near the middle of the nest in the center of a hard nodule.

Termites are highly susceptible to changes in their environment and need to maintain a constant temperature, humidity and atmosphere. Their nests provide varying degrees of insulation from the outside air. Subterranean habitats provide the best insulation. Mounds are more likely to be affected by the external weather, but species that live in tropical forests are less likely to need to regulate the temperature inside their nests because the trees usually shield them from the sun, wind and rain.

Termites control the temperature inside their large mounds with great precision, keeping it constant with the heat from their bodies. In the middle of a nest, it is 86°F throughout the year (fluctuating by about 6 degrees in each 24-hour period when the outer surface of the nest is soaked by rain).

Humidity

The majority of termites are poorly protected against dehydration and require considerable amounts of water to survive. Most can use the water produced

by their own metabolism to maintain a 95 percent humidity in the nest. However, some species build the middle of their nests out of a water-absorbing substance. The outer walls are thick and nonporous. Species that keep fungus gardens need considerable water to keep it growing, increasing the relative humidity of the nest. Some termites that live in arid conditions dig tunnels deep into the earth in search of underground water that they bring up and deposit on the interior walls of the nest.

Atmosphere

Some termite nests contain as many as three million individuals, all breathing in the same enclosed area. They need appropriate levels of oxygen and carbon dioxide and an outlet for the intestinal gases they emit. Without some form of ventilation, they would rapidly die.

Gases probably diffuse through the walls of some simple nests. In more complex structures, the method of ventilation is not clear. Chimney-like structures have been found on mounds, but they cannot serve as ventilator shafts because they are isolated from the actual nest. It is possible that heated air containing waste gases rises to the top of the nest and reaches special chambers from where it slowly diffuses out through the walls of the nest. The upward movement

ABOVE When the queen termite first starts laying eggs she resembles all the other members of her species, but as her ovaries grow and her egg production increases, her abdomen stretches and swells. In some species, by the end of the third year, the queen termite can be almost 200 times her original size and measure about 5.5 in. in length. All that remain of her original appearance are her head (on the left in the picture) and the hardened plates of her swollen abdomen that appear as short, brown stripes along the top of her body. By this stage, the queen may be producing as many as 86,400 eggs a day.

of the warm gases then sucks fresh air in through the bottom of the mound.

Swarming termites

New termite colonies begin in ways that vary greatly from one species to another. However, the most common method is the swarm. When a termite nest reaches a certain size, and the weather is right for the particular species, large numbers of specially produced, sexually mature, winged males and females leave the nest in huge numbers, swarm, mate and start new colonies. The number of winged adults or reproductives that are produced varies with the species of termite and age of the colony. Some termite species produce

ABOVE Not all species of termite have soldiers with biting jaws. In the harvester termites, the soldiers (upper left and far right) have lost their powerful jaws and have developed instead a long, hollow spike that protrudes from the top of their heads. When threatened, these soldiers squirt a white, sticky liquid from the spikes over their enemies, making them immobile.

only a small number of winged adults, while others produce tens of thousands each year.

Development of the primary reproductives

The start of this process is quite unremarkable. It involves the laying and hatching of apparently ordinary eggs, into larvae (or nymphs) that are indistinguishable from the others. However, after their first molt, small wing buds can be seen on the nymphs' backs. At the same time, their sexual organs begin to develop. As the nymphs approach their seventh molt their wing buds become larger and their compound eyes form. Eventually their body covering becomes harder and darker in color. In most species this transformation takes about five or six months.

In the early stages of their development, termite nymphs are completely dependent on the worker caste for their food, which comes in the form of a salivary secretion. As they get older they become more active and begin to eat solid food regurgitated by the workers. In some species, the nymph at its last stage of development feeds itself.

When the winged termites cast off their last larval skin, their wings are folded and contracted. Different species take different periods of time to stretch their wings—a process that involves the termites pushing air into their trachea and distending the ducts that run in their wing veins. The winged termites remain in the nest for up to two months.

Awaiting departure

Before the flight, all members of the nest begin to behave differently. In the more primitive species the workers dig tunnels to the surface of the nest. Some species build special "waiting chambers" to house the large number of winged adults. Other species use the abandoned tunnels of wood-boring beetles as exit points. The workers of certain species of subterranean termite build special "launch pads" that help the winged adults to take off. These structures take many forms and can be shaped like cones, craters, funnels and walls.

Defending the swarm

During all this activity, the soldier termites begin to gather at the newly created exits. Just before the swarm takes place, the soldier termites, with their heads raised and their mandibles open, move out into the open to stand guard. In some species, the soldiers climb onto blades of grass, while others wander off into the surrounding area to act as diversions for any ants that might be lurking about. (Once the swarm has left, the termites reseal the nest and these soldiers are often left outside.) Another of the soldiers' roles is to prevent adults that have already swarmed and lost their wings from reentering the nest.

As the swarming time approaches, the older termite nymphs and winged adults start to gather in groups. The reason for this may be either a need for higher temperatures or a response to increased hostility from the rest of the colony. If the weather is unsuitable, the winged adults remain in the nest, and if the weather does not improve they may not leave the nest at all. In some termite species small numbers of winged adults remain in the nest after the swarm has left. They eventually lose their wings, and their sexual organs cease to function. However, they continue to feed. These individuals play no part in the running of the nest, yet the other members of the colony tolerate them. In other species, the winged adults that remain in the nest either die of natural causes or are killed by the soldier termites.

The flight

If the weather conditions are right, often after a heavy storm, the termites start to swarm. The reason for this swarm is to disperse as far as possible from the parent nest. The winged adults disperse in several different ways. Sometimes the swarm contains only a few individuals that leave the nest over a short period of time. In other species many thousands leave the nest over several hours. Some species of termites do not fly at all and the primary reproductives simply crawl from the nest and mate almost instantly.

In warm climates the winged adults take to the air immediately, but in colder weather they have to warm up first. Once in the air or on the ground, the swarming termites are easy prey for many animals including spiders, ants, lizards and birds. In many parts of the tropics, people eat flying termites. Of the many thousands of termites that leave the nest, only a small number survive to raise new colonies. Termites are not accomplished fliers, and their flight is an ungainly, undulating motion in an apparently random

direction. The swarming often lasts up to two or three hours. Although they take a long time to reach their destination, the flying termites do not travel a great distance. Most termite species swarm at the same time of year, and members of different species do cross mate. Those species of termites that travel only a short distance from their home nest are more likely to mate with members of their own nests, or with members from nearby nests of the same species. In this way they can maintain many of their hereditary characteristics.

Shedding their wings

Mating does not usually occur in flight, but in one species the male discards his wings after attaching himself to a female who carries him with her. Generally though, the winged males fly low, seeking out females on the ground. It is thought that they use their eyes to spot the glinting wings of the females. When a male termite finds a female he performs a short courtship ritual, which, if successful, ends with the wing loss of both partners. All termites shed their wings before they mate and build a new nest. Again, the wingless termites are in great danger from predators. To avoid becoming a meal for a bird, some

BELOW A cross-section taken from the nest of the fungus-growing termites _Macrotermes bellicosus_ shows the source of certain fungi that may be seen growing out of the walls of the nests during the wet season. Like many termites, this species feeds on wood, but because they have lost the kind of wood-dissolving protozoa that live in the gut of less advanced termites, they have taken to growing fungi that break down wood and convert it into an edible food.

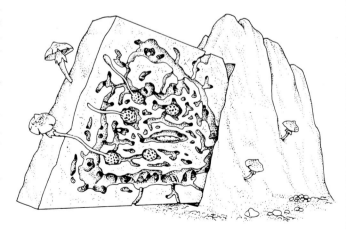

ABOVE Termite nests assume a variety of shapes and sizes. Some are simple mounds, while others are mushroom-shaped—the "caps" are thought to serve as shields against the sun and rain. The wedge-shaped nests of the compass termites of northern Australia reach 8 ft. in height, and are angled in a north-south direction—thus the broadest sides receive the warmth of the morning and afternoon sun, leaving the knife edges to face the hot noonday sun.

termite species feign death. However, this ploy is of little use against other invertebrates, especially ants.

Those termites that have survived the flight from the nest and met a mate then perform an extended courtship ritual. With both termites now wingless, the female searches out a prominent position and raises her abdomen in her "calling" posture. The male excitedly advances upon the female and touches her with vibrating antennae. If accepted, the male strokes the female with his mandibles. The female lowers her abdomen and strokes the attentive male. Turning away from the male, the female moves off. The male follows her, never letting her get out of reach of his antennae. If the male loses contact with the female, she calls him until he locates her again.

The termite pair try to find a nesting site as quickly as possible. Most species find a suitable place within a few hours, although some species search for several days. The species of termites that live in wood find a suitable crack or crevice in a log in which to build their nest. Once inside, the female seals the opening with a quick-drying, liquid excretion. When she has completed the job, the pair usually rest for a few days before they start to feed themselves and enlarge the chamber. It is the female who does most of the digging.

Building a new nest

The termite species that live underground usually excavate a chamber that is either next to some wood or actually in wood. Some species begin digging before they have lost their wings. The female completes the initial chamber in about 10 minutes, but she takes about two days to complete the nest, which consists of several chambers or cells. When completed, the termites mate. Known as the king and queen, the royal pair mate repeatedly throughout their lives. The female lays her eggs in a nuptial chamber. The first young to hatch are mostly workers. The parents tend them until they (the workers) are able to look after the next generation of young. After they have completed their parental duties, the king and queen continue to mate. The succeeding generations gradually complete the population of the nest, while the queen progressively grows to her final enormous size. But it takes many months for a new colony to reach full size.

Another method of nest formation, called "sociotomy," is a process that is similar to a bee swarm. A fraction of an established colony break away and march off in search of a new home. Sometimes the queen and king join this exodus, leaving supplementary reproductives to head the orphaned colony.

Fungus gardens

When zoologists first came across the giant termite mounds of tropical Africa, not only were they struck by the gigantic size of the nests and the remarkable differences in the shape of their inhabitants, but they were particularly puzzled when they discovered a strange, spongy, dark, reddish brown coral-like comb inside the nest. The cells containing this mysterious substance gave off a typically fungal smell.

Many years later scientists established that these were gardens in which the worker termites grew and tended special types of fungi. These fungal gardens occur most often in the nests of the tropical African termite species and in the nests of a few species in southern Asia. The gardens are usually found in the part of the nest that is above ground, although they sometimes occur throughout the nest. The workers build a system of round chambers that interconnect via a dense network of galleries. These chambers contain large amounts of undigested wood that the termites expel in their feces, as well as tiny fragments of wood that have been finely ground by their mandibles. The termites regularly stir up these wood deposits and keep them damp with saliva until a kind of soft, spongy ball develops that acts as the bed in which the fungus spores grow.

A specialized environment

In almost all cases, the fungi that the termites grow belong to the same genus, *Termitomyces*, but each farmed fungus is unique to each group of termites. Furthermore, the fungi cannot survive outside the nests. The temperature in the garden area is strictly regulated and kept humid, so that the spores begin to germinate within a short space of time. A fine network of filaments, known as mycelium, gradually covers the entire fungus bed until it takes on a soft, velvety appearance. The termites feed on the small white nodules that appear on the garden bed—these are the fruiting bodies of the fungus.

At certain times of the year, and in particular during the rainy season, the fungus pushes outside the walls of the nest. The mycelium of some species of fungi have specially hardened tips that help it force its way through the termite mound. Many theories have been put forward as to the exact role of fungus within the termite colony and recent discoveries, made by zoologists, suggest that the fungi fulfill several different functions simultaneously.

Breaking down the wood

Through the action of its enzymes, the fungus breaks down the tough indigestible wood, releasing the large amounts of cellulose that the wood contains. Cellulose is one of the main food sources of the wood-eating termites (termites given a diet of the complete fungus comb develop normally, while populations kept on a diet consisting of fungus alone die within a short time). The fungus is thought to be a source of a vitamin, known as "vitamin T," that is capable of accelerating growth in insects and vertebrates. Some

entomologists believe that "vitamin T" influences the caste formation within the colony.

The fungi also act as controllers of heat and damp, both of which the termites need to survive. Although most of the heat in the nest comes from the termites' own metabolism, the fungus produces substantial amounts of heat as it ferments its food. Fungus also thrives in a damp atmosphere, and dampness is one of the by-products produced when the fungus breaks down wood. The fungus gardens act as nurseries for termite larvae because of the increased warmth and humidity.

Termitophiles

Although termite mounds are almost completely isolated from the outside world, they are vulnerable to attack by both large and small animals. Various invertebrates, known as termitophiles, live semi-parasitically in termite nests, relying on them for protection or food—sometimes both. Included among the termitophiles are certain species of wood lice, millipedes, centipedes, mites, spiders, ants, flies and beetles. Some of the lodgers pay for their accommodation by producing secretions that termites find useful; others are scavengers or predators, and still others are simply ignored by their hosts.

To avoid eviction from their termite nests or death at the hands of their hosts, termitophiles have evolved several different defense strategies, three of which are particularly common.

Phoretic termitophiles or hitching guests live inside termite nests and ride on the backs of their hosts. Other species have evolved specialized body shapes to protect them from hostile termites, since without their natural defensive armors, they risk deadly attacks from termites. "Armored" termitophiles have tear-drop-shaped bodies, greatly enlarged thoraxes that cover their entire heads, short, compact antennae, and protective flanges, behind which they can fold their legs.

Physogastry

Certain species of flies and beetles that associate with termites develop swollen abdomens—a process called physogastry. Like queen termites, they have evolved highly elastic membranes between the plates of their abdomens: the swelling is caused by enlarged reproductive organs, fat deposits and sometimes by both.

Mounds of compass termites
(*Amitermes meridionalis*)

Nest of a tree termite (*Nasutitermes arborum*)

Mound of a fungus-growing termite
(*Macrotermes natalensis*)

Mound of an Ethiopian umbrella termite (*Cubitermes sp.*)

Mound of an Australian termite species

RIGHT Termites often build their mounds against the sides of trees. They do this for two reasons: the first is that the wood of the tree supplies a ready source of food for the growing colony, and the second is that it provides a certain amount of shade during the day. These types of nests can reach more than 42 ft. in height.

Zoologists agree that physogastry safeguards a termitophile against eviction from a termite nest, but they do not fully understand why. Because termites lick at the swollen abdomens of termitophiles, it is possible that they are attracted to a secretion on their bodies. Zoologists theorize that termites and termitophiles enjoy a mutually beneficial relationship in which termites provide a home for a termitophile in exchange for its desirable secretion. Unfortunately, there is no conclusive evidence to support the theory, since most observations of termite/termitophile interactions have been carried out in artificial laboratory conditions.

Recent field observations show that termites feed termitophiles, as well as receive food from them. Some termitophile species rely so much on their hosts for food that—through the process of evolution—their mouthparts have changed shape, making them unable to catch prey. Such species are wholly reliant on termites for their sustenance; if they lose their hosts' support, they die.

Information from field observations of termitophiles is confused, with different studies often contradicting each other. Early reports suggest that termitophiles were not only tolerated, but allowed to groom termites and feed in their fungus gardens. However, more recent studies have found that termitophiles are intimidated by termites, and they stay in fungus gardens for safety, not as a result of their hosts' goodwill.

Big trouble

Termites are plagued by large predators as well as by invertebrate parasites. In central and southern Africa, one of their prime enemies are the aardvarks—mammals whose diet consists mainly of termites. After aardvarks have detected termite movements with their keen senses of hearing and smell, they use their long, sticky tongues to scoop dozens of the insects from their mounds. In Australasia, termites are the prey of anteaters: the mammals sniff out termites and ants with their long, slender snouts and pick them up with their sticky tongues.

The greatest enemies of termites are ants, which evolved independently of termites. Some species of ants even specialize in attacking parties of foraging termites. The distance that termites travel in search of food varies according to species: some travel over 164 ft. through temporary tunnels to search for food, while dry-wood termites never leave the branches where they nest. Termites defend themselves from ants by reinforcing their nests, using specialized soldier castes, or by covering their food with protective sheets of mud.

Caste determination

A termite nest contains one truly fertile pair—the queen, acting as an immense egg factory, and the king, the provider of spermatozoa for fertilization. Many zoologists believe that a termite queen regulates at will the production of individuals for different castes.

ABOVE Termite nests such as this one built high up a tree trunk in Ecuador, South America, are common sights in tropical forests around the world.

By living in trees, these termites avoid large ground predators—anteaters in South America and aardvarks and pangolins in Africa.

The social insects in the order Hymenoptera—wasps, bees and ants—produce differentiated eggs that are sometimes fertilized and sometimes not. If conditions are right, the caste of a young ant, bee or wasp is determined before it hatches. Termites, however, lay only fertilized eggs that are identical to each other, lacking any indication as to their caste. Therefore, it is probable that caste determination occurs early in a larva's life, before it hatches: remarkable experiments have shown that the production of workers, soldiers and winged breeders reflects precisely the current needs of a termite colony.

Social organisms

Termite communities are considered to be single, highly complicated social organisms, rather than mere colonies. A termite is as ill-suited to survival outside its colony as an individual animal cell is incapable of independent life once separated from the organism of which it forms a part. Termite social organisms are made possible by the operation of pheromones—chemicals that regulate the exchange of information within the colonies. In the same way that hormones control the biological processes of a single organism, pheromones control the internal functions of a termite social organism.

Pheromones are complex chemical substances that are released by animals to influence the behavior and development of other individuals of the same species. The way they work is best demonstrated by a pheromone variety that is secreted by queens: worker termites pick it up when they groom their queen, and pass it to others during the exchange of regurgitated food; larvae receive pheromones when adult worker termites feed them. The pheromones inhibit the development of larvae's reproductive organs and determine whether they develop into worker or soldier termites. If these pheromones are not released, their absence allows the larvae to develop into reproductive castes.

Royal succession

Royal termites, in particular the queens, are very long lived—some individuals reach the age of 10 years, although the majority fall foul of disease, parasites or predators at a much earlier age. Some termite communities, however, outlive their founding queens by as much as 15 years. The phenomenon is linked to the circulation of the queen's pheromones among the inhabitants of a termite nest: the pheromones contain all the information necessary to the continued functioning of the termite community.

Developing reproductives

Pheromone circulation stimulates the development of special termite nymphs that are reared in special cells in the most outlying areas of the nest. These nymphs are unusual creatures, often possessing tiny wing buds and compound eyes. They also have a latent ability to reach sexual maturity. If a termite community does not need new adult breeders, a complicated series of changes triggered by hormonal factors turns the nymphs into workers. However, in the absence of the king and queen, the nymphs rapidly transform into secondary breeders, known as replacement royals. Immediately, the new royals take command of their nests, producing eggs and secreting the pheromones specific to their species.

AT HOME ON A HOST

Lice are tiny, wingless insects that live as parasites on humans and animals. They are often detested for the skin irritations, disease and infections they can bring to their hosts

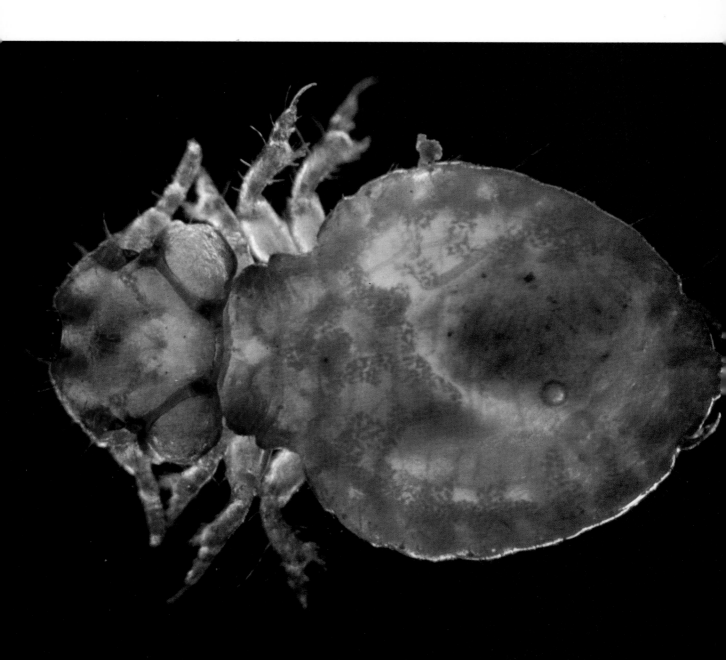

There are 3150 known species of parasitic lice, and they all belong to the superorder Phthiraptera, whose ancestors date from the Cretaceous period some 130 million years ago. The superorder contains two orders—Mallophaga, or biting lice, and Anoplura, or sucking lice.

All species of parasitic lice spend their entire lives in the skin and fur or feathers of their hosts and closely resemble one another. They are tiny and wingless, with flattened bodies, large segmented abdomens and clawed legs. Biting lice, however, have chewing mouthparts suitable for feeding on the skin and feathers of birds and some mammals, while sucking lice have piercing mouthparts adapted for sucking the blood of humans and other placental mammals.

Biting lice

Biting lice vary in length from 0.04 to 0.4 in. They have small eyes, short antennae and hooked limbs. Many have grooves on their antennae and large sucking pads on their feet, enabling them to move along their host's body at incredible speed. Others have short, inwardly curved legs adapted for climbing.

Biting lice that live on birds have two claws on each leg for gripping the tangle of barbs and barbules on their hosts' plumage. By contrast, those that live on mammals possess a single claw on each leg, with a pad at the end, to gain a pincer-like grip on their prey. The elephant louse, which lives on elephants, wields its claw like an ice-axe to attach itself to its host's tough skin. It also has claws on its mid and hind legs to help it grip, although they are less robust than the ones in front.

Biting lice feed on tiny pieces of feather, skin and skin secretions. If their host has a wound, they also drink any blood that seeps out of it. Some species, such as chicken lice and elephant lice, use their sharp, pointed mandibles to make small wounds in their host so they can feed on its blood. A species of South American guinea pig louse has serrated mouthparts for cutting its host's hair follicles and extracting the oils and waxes.

The seasons have no effect on the reproductive cycle of biting lice, but when they are exposed to light, biting lice immediately seek shade. If the body temperature of their host increases, biting lice do not appear overly bothered, and they continue to feed regularly. However, if they can, they will move to another animal whose temperature is normal.

INSECTS CLASSIFICATION: 9

Lice

All lice belong to the superorder Phthiraptera which consists of two orders: the Mallophaga (biting lice) and the Anoplura (sucking lice). The order Mallophaga consists of three suborders: Rhyncophtherina contains one family and only two species—the elephant louse, *Haematomyzus elephantis*, and the wart hog louse, *H. hopkinsi*; suborder Ischnocera contains five families and 1800 species, which include the dog louse, *Trichodectes canis*, and the sheep-chewing louse, *Bovicola ovis*; and the suborder Amblycera whose seven families contain 850 species. These include the guinea pig louse, *Gliricola porcelli*, the hummingbird louse, *Trochiloecetes sp.*, the curlew quill louse, *Actornithophilus patellatus*, and the rodent louse (family Gyropidae).

The order Anoplura (the sucking lice) contains 15 families and 500 species. They include the human crab or pubic louse, *Pthirus pubis*; the human body louse, *Pediculus humanus vestimentorum*, which lives in clothing; the human head louse, *Pediculus humanus capitis*; and the seal louse (family Echinophthiridae).

Thrips

Thrips belong to the order Thysanoptera which consists of eight families grouped into two suborders: the Terebrantia and the Tubulifera. The suborder Terebrantia has seven of the order's families, which total 1500 species. They include the greenhouse thrips, *Heliothrips haemorrhoidalis*; the pine-tree thrips, *Oxythrips bicolor*; and the thunderfly or grain thrips, *Limothrips cerealium*.

The suborder Tubulifera consists of one family, the Phlaeothripidae, which contains approximately 2700 species divided into two subfamilies: the Idolothripinae includes the Gustavia thrips, *Anactinothrips gustaviae*; and the Phlaeothripinae, which has the laurel thrips, *Gynaikothrips ficorum*, and the wheat thrips, *Haplothrips tritici*. Thrips are minute insects that measure 0.002-0.3 in. in length. Most of the 5000 or so species feed on the sap of plants or on arthropods such as mites and apids.

Biting lice most often infect birds, causing weakness and vulnerability to disease, and they can create a substantial health problem for domestic animals such as sheep and hens. The seven species of biting lice that infest hens can cause the death of young birds and adversely affect the health of adults. Heavily infested hens also produce fewer eggs. As many as 35,000 chicken body lice can prey on a single bird.

Sucking lice

Sucking lice vary in length from 0.014 to 0.24 in. They have sharp mouthparts that are especially for sucking the blood of mammals, including egg-laying mammals and marsupials. Many species infect the scalp, pubic region and clothing of humans. Lice usually infest people who live in crowded, unsanitary conditions. They also prefer cool climates where people wear woolen clothing.

There are about 500 species of sucking lice, and they are extremely well adapted to their parasitic existence. They lack wings, but they have short, inwardly curving legs that end in maneuverable claws. Sucking lice fold their claws back against their fourth leg segments and use them like pincers to fasten themselves securely to the fur or hair of their hosts.

Sucking lice have radically modified mouthparts. Their mandibles are useless as biting instruments. Instead, they have three sharp, tusk-like stylets with which to bite. Two of the stylets are situated around the top of a louse's alimentary canal, and the third lies underneath it. A salivary channel runs between them. The third stylet forms a pipe-like structure with four serrated appendages at its tip, and sucking lice use it to saw holes in the skin of their hosts.

Sucking lice feed exclusively on blood. However, blood does not contain all the vitamins that the lice require in order to survive. They obtain the remaining vitamins from bacteria that live inside them, either inhabiting the area between their intestinal cells or living inside certain organs.

Several species of sucking lice are parasitic on various animals, including horses, sheep, goats, pigs, calves and dogs. Usually, a single species of louse restricts itself to a particular animal. Among humans, however, different species infest different parts of the body. They cause intense irritation and itching, and occasionally their bites produce pus-filled pimples on their host's skin. By transmitting such diseases as

PAGE 2427 Biting lice are mainly ectoparasites of birds, but can infest cattle, horses and dogs. They usually attach themselves to the head or back of their hosts, where they are difficult to remove during cleaning or preening. Biting lice cannot survive if they are dislodged from their hosts.

ABOVE Like other insect ectoparasites, human head lice are wingless, flattened creatures. They have well-developed claws at the ends of their legs that they use to cling to their hosts. A severe infestation can involve thousands of lice and can cause weeping of the skin, redness, swelling and a low fever.

typhus and relapsing fever, they also bring about human deaths.

The sucking lice that infest humans are pale-colored insects with dark markings along their sides. Their abdomens are flattened and divided into nine segments that can extend when filled with blood. The males are 0.08-0.1 in. long, and the females are 0.1-0.16 in. There are three varieties of human louse: the human crab louse, the human body louse and the human head louse.

The human crab louse usually lives among the coarse hairs of the pubic and anal areas, but it also inhabits other hairy parts of the body, such as the armpits. In rare cases, it spreads to the beard, eyebrows and eyelashes. The human crab louse is

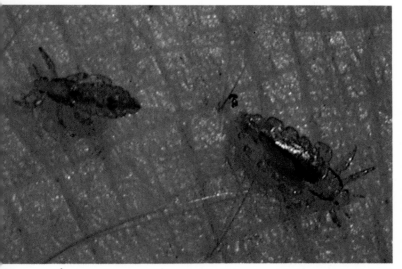

ABOVE The mouthparts of the head louse are adapted to suck the blood of its human host. Like other external parasites, the head louse is wingless, flattened in shape and almost blind. Its front legs end in well-developed, grasping claws that it uses to cling to the hairs on the head of its host. During ovulation, the female head louse cements her eggs individually to strands of hair. Head lice are notorious for spreading the microorganisms that cause typhus and rickets.

grayish white, with a broad, short body and clawed appendages that give it a crab-like appearance. It is 0.06-0.08 in. in length and moves from host to host by direct contact.

Human body lice live in clothing, laying their 200-300 eggs in the folds of material. They only move onto the skin of their hosts to feed and can survive for up to 10 days away from their host. Sometimes, however, they also live on necklaces and other types of jewelry. These are the most dangerous of all the sucking lice. Although their bite only causes a reddening of the skin, it carries pathogenic (disease-bearing) germs that produce exanthematic typhus and five-day or French fever. Human body lice have been called the "carrier of some of the great human scourges." In the USSR, between 1918 and 1922, 10 million people caught exanthematic typhus and at least 3 million people died from the disease.

The female human head louse lays about two eggs (or nits) a day, amounting to some 40 eggs in total during her lifetime. She attaches each egg, individually, to a strand of her host's hair. The young hatch in six to nine days and undergo several molts before reaching maturity in about 18 days. The louse dies after about three or four weeks.

Thrips

Thrips belong to the order Thysanoptera. There are about 5000 species, and most measure no more than 0.04-0.08 in. in length. Thrips are tiny and difficult to see. They occur in large numbers in flower heads. They also live in dry hay and in decaying matter. One South African species lives in tunnels dug by other insects, such as termites. Thrips occur in almost every region of the world, including subpolar and desert areas, and at altitudes of 10,000 ft. above sea level.

Some species have two pairs of wings, each consisting of a narrow strap fringed in front and behind with long, delicate hairs. In some species, it is either the male or the female that possesses wings. They cannot fold their slender wings, and when at rest, thrips hold them horizontally, one above the other, over the abdomen. They have slender cylindrical or flat bodies terminating in a tapering abdomen. Their exoskeletons are tough and usually brown, black or yellow in color. They have piercing and sucking mouthparts on the lower part of their heads. They feed for the most part by sucking the sap from plants, while a few species are carnivorous, feeding on the body liquids of mites, aphids and their larvae. Some live off fungal spores or pollen from which they suck the fluids. Their right mandible is much less developed than their left one, giving their mouthparts and the rest of the lower part of their head an asymmetrical appearance.

Sensory antennae

Some thrip species have small compound eyes, with as few as four cells or ommatidia, situated at the side of their heads, while other species have large centrally positioned compound eyes with up to 300 ommatidia. Winged thrips have three frontal simple eyes that are absent in the wingless species. Their antennae have four to nine segments, some of which have sensory organs; the legs bear appendages (tarsi) with a type of retractable sucker; the abdomens are divided into 11 sections, the last section being so small that it is often invisible. They have breathing tubes or tracheae that open onto the outside via three or four spiracles (breathing holes).

After reaching sexual maturity, most adult thrips live between 20 and 70 days, although the species that have to live through the winter can last for seven or eight months. Females lay an average of 20-40 elongated eggs. They either lay their eggs in slits that they make in the plant tissue with their egg-laying tubes, or they place them singly or in groups on the leaves, stems, or bark of plants.

A serious pest

When thrips suck the sap of plants, they kill the plant cells and disrupt the plants' internal processes. If a large number of thrips inhabit a particular area they can cause serious damage to the vegetation. In addition, some thrip species carry viruses that can kill the plants. Although regarded as serious pests, many species of thrips feed on uncultivated plants, weeds and fungi and are completely harmless. Some species of thrips are beneficial to humans since they eat aphids that can cause extensive damage to plants, such as roses.

Psocids

The order Psocoptera contains about 1700 species of insects known as psocids. They are more commonly called book lice after some of the members of the order. Most psocids are under 0.25 in. in length. They have highly developed heads, slender antennae, chewing mouthparts with pointed maxillae and a lower lip bearing the openings of two silk-producing glands. Some psocids, including book lice, lack wings, others have membranous wings with few, if any, veins. They are poor fliers but some species are capable of jumping. Their abdomens bear cerci or sensory appendages.

Most species of psocids live outdoors. They live mostly on leaves or under tree bark, often in orchards and vineyards. But they also live in birds' nests, in the dens of mammals, in wasp and ant nests and in crops.

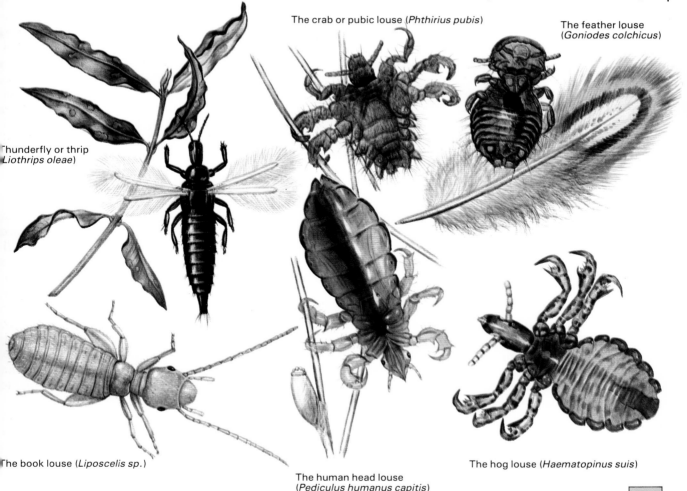

The crab or pubic louse (*Phthirius pubis*)

The feather louse (*Goniodes colchicus*)

Thunderfly or thrip (*Liothrips oleae*)

The book louse (*Liposcelis sp.*)

The human head louse (*Pediculus humanus capitis*)

The hog louse (*Haematopinus suis*)

ABOVE Book lice mainly live in trees, shrubs or under bark and stones, but some species occur in houses, barns and among old papers, books and other debris. They are small, soft-bodied insects with modified mouthparts that enable them to feed on fungi, lichens, pollen and even paper. The majority of species have two membranous wings that they fold over their abdomen when at rest.

INSECTS CLASSIFICATION: 10

Book lice and zorapterans

Book lice are small, soft-bodied insects that belong to the order Psocoptera. Although they sometimes give their name to the entire order, they properly constitute a group within the Psocoptera—an order whose approximately 1700 species are more scientifically known as psocids. Psocids are named according to the type of food they eat: for example, book lice feed on the mold that grows in old, damp books, while bark lice feed on tree bark. They are divided into three suborders and 21 families (one of them, the family Liposcelidae, contains the common book louse, *Liposcelis divinatorius*).

Discovered in 1913, the zorapterans belong to the small order Zoraptera and number only 23 species; these are all contained within the family Zorotypidae and the single genus *Zorotypus*. Zorapterans measure under 0.1 in. in length, live mainly in hot and humid areas, and can be found in rotting logs and tree stumps, under bark and in leaf litter and sawdust.

They feed mainly on dry leaves and mildew. Some species even live in beehives, where they feed on honey. Most psocids live outdoors, feeding on dry leaves and mildew. Other species of psocids live indoors, often in human habitations and especially in warehouses where they feed on cereal products, vegetable and animal debris, dead insects, paste, glue and molds of all kinds. They also live in moldy areas of cupboards, unused rooms, old upholstery and inside old books. Nevertheless, it is not only old and neglected objects that attract these tiny animals. Since the main sources of psocid food are fungi (mold), psocids occur wherever there is sufficient humidity for mold to form, such as under the flooring and wallpaper of new houses that remain slightly damp, and in stored food.

The developing larvae

During incubation, psocid eggs stick to the surface on which they are laid. They usually take one to three weeks to hatch; the newly hatched larvae of wingless psocids resemble the adults while the larvae of winged species begin to resemble the adults after five to eight months. Psocids develop quickly, and many generations are produced during the course of a year. Indoor species reproduce throughout the year, whereas the eggs of the outdoor psocids remain dormant during the winter.

Zoraptera

The order Zoraptera contains minute insects all less than 0.1 in. in length. They are rare insects, living in small colonies in vegetable detritus and under dead wood. They occur in the tropical regions of the world. There are both winged and nonwinged adult forms. Soft-bodied insects resembling termites, they have oval heads that are separated from their thoraxes. They have chewing mouthparts, long antennae with ball-like segments like strings of pearls, and two sense organs at the end of their abdomens. The wingless forms are blind, with only occasional traces of compound or simple eyes. However, the winged species do possess compound eyes as well as pronounced simple eyes. Winged zorapterans have two pairs of delicate wings that they shed, in a similar way to termites. Zorapterans are not highly advanced insects, and they undergo gradual metamorphosis.

SUCKERS OF SAP AND BLOOD

Distinct from all other insects by virtue of their piercing beaks that they use to suck plant or animal juices, bugs range from the delicate pond skaters and water boatmen to the aphids and blood-sucking bedbugs

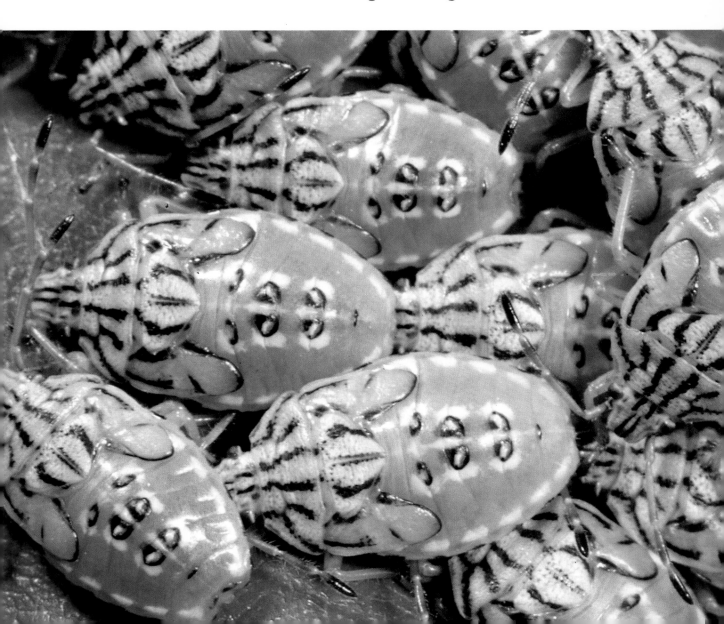

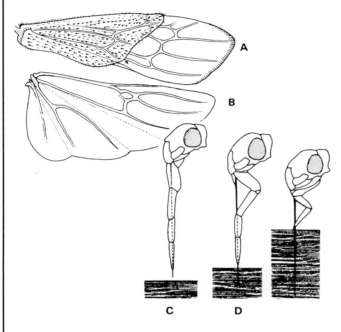

LEFT True bugs, such as bedbugs, of the suborder Heteroptera, have wings that are different in texture. Their forewings (A) are typically thickened at the base and membranous at their tips. Their hind wings (B) are totally membranous. Members of the suborder Homoptera, such as aphids and cicadas, have forewings that are either entirely membranous, like their hind wings, or completely thickened. Bugs have specially adapted mouthparts that consist of stylets or maxillae (dotted line) containing salivary and feeding canals. They are contained in the rostrum or labium (C). As the stylets enter the food (solid black and dotted line), the labium retracts (D). Once the stylets have fully penetrated the food, enzymes are pumped into it, and semidigested food is drawn back up the food canal.

RIGHT The assassin bug, *Playmenis bigottata*, lies concealed among flowers and leaves to ambush insects, such as beetles, millipedes and mosquitoes; certain species exude attractive odors to entice bees to their death. They can inflict painful bites on humans, and, in South America, assassin bugs transmit Chagas' disease to humans.

PAGE 2433 The shield bug, *Elasmucha grisea*, has a large, camouflaged plate over its thorax and long, thin antennae that divide into five segments.

Bugs belong to the order Hemiptera—one of the largest orders in the class Insecta. With 67,500 species, Hemiptera comprises more life forms than all the species of vertebrate creatures combined. Bugs are unpopular among humans since they include bedbugs, plant lice and other pests. However, their parasitic habits and important roles in ecological systems are of great scientific interest. No other insect group has evolved through a greater variety of structural and physiological changes, and few have undergone changes as unusual as those experienced by bugs.

Heteroptera and Homoptera

The name Hemiptera means literally "half wing"—it refers to the membranous and hardened sections of bugs' wings. Most species of bugs fly with their transparent second pairs of wings, folding them beneath their first wings when they are not flying. However, the name Hemiptera is not appropriate for all bugs, since many species have two pairs of completely membranous wings. Bugs with differentiated wings are true bugs or Heteroptera ("unlike wings"), while ones with four membranous wings are called Homoptera ("like wings").

Modified mouthparts

Hemiptera have an alternative name, Rhyncota (after the Greek *rincos*), to stress that they have rostra, or beaks, containing the piercing and sucking mouthparts that distinguish all bugs from the other insect orders. The diets and life-styles of bugs are determined by their mouthparts, which contain two pairs of thin threads or stylets. The outer pair are two rapier-like instruments (mandibles) that are tipped with sharp teeth for making openings in plant or animal surfaces, while the inner pair of stylets (maxillae) form the food and salivary ducts. Bug mouthparts are, in fact, modifications of the movable mouthparts with which all insects are equipped.

When feeding, bugs dig their mandibles into their food source and immediately afterward insert their maxillae. One duct of the maxillae injects a liquefying saliva containing enzymes, while the other carries the liquefied food into the mouth. A labium—a sheath-like extension on a bug's lower lip—guides the maxillae and mandibles toward a food source, but does not penetrate its surface. When the bug is not feeding, it retracts its stylets within its labium.

True bugs on land

The foul-smelling secretions of their stink glands distinguish land bugs from other insects. In the larva

ABOVE **A bedbug in one of its larval stages, feeding on human blood. A bedbug's skin is partly transparent and as the insect takes its fill, its skin becomes a red color. The dark area at the tip of its abdomen** shows the remains of its last meal. Newly hatched larvae have to feed on blood before they can molt. Bedbugs do not feed solely on humans, they also attack mice, rats, rabbits, poultry and other birds.

stage, stink glands open onto the back of their abdomens, while adult bugs have stink glands on the sides or undersides of their thoraxes.

Land bugs reproduce in fascinating and unusual ways. Unlike many insect species, male bugs deposit their sperm in special pockets on the undersides of the females' bodies, rather than in their vaginal openings. These pockets are not linked to the internal organs, so sperm enter a female's bloodstream by penetrating her cuticle. Sperm fertilize the eggs once they have reached them by way of the circulatory system.

Development

Female land bugs lay approximately 200 eggs that develop after eight days or more—depending on the temperature of the air. Many bug nymphs break out of their eggs using detachable spines on their bodies, called "egg bursters." Newly hatched nymphs are pale in color but otherwise resemble their parents. They feed in the same way as the adults, sucking blood from living prey with their rostra.

Land bug nymphs molt five times during their development, and, if conditions are reasonably warm, they reach full maturity after two months. Adult land bugs feed approximately once a week—more often if the weather is very hot. They live for about a year.

Flower bugs

Flower bugs or Anthocoridae (*antos* is Greek for "flower" and *coris* means "bug") comprise several herbivorous and predatory species. Some species live in flowers, feeding on protein-rich pollen grains, while others live among decaying vegetation, in tree bark or in animal dens and nests. They have highly developed eyes. Predatory flower bugs are useful to humans since they consume many caterpillars, aphids and plant lice. A few particularly aggressive species are considered pests as they suck the blood of cattle, and even people, if other insects are scarce.

Blood-sucking bugs

Typical species of blood-sucking land bugs are *Cimex pipistrelli*, found on bats; *Cimex columbarius*, an inhabitant of dovecotes that feeds on the blood of doves and chickens; and *Oeiacus hirundinus*, a parasite of swallows. When their hosts migrate, parasitic land bugs hide in their nests, spending the winter without food; like all blood-sucking creatures such as ticks and leeches, land bugs can withstand long periods of fasting.

Resident bacteria

Blood-sucking land bugs are hosts to symbiotic bacteria that inhabit special areas of their bodies known as mycetomes (symbiosis is a mutually beneficial relationship between two living organisms). Bacterial symbiosis is not exclusive to land bugs, but occurs in all insects that feed only on blood. Although blood is rich in nutrients, it contains no vitamin B—a substance vital to animal life. Bacteria need no external source of vitamins, since they produce their own. Thus, the bacteria in a bug's mycetomes provide their host with life-sustaining vitamin B in exchange for a habitat.

Bedbugs

Bedbugs belong to the family *Cimicidae*, a small family well known for its parasitic habits; all bedbugs feed on the blood of reptiles, birds or mammals. Their bodies are wide and very flat, with tiny stumps of wings. Bedbugs avoid daylight, hiding in cracks in rock, animal dens or chinks in walls. They emerge at night and actively search for prey with their highly developed sense of smell.

Bedbugs of the species *Cimex lectularius* plague Europeans, while *Cimex rotundatus* is common throughout Africa and southern Asia. Bugs of the genus *Cimex are*

RIGHT The assassin bug, *Triatoma infestans,* inhabits tropical and subtropical regions of the world. Like other assassin bugs, it is an extremely active and efficient hunter, with powerful, jackknife forelegs for grasping its prey. It has adhesive pads on the end of its legs that consist of thousands of tiny hairs. Each hair has a film of oil that sticks to the victim like a prickly burr. Some species have evolved stickier pads to grasp hairy prey, such as bees.

about 0.24 in. in length; however, their typically flat bodies undergo an enormous increase in size when feeding. The species *Oeiacus hirundinus* enters human households and sucks blood from the occupants.

The Polyctenidae: an unusual family

Bugs of the family Polyctenidae are unusual, since they spend their lives constantly attached to their hosts. Their name, which means "many combs," refers to the short, thick spines arranged in regular rows along the edges of various parts of their bodies. The "combs" are microscopic in size, since the bugs are less than 0.2 in. long. Polyctenidae are eyeless, and their antennae and wings are tiny. They live hidden in the fur of bats, feeding on their blood. Their young are born live and at an advanced stage of development. Polyctenidae are widespread in Africa, Asia and America.

Capsid bugs

The largest family of true bugs is the *Miridae*, which contains 6000 species of capsid bugs, or plant lice. Capsid bugs are common in Europe, where there are more than 300 species. Their elongated bodies are oval in shape and sometimes brightly colored—the species *Lopus lineolatus,* for example, has black and reddish body stripes.

Although capsid bugs can cause enormous damage to crops, a small parasitic wasp called *Teleonomus lopicida* ensures that they are not a serious threat. Enemies of the species *L. lineolatus,* the wasps lay their minute eggs inside the 0.06-in.-long bug eggs. When the young wasps hatch, they devour the bug embryos before abandoning their eggs.

Unfortunately, other species of capsid bugs cannot be controlled by their natural enemies alone. Consequently, they cause extensive damage to vines, bean plants, coffee, cocoa and tobacco plants.

Predatory capsid bugs

Not all capsid bugs are herbivores. Several species prey on other insects, such as ants or termites, and some actually dwell in their victims' nests. Before capsid bugs are allowed to enter ant or termite colonies, they are closely scrutinized by the soldiers and workers. However, most penetrate successfully and achieve acceptance as members of a colony, since they closely resemble their hosts in smell and appearance.

Assassin bugs

The family *Reduvidae,* or assassin bugs, consists of over 3000 species. Assassin bugs are predominant in the tropics, although they also inhabit colder regions. They are large, aggressive creatures. Some hunt flies, wasps and other insects, while others are parasites that feed on the blood of large mammals. Assassin bugs

INSECTS
CLASSIFICATION: 11

Bugs

Although most people call any small insects "bugs," entomologists regard only those insects in the order Hemiptera as "real" bugs. Comprising 67,500 species, the bugs are divided into two suborders: the Heteroptera (true bugs) and the Homoptera (which include cicadas and aphids).

The suborder Heteroptera contains 25,000 known species in about 60 families—these are grouped into "land bugs" (of which a few have adapted to life on the water surface) and "water bugs." Some of the main land-bug families are the Anthocoridae (flower bugs); the Cimicidae (bedbugs, including the European species *Cimex lectularius* that feeds on human blood); the Miridae (capsid bugs) whose 6000 species include *Lopus lineolatus* of Europe; the Reduvidae (assassin bugs, such as the 0.12-in.-long tropical American species *Triatoma megista*); the Gerridae (pond skaters, including the marine genus *Halobates*); the Veliidae, whose 200 or so species include the marine genus *Holvelia*; the Hydrometridae (water striders); the Pyrrhococoridae (fire bugs) including *Pyrrhocoris apterus* of Europe, Asia and America; the Tingidae (lace bugs); and the Pentatomidae (shield bugs) with over 5000 species.

The water-bug families include the Naucoridae (saucer bugs); the Belostomidae (giant water bugs of North America, southern Africa and Asia); the Nepidae (water scorpions); the Notonectidae (water boatmen); and the Corixidae (lesser water boatmen).

The suborder Homoptera contains 42,500 species. Some of the main families are the Fulgoridae (lantern flies); the Delphacidae (plant hoppers, including the sugarcane plant hopper, *Perkinsiella saccharicida*); the Cicadidae (cicadas) including the 17-year cicada, *Magicicada septemdecim*; the Cercopidae (froghoppers); the Aleyrodidae (white fly); the Aphidae (aphids or greenfly); and the Coccidae (scale insects), which includes the cochineal insect, *Dactylopius coccus*.

hunt at night, attacking their prey by piercing the skin and causing a painless bite.

Deadly disease carriers

Although bugs do not have poisonous bites, some species carry harmful poisons in their feces. One such species, the dangerous South American *Triatoma megista*, measures approximately 1.2 in. in length and has brilliant red and black markings. It commonly inhabits rural homes and the dens of mammals. Both immature and adult members of the species suck blood from prey with their rostra. The bites are not painful, but their annoying itch causes victims to scratch themselves and open up tiny wounds in the skin. Parasitic protozoa of the genus *Trypanosoma*—which are contained in the insect's feces—may enter a victim's bloodstream through a wound and cause a fatal illness known as Chagas' disease. Charles Darwin caught the disease on a visit to South America, and he remained a sick man for the rest of his life.

Pond skaters: true bugs on water

Pond skaters are hemipterans of the family Gerridae. They live on ponds and other still bodies of water where they slide across the water's surface without sinking.

Pond skaters have long, narrow bodies of approximately 0.2 in. in length. Their second and third pairs of limbs are long and splayed out in an X-shape, allowing them to rest on the water's surface. Water-repellent hairs cover the limbs' tips, keeping the pond skaters completely dry and preventing them from sinking. Their first pair of legs are short, and held up and forward to strike at prey.

Aquatic hunters

Pond skaters prey on small, aquatic creatures that rise to the surface to breathe, as well as on ants and other insects that fall into the water. They impale their victims on their beaks and paralyze them with their digestive saliva. After a few minutes, they suck in their prey's liquefied tissues, leaving only the empty cuticle.

Diactor bilineatus

Plisthenes ventralis

Mozena lunata

The rose aphid
(*Macrosiphum rosae*)

A species of shield bug
(*Graphosoma italicum*)

A species of lace bug
(*Stephenitis pyri*)

The horned tree hopper
(*Centrotus cornutus*)

...es of tree hopper
...nia spinosa)

The vine phylloxera
(*Phylloxera vastatrix*)

The lantern fly (*Centrotypus amplicornis*)

2439

LEFT Male and female pond skaters of the species *Gerris lacustria* breed twice each year in temperate climates. The second generation of offspring hibernate on land, but occasionally take to the water on warm winter days. They mate in the spring, and the female lays approximately 100 eggs on submerged and floating plants.

BELOW LEFT The sloe bug, *Dolycoris baccarum*, a species of shield bug that feeds on berries and fruits, has a flattened shape. Its colorful forewings, divided into two parts, a thick basal part and a thin, membranous area toward the tip, act as a protective covering for the hind wings, which they use for flying.

female that responds to the "proposition" skates toward the male emitting faint high-frequency signals as she does so; the male responds by emitting similar high-frequency signals. Courting pond skater couples meet, and mate for about a minute before separating. The female immediately lays her eggs on an aquatic plant, piece of wood or other object, while the male remains nearby to protect her from other males.

Pond skaters spend their lives on the surface of the water, taking shelter only in winter or when it rains. Many species are capable of flying away to search for new homes if their ponds dry up, and thus they are found in bodies of water all over the world.

The family Gerridae includes the genus *Halobates*—one of the few examples of marine insects. Members of the genus live on the Atlantic, Pacific and Indian oceans, spending their entire lives skating on the high seas. They are tiny, wingless creatures that usually lay their eggs on floating feathers.

The family Veliidae

Members of the family Veliidae are similar to Gerridae, but have stockier bodies. Unlike the Gerridae, all six of their legs touch the water's surface, although they move only the middle pair when skating. As they move across the water, they catch small creatures that they then carry to the bank to feed on at leisure.

Water striders

The water striders or Hydrometridae are a family of aquatic true bugs. They live on water, but since they prefer to rest above its surface, on wet mud or parts of aquatic plants, their habits are similar to those of land-based creatures. Although they can walk on

Pond skaters detect prey with their large eyes and the sensitive organs at the tips of their skating limbs. With their limbs they sense even the slightest vibrations on the water's surface. Thus, when an insect accidentally falls into a pond, pond skaters immediately detect the waves made as it thrashes about.

Mating waves

Water vibrations allow pond skaters to communicate with each other, and play an especially important role when males and females are ready to mate. After a male has found a suitable place for egg-laying, he calls to females by beating his legs against the water's surface—sending out messages that begin with high frequencies (many beats per minute) and end at lower frequencies (few beats per minute). A

the water's surface, they usually move very slowly (their scientific name means "water pacers"). Water striders are different from all other aquatic bugs in that they have long antennae, stick-like bodies and slender "pacing" legs. They suck out the body fluids of live or dead insects, but do not use their forelegs to grasp their prey.

Ground and seed bugs

Over 2000 species of ground and seed bugs, of the family Lygaeidae, occur throughout the world. They are tiny creatures that feed mainly on plant sap, puncturing and damaging many types of wild and cultivated plants, including cereal plants and apple trees. In 1912, ground and seed bugs destroyed about a third of the vineyards in southern France, and a South American species has caused considerable damage in Canada. Seed bugs continue to have a disastrous effect on cotton crops in northern Africa.

Fire bugs

The fire bugs of the family Pyrrhocoridae comprise over 400 species that are similar in behavior and structure to the Lygaeidae. Their name, derived from the Greek *pyros* meaning "fire," refers to the brilliant red-and-black colorings of the creatures.

Some species of fire bugs gather in groups of between a few dozen and a few hundred individuals, clustering around the bases of tree trunks or underneath large stones.

Fire bugs of the species *Pyrrhocoris apterus* have red bodies marked with black spots—the most familiar example being the common ladybugs. The species is almost unique among insects in that its body colors and markings vary among individuals. *P. apterus* fire bugs are widespread in Europe, Asia and America, where they feed on plant sap, fruit and small insects. Although they are found on cultivated plants, they do not damage crops.

Some fire bug species cause serious damage to plant life, attacking cotton and other herbaceous plants and trees. Many species are carnivorous, and prey on ants and termites.

Lace bugs

Lace bugs belong to the family Tingidae, which contains over 700 different species. Although lace

BELOW Some insects that live on the surface of the water: Gerridae or pond skaters (A) have water-repellent hairs on the ends of their second and third pairs of legs that enable them to move on the surface film of the water; Gyrinidae, the whirligig beetles (B), have flattened legs fringed with hairs that act as oars; the Notonectidae, or water boatmen (C), live just below the water surface. They swim on their backs and breathe by trapping bubbles of air on the undersides of their bodies.

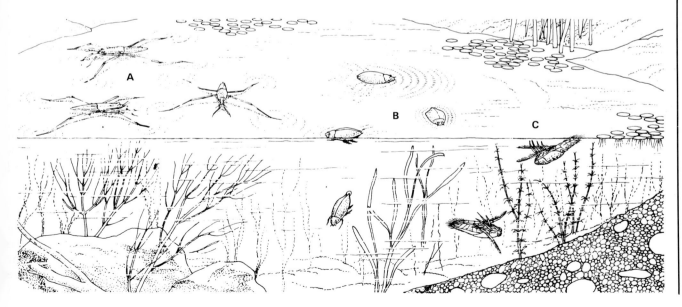

bugs are common creatures, their 0.08 to 0.12-in.-long bodies ensure that they remain an obscure family. They have flat, almost transparent bodies covered in net-like cuticles with the appearance of fine lace.

Shield bugs

Shield bugs constitute the Pentatomidae, which is one of the largest families of bugs, containing over 5000 species. Shield bugs are distinguished from all other families by their wide, pentagonally shaped bodies. Their conspicuous forms are vividly colored in reds, blues, greens or browns, often with metallic flecks. Like all other families of true bugs, shield bugs emit foul-smelling vapors from special openings in their thoraxes.

True bugs underwater

Water bugs comprise several families of true bugs that spend considerable lengths of time underwater—there are over 1100 species. They are characterized by very short antennae, spade-shaped limbs and an absence of stink glands or poison glands. During evolution, water bugs have had to deal with the problem of underwater respiration, since none possess gills. Some species swim to the surface of the water from time to time to replenish their air supplies, while others, such as the water scorpions, breathe through long, respiratory siphons at their tail ends.

Saucer bugs

The family Naucoridae contains the saucer bugs—small bugs that resemble water beetles. The membranous tips of their front wings, however, identify them as true bugs. Saucer bugs live in stagnant water that contains an abundance of submerged vegetation; they swim at great speed with their backs suspended below the water's surface. Their front legs are shaped like penknives, for grasping prey.

A coat of fine hairs covers a saucer bug's body, each hair being curved at the tip to trap a tiny pocket of air. Consequently, a thin layer of air constantly surrounds the creature, giving it an attractive, silvery appearance. The air covering functions as a sort of external lung: as a saucer bug draws oxygen from it, dissolved oxygen in the water passes into the layer of air and sticks to the body's surface. Occasionally, saucer bugs surface to completely replenish their air supplies.

TOP The shield bug, *Picromerus bidens*, common to Britain and northern Europe, is a predatory insect that feeds on the larvae of beetles, butterflies and moths. It is useful to humans because it eats insects that can cause damage to crops.
ABOVE The fully aquatic *Belostomidae*, or giant water bugs, are capable of immersing themselves totally in the water, although they often float at the surface. They breathe through two retractable respiratory tubes situated at the rear of their abdomens. They are voracious aquatic insects that often attack frogs and fish.

Giant water bugs

The family Belostomidae contains the giant water bugs or toe biters, and consists of about 100 species that are widespread in North America, southern Africa and Asia—a few species live in eastern Europe. True to their name, giant water bugs are often huge, some species being nearly 4 in. long. They are some of the most ferocious of all insects and readily attack prey much larger than themselves. Giant water bugs antagonize not only other water insects but also frogs, salamanders and fish—in some cases, they have even attacked water snakes and birds that paused to drink at the water's edge. Like other bugs, they liquefy the internal organs of their prey before sucking up the contents through their beaks.

Apart from being strong swimmers, giant water bugs are proficient fliers. If the hunting in a particular pond is poor, they fly away in search of a more suitable habitat. During flight, they breathe like other insects, through stigmata on their thoraxes. Underwater, however, they use two retractable respiratory tubes at the rear ends of their abdomens.

Reproduction

Giant water bugs have an unusual method of reproduction. After mating occurs, the female climbs onto the back of the male and deposits over 100 eggs onto his wings, bonding the eggs to the surface of the wings with secretions that do not dissolve in water.

The added burden of the secretions and eggs prevents the male from opening his wings to fly, forcing him to remain in the pond until the eggs hatch a week later. The newly hatched larvae disperse into the water immediately or remain attached to the male's back for a little longer. After the larvae disperse, the female cleans the remains of the egg shells from the back of the male so that he is able to receive the next brood.

Aquatic bugs

The 150 species of the family Nepidae are aquatic bugs. Commonly known as the water scorpions, they are active hunters, usually lying in ambush for their prey. They have distinctive, raptorial (snatching) front legs that divide into two segments; the bugs stretch and contract the segments like the blade of a penknife as it opens and closes. The abdomen of the water scorpions terminates in two segments of varying

ABOVE The female of the giant water bug, *Belostoma foveolam*, cements her eggs onto the back of the male with adhesive secretions that do not dissolve in water. The male is unable to fly because of his cargo and carries the eggs until they are ready to hatch. He then floats at the surface of the water and dips his body as each egg hatches, so that the young can slide into the water.

length that lie against one another to form a breathing tube, supplying the insects with air during their regular visits to the surface.

Nepan species are carnivores, and lie motionless for hours waiting for a victim to pass within reach of their grasping claws. They prey on insects, tadpoles and small fish, impaling them on their beaks and paralyzing them immediately with their saliva. While lying in wait, they breathe through a long, respiratory tube that occurs at the end of their abdomen. Occasionally, the bugs rise toward the surface, letting the tip of their respiratory tube emerge above the water, so that they can inhale air.

The water scorpion, *Ranatra linearis*, commonly known as the water stick insect, has a long, thin body that grows to 1.6 in. in length. Like the water scorpions of the genus *Nepa*, the water stick insect has a long, slender breathing tube at the end of its abdomen. It inhabits the same habitat as Nepan water

ABOVE The water stick insect, *Ranatra linearis*, has a long thin body and a breathing siphon that is nearly as long as the rest of its body. Its coloring provides good camouflage in ponds and ditches. Resembling vegetation, it spends its time hidden among the waterweeds waiting for prey, but every so often it approaches the surface to take in air.
FAR RIGHT When traveling through the water, the water boatman *Notonecta glanca* swims on its back with powerful strokes of its hind legs.

scorpions, but prefers to live among water weeds, using its stalk-like camouflage for protection. The water stick insect hunts insects, tadpoles and small fish.

Water boatmen

Water boatmen of the family Notonectidae are among the strangest of all the water insects. They use an extraordinary form of backstroke to swim, plowing through the water on their backs with powerful strokes of their hind legs. The convex shape of the water boatman's back acts like the keel of a ship to enhance its passage through the water. Its classification name comes from the Greek *noto* ("back") and *necto* ("swimming").

Since they swim upside-down, water boatmen have a dark underside and a light-colored dorsal or upperpart to camouflage them against the surrounding water. In this way, they are difficult to see both from above and below, because the surface of the water forms a dark background from above and a light background from below. A layer of water-repellent hairs covers their bodies, trapping a layer of air bubbles around them. The trapped oxygen reflects the rays of light and gives the insects their silvery sheen. As they break the surface of the water, the water boatmen turn over onto their legs and "skate" across the surface in an action that resembles the pond skaters—they press their legs against the water surface, but the water-resistant hairs on their legs prevent them from breaking the surface film.

Water boatmen also feed on crustaceans, tadpoles and fry (young fish). They hunt the aquatic larvae of mosquitoes, including the *Anopheles* mosquito that carries the disease malaria. The voracity and aggressiveness of water boatmen make them completely asocial, unlike the pond skaters, which live in groups. When food is scarce, adult water boatmen hunt the young of their own species, even their own offspring. If their habitat becomes unsuitable, they move off in search of another pond.

Lesser water boatmen

Commonly known as the lesser water boatmen, the members of the family Corixidae resemble water

TOP The vegetarian, land-based, European lantern fly, *Dictyophara europaea*, sucks sap from a plant using its specially adapted mouthparts. Lantern flies dwell among the foliage of trees and bushes, feeding upon the sap.

ABOVE The lantern fly, *Lanternaria candelaria*, is a tropical species belonging to the family Fulgoridae. It has a grossly extended head that is almost as long as its body. Its large, highly decorated wings give it a reptilian appearance.

boatmen in appearance, but they behave differently: they do not position themselves upside-down when they swim and they use the upward thrust of the water to travel from the bottom to the top, breaking the surface at high speed. They are predominantly vegetarian, and, when they feed on animals, they choose small, planktonic organisms or the larvae of aquatic insects. They have small, spike-like mouthparts that function like forks, tearing the prey apart.

Because their bodies are lighter than water, the lesser water boatmen tend to float upward. To remain at the bottom of the pond, they use their limbs to anchor themselves down, only rising to the surface to renew their supply of air. Unlike water boatmen, they store air bubbles in two furrows on the ventral surface of their bodies.

Homoptera

Homoptera are typically land-based, vegetarian insects. Some, such as aphids, cause serious damage to crops. They pierce the veins of plants with their beaks and suck out the sap. Sometimes, they do not have to go to the trouble of sucking it out—the sap oozes out under pressure as soon as the insects perforate the veins.

The probing mouthparts of homopterans enable these insects to take full advantage of the vast quantities of plants at their disposal, and they spend all their lives sucking sap from them. The sap contains the all-important proteins that the aphids need, as well as water and sugar. But since there is very little protein in sap, homopterans must take in large amounts of sap. The result is that they absorb too much sugar; this excess sometimes condenses into a waxy substance that collects on the surface of the insects' bodies or forms a sweet honeydew that oozes from the insects' cuticles. The sugary liquid either disappears into the soil or is lapped up by ants.

Masks and long tails

The Fulgoridae comprise one of the main families in the suborder Homoptera, and they include creatures commonly known as lantern flies. Their name derives from the fact that Fulgoridae were once thought to emit light. All species in the family dwell in tropical or hot climates; very few can be found in Europe.

The strangest, most conspicuous characteristic of the Fulgoridae is its head. It is distinctive and monstrous in shape, and sometimes it is almost as

long as their body. Some species of Fulgoridae have heads that protrude forward, forming a mask that resembles a crocodile's jaws.

Fulgoridae dwell among the foliage of trees and bushes, feeding upon the sap. They lay their eggs on branches or leaves, often covering them with grains of earth that they stick together with their secretions. They fly or leap, depending on the species, and are rarely harmful to cultivated plants.

Crop pests

The family Delphacidae, or plant hoppers, includes several crop pests. The species *Perkinsiella saccharicida*, which was imported to Hawaii from Australia at the beginning of the 20th century, seriously damages sugarcane crops by injecting them with parasitic viruses. It almost destroyed the Hawaiian sugarcane industry. However, rather than relying on chemical insecticides to control the plant hopper population, a natural enemy of the plant hopper was imported. A capsid bug of the Miridae family ate the plant hoppers' eggs and soon reduced the population of these plant pests.

The loudest insects

In warm climates, cicadas are undoubtedly the best-known homopterans. There are over 3000 species of cicadas, mainly distributed throughout hot climates. In Europe, they most commonly inhabit Mediterranean areas, although one species—*Cicadetta montana*—does occur in limited parts of Britain.

It is the chirruping of the males that is so characteristic of cicadas. In some species, the females also emit vibrations, but they are not audible to the human ear. While an organ comparable to a string-resonating instrument produces the song of the cricket, one similar to a drum makes the cicada's call. It consists of two convex plates, called tymbals, situated on either side of the first abdominal segment. Two powerful muscles make the plates vibrate, and the surrounding space acts like an amplifier. The resulting sound is the loudest known insect noise.

Subterranean larvae

Cicadas die before the onset of winter, but just before they end their life cycle they mate and lay their eggs. The female deposits her eggs in long, regular rows, fixing them to the branch of a tree. They hatch

ABOVE An adult cicada sitting high up on the trunk of a tree where it spends a great deal of its time, singing intermittently. Related to the aphids, frog-hoppers and scale insects, cicadas have broad, flattened bodies and two pairs of large wings with a characteristic pattern of veins that do not extend to the outer rim of their wings, but stop short leaving a narrow margin along the outer border of each wing. As in this cicada, their wings are usually transparent.

LEFT After feeding underground, the cicada larva digs its way to the surface of the soil and scales a nearby tree. It then metamorphoses into its winged, adult form.

BELOW LEFT The tree hopper, *Ceresa bubalus*, shaped and colored like a leaf, is extremely well camouflaged against predators when feeding in the foliage.

into tiny larvae enclosed within delicate transparent sacs. Once the larvae have freed themselves from the sacs, they dry in the open air and drop to the ground. Then they search for a place to dig, and so begins the subterranean, or underground, phase of their lives.

Cicadas remain in the larval stage for varying lengths of time, depending on the species. When they have finished growing, the larvae wait for a hot summer's day and come to the surface to begin their life among the trees. When they first emerge from underground, their eyes and wings are not properly developed. They climb onto the lower part of a tree trunk and molt for the last time before reaching adulthood.

The 17-year cicada

One species of cicada that lives throughout North America takes at least 17 years to develop. It measures about 1.5 in. in length and is appropriately called *Magicicada septemdecim* or, more commonly, the 17-year cicada. There are, in fact, two types of 17-year cicadas. The northern variety lives up to its name and takes 17 years to develop, but individuals that range further south have a larval stage that lasts for 13 years.

Froghoppers

The family Cercopidae contains about 2500 species of insects known as froghoppers and spittlebugs, that live in both hot and temperate climates. The green, moist froghopper larvae live inside a frothy mass, known as "cuckoo spit," that they produce and attach to plants. The larvae have a deep, gutter-like furrow along the underside of their abdomens, bearing the openings of their tracheae or respiratory tubes. The mixture that forms the froth emerges from the anus and runs along their abdominal fold and over their tracheal openings, where it mixes with streams of air and forms bubbles. Slowly, the froghopper larvae surround themselves with a mass of foam. Inside the spittle mass, sheltered from predators and from drying out in the sun, the developing larvae feed on the xylem sap of the plant on which they hatch.

RIGHT The froghopper larva intent on making its shelter of bubbles or "cuckoo spit." The larva excretes the liquid through its anus. The liquid passes underneath the larva, where air from the respiratory tubes turns it into bubbles.

BELOW RIGHT The mass of white foam hanging from the stalk of a plant contains the froghopper larva. The bubbles or cuckoo spit protect the larva from predators and parasites and also prevent it from drying out while it sucks the sap of plants.

Although the "cuckoo spit" shelter is effective, it is not totally secure: certain types of wasp of the family Sphecidae remove the larvae from the foam and eat them. Some froghoppers are willow tree parasites, and when the wind blows, their bubbles scatter like small flakes, creating a "weeping" effect.

Brightly colored bugs

Unlike their larvae, the adult froghoppers do not live in a spittle mass and are extremely mobile, rapidly leaping about among the plants and bushes. They are difficult to capture: if startled or hit by a predator, they drop down into the grass, feigning death. Many adult froghoppers have red-and-black markings and many have brightly colored wings. Froghoppers live on a range of plants and herbs, such as willows, poplars, alders, pines, sage and rosemary. However, the meadow spittlebug *Philaneus spumarius* (the most common and widespread species in Europe and in the USA) feeds on a much wider range of plants. Meadow spittlebugs occur in a range of colors, from entirely dark to pale varieties.

Leafhoppers

The family Cicadellidae contains 15,000 species of insects commonly known as leafhoppers. Although related to the froghoppers, adult leafhoppers are smaller, and have their antennae between their eyes. The sexes usually have different coloring. For example, females of the species *Cicadella viridis* are green, while the males are sky-blue. Leafhoppers live among herbs and bushes, where they sometimes collect in large numbers. Most leafhoppers feed on phloem sap, the nutrient-bearing liquid in plants. They damage plants by sucking the sap and by laying their eggs in the young shoots. They carry viruses that cause yellowing in peach trees and shriveling in sugar-beet leaves. Leafhoppers also pose a threat to potatoes, cereals, vines, cotton, rose bushes and other herbaceous plants. Although a large number of plant families play host to leafhoppers, most leafhopper species feed only on a narrow range of plants, and many on just one genus or group of plants.

Tree hoppers

The family Membracidae or tree hoppers consists of 2500 species that live in tropical areas. Many of these creatures have large, strangely shaped outgrowths resulting from the unusual development of the first segment of their thoraxes (the pronotum), which results in a broad, hood-like covering. In the rose-thorn tree hopper *Umbonia spinosa* of Central and South America, the pronotum takes the form of a thorn that is believed to be a defense against predators. Tree hoppers live in small groups, often in association with ants. The tree hoppers produce

LEFT *Ledra aurita*, a leafhopper with an extremely effective camouflage. It is just under 0.7 in. in length. Leafhoppers often live in herbs and bushes and can damage plants by sucking the sap and laying their eggs in the young shoots.

BELOW LEFT *Psylla pyricola*, a species of leaf sucker that infests orchards. Its transparent wings have few veins, and they hold them over their bodies when at rest. They have small, soft bodies and rostrums resembling those of aphids.

eggs. Most leaf-sucker species are adapted to living on a single, specific host.

The leaf-sucker larvae secrete large quantities of wax, in the form of flakes or strands, that cover their bodies to varying degrees. In some cases, the wax forms a small receptacle resting against the back end of their bodies that collects their sugar-rich excrement.

Whiteflies

The family Aleyrodidae consists of 1200 species of insects known as whiteflies. They attach their eggs to the undersides of leaves by means of a tiny stalk inserted in the leaf tissue. Initially, the larvae are mobile, but after the first molt, their limbs become reduced to stumps and their wax glands begin to function.

By the time the larvae have developed fully, the wax glands have produced a skein of waxy threads that completely surround the insects. Even the adults are permanently coated in a white, waxy powder—their classification name derives from the Greek word *aleuron* meaning "flour." After their third or fourth molt, the larvae begin to suck the sap of the plants to which they are attached, and gradually transform themselves into adults inside their coatings of wax. The final larval stage, called the puparium, has similarities to the chrysalis of higher insects.

Adult whiteflies are between 0.04 and 0.1 in. long. Although they resemble aphids, they are slimmer and more elegant. They live on the underside of leaves, clinging on with their tiny but robust claws. When moving from one leaf to another, they take a leap that launches them into flight, and they soon come to rest on a new leaf. Some females reproduce parthenogenetically—that is, without fertilization by males.

Whiteflies suck the sap of citrus trees, tomato plants, fig trees, tobacco plants, sugarcane and other types of plants. The cabbage whitefly lives on cabbages and related crops, but it causes little damage to them.

honeydew that the ants collect and feed on; in return, the ants protect the tree hoppers against predators such as spiders.

Leaf suckers

The family Psyllidae, or leaf suckers, consists of about 1000 species. They have the same general appearance as froghoppers and tree hoppers, with wings that fold over their bodies to resemble roofs. However, psyllidaeans have small, soft bodies like aphids.

Leaf suckers are sometimes called jumping plant lice, and their ability to leap distinguishes them from aphids. It is only the adults that have this ability, for the immature stages are almost immobile. They fly well and their wings have few veins. Leaf suckers disperse on the wing, and the females take great care when choosing the plant species on which to lay their

RIGHT **The aphid or greenfly,** *Macrosiphum rosae*, **a parasite that attacks roses, is commonly called the rose aphid. The female is giving birth to live young, and the offspring are just free of her body. She may produce as many as 25 daughters in one day. Aphids have two pairs of transparent** wings, the first pair being much longer.
BELOW RIGHT **A group of aphids (greenflies) on the stem of a plant. They reproduce rapidly, and because they are major crop pests, farmers regularly monitor their levels and take action when their numbers increase dramatically.**

Aphids

The family Aphidae contains 4000 species of true aphids or plant lice. Extremely common on every kind of plant and tree, these insects, commonly known as greenflies or blackflies, are among the most widely distributed insects in the world. (They occur in greater numbers in temperate than in hot climates.) They are among the most harmful of all insects, as far as crops are concerned. They normally only measure about 0.08-0.12 in. in length, although a small minority of species grow as long as 0.3 in. Some species have four lightweight and transparent wings, while other species lack wings (depending on sex and biological cycle). Their bodies have a thin, soft cuticle. On each side, toward the end of their abdomen, they have two horn-like protuberances that produce and secrete the sugary substance known as honeydew. The family Aphidae is divided into four subfamilies: the Aphidinae, the Eriosomatinae, the Phylloxerinae and the Chermesinae.

The subfamily Aphidinae contains more species of aphids than any of the other subfamilies. The species resemble each other in shape and color, and it is often difficult to distinguish them.

Aphids have long, thin beaks, or rostrums, adapted for penetrating tough plant tissues. Some species have beaks that are longer than their entire body. Aphids nearly always have sober, uniform coloring that may be green, black or reddish. Some feed on the sap of one specific plant, while others change from one type of plant to another at different stages of their lives.

A female population

The aphid eggs hatch into agile individuals in the spring, and they seek out plants on which to suck the sap. When fully developed, these young aphids lay eggs or give birth to live young by means of parthenogenesis.

These in turn give rise to more females that may or may not be winged, depending on the species, and that lay yet more unfertilized eggs. The process continues throughout the summer, producing many generations of aphids. When the weather begins to turn cold, the many females give birth to live young of both sexes. The males almost always have wings and, in some cases, the females too. The new generation returns to the same species of plant—usually trees—upon which their life cycle began in spring, and mate. The females lay a limited number of eggs that are extremely rich in yolk, enabling them to survive the winter. The whole cycle recommences in the spring.

Eriosomatinae

The subfamily Eriosomatinae consists of aphid species that, although very similar to those in the

ABOVE The life cycle of the whiteflies is similar to that of the jumping plant lice. The adults are covered in a white wax, and the immature whiteflies are largely immobile and scale-like in appearance. They feed on plants and, when disturbed, jump and fly about in large groups. Because of their feeding habits, whiteflies can prove destructive, attacking cabbages, house plants and greenhouse crops.

subfamily Aphidinae, have a stockier appearance and produce enormous amounts of wax. Sometimes the flakes of wax, which resemble woolen flock, cover not only the creatures themselves but the entire branch to which they are attached. The species *Erisoma langerum*, originally from America, measures only 0.08 in. in length. It attacks elms and apple trees, causing massive damage by provoking growths known as galls on the leaf blades and stalks that often cause the plants' death.

Phylloxerinae

The subfamily Phylloxerinae consists of aphid species that differ from the subfamily Aphidinae in that they are tiny and have bulky bodies. They have comparatively large, but extremely light wings, and a complex life cycle in which species that reproduce parthenogenetically alternate with species that contain both males and females. Phylloxerinae live on willow trees, oak trees, walnut trees and other plants.

The vine parasite *Phylloxera vastatrix* arrived in Europe from the United States about 1863. Unlike the American vines, the roots of European vines proved to be highly sensitive to these insects, which in 1938 destroyed about half of Italy's vineyards. To combat them, European vines were grafted onto the more resilient American vine rootstock.

Chermesinae

The aphid subfamily Chermesinae resembles that of Phylloxerinae. It contains many species that live on conifers. Their wings, when present, tend to be arranged like a roof over their backs. Larvae (hatched from the eggs laid early in the spring by a parthenogenetic female) induce pineapple-shaped swellings or galls about 0.8-1.2 in. in length on the twigs of fir trees, larches and pines. The larvae grow inside the galls and, in turn, produce a generation of winged parthenogenetic females. The cycle continues for two years, through a succession of complex stages until, finally, the males appear. Chermesinae occur throughout the world.

Scale insects

The family Coccidae contains about 6000 species of insects commonly known as scale insects. They rarely measure more than 0.12 in. in length. Male scale insects resemble Aphidinaenas. They have a brief adult life and do not feed, devoting their lives to reproduction. The females have oval bodies with little distinction between their heads, thoraxes and abdomens. They have no wings, and in many cases, no limbs either. They have glands that produce wax, silk and lacquer; the lacquer, known as shellac, is a dark red resin particularly associated with certain species, such as *Laccifer lacca*. In southern Asia it is reared especially to produce this valuable substance, which is used as a varnish.

Crawlers

The newly hatched larvae, active creatures called "crawlers," are the stage where dispersal occurs. Crawlers of some species can survive being blown about by the wind, traveling a considerable distance before settling down on a plant to commence feeding.

Another common species, *Dactylopius coccus*, lives on cactus plants in the West Indies and in Mexico. Before the invention of synthetic dyes, the dried, crushed bodies of these creatures made the valuable cochineal dye.

The common scale insect that inhabits citrus trees hardly even resembles an animal. It often lives on oranges, and clinging to the peel, it looks like a flat, dark scale, measuring about 0.12 in. long. There are many other species of scale insects, the majority being plant pests.

NATURE'S TANKS

Often seen lumbering along in their tough, protective wing casings, the beetles are actually the most diverse of all the insects— including in their vast number both the tiniest and largest of insect species

LEFT The devil's coach-horse beetle lives under rotting plants where it hunts maggots and other insect larvae. It is a dull black color, and its upper surface is covered with fine dots. Unlike most species of beetle, the devil's coach-horse beetle has short wing cases that cover the first two segments of its abdomen.

PAGE 2453 The pollen-eating chafer beetle has a dense covering of light-colored hair all over its body, except on its yellow and black wing cases. While the beetle feeds, pollen collects on its hairs, and when the beetle flies to another plant the pollen is transferred from one flower to another, pollinating them.

are also many unusual species, such as blind, colorless, cave-dwelling beetles that feed on organic debris or mold, and species that have evolved an aquatic way of life, living in the calm waters of lakes and ponds or in the swift currents of mountain streams. Beetles are one of the few forms of life that are able to live on mountains more than 16,400 ft. high.

Tricks of survival

Some beetles have adapted to life in scorching desert sand, often emerging only at night. To survive the desert environment these beetles have developed the ability to collect and store every drop of water that is available. Plants are often scarce in the desert, and so many of the beetles living there feed on the excreta or the decaying bodies of other invertebrates. Many nondesert beetle species have a similar diet. These beetles have an amazing digging ability and work ceaselessly, burying large quantities of dung or tiny corpses that they will feed on later. Since the uneaten remains of their meals eventually decay, the beetles play a vital role in releasing essential nutrients back into the soil.

Certain beetle species have evolved to resemble ants and termites. So accurate is their mimicry that they are able to move among them, exploiting the food of their hosts to the full. In some cases the beetles are accepted because of their perfect mimicry, but other species, such as the rove beetles, go so far as to offer their hosts intoxicating liquids.

Very few beetles have a parasitic life-style, and they are never parasitic on higher animals such as mammals and birds. However, some beetles do live alongside higher animals. For example, the beetle species *Platyspsyllus castons* lives in the fur of beavers where it hunts for parasitic mites to the benefit of the

The beetles are the most numerous group of animals in the world. There are approximately 350,000 recorded species of beetles, accounting for almost half of all known insects. In addition, a few hundred new types of beetles are described every year, adding bit by bit to the already impressive range of known species. In fact, recent survey work in rain forest areas suggests that there are millions of species of beetles awaiting discovery—that is, if they are not wiped out by the remorseless destruction of the rain forests.

The huge success of the beetles is due largely to their ability to adapt to so many environments. Beetles are found in almost every habitat and are able to survive and multiply even in the harshest conditions. Nevertheless, only a few species live in a marine environment. One of them, a water beetle from the family Hydrophilidae, lives in the extremely changeable and restricted environment of rock pools. Here, individuals manage to survive in water containing high levels of salt. When the conditions become too harsh, the beetles fly off in search of new shores and new pools. However, the open sea still remains an insurmountable barrier as far as beetles are concerned.

Most beetles live in habitats where there is plenty of vegetation on which to feed—for example, in forests, woods, scrub or open fields and meadows. But there

beaver. Another species lives in birds' nests, particularly those of birds of prey, and functions as a cleaner by feeding on bird droppings and food remains.

The human connection

Although the majority of beetle species are indirectly beneficial to man, a few species are notorious as pests of agriculture, forestry and households, and have a serious economic impact.

Insect pests often occur where large areas of land have been planted with a single crop. The huge crop yield provides an increase in the insect's food supply, enabling its population to multiply rapidly. Both adult beetles and their larvae collect in huge swarms to feed upon a whole range of vegetable matter, tearing away relentlessly at wood, leaves, buds, flowers, fruits, seeds and roots. Such infestation causes immense damage.

The most serious beetle pests of cereal crops are the wireworms, whose larvae eat the seeds of the plants and tunnel into their roots and stems. Wireworms are usually present in grassland long before the land is cultivated, but they become pests when the land is plowed up and planted with cereals.

The Colorado killer

Many crop pests are leaf feeders. The most notorious and destructive of them is the Colorado beetle, which attacks the leaves of potato plants. Only about the size of a ladybug, it was discovered in 1823 in the Rocky Mountains of Colorado, where it fed on the wild plants of the potato and nightshade family (such as buffalo burr). When cultivated potatoes began to be introduced into the West, the beetles began to attack them. By 1874 they had spread to the Atlantic coast and were considered a potato pest. In the early 1920s the Colorado beetle was accidentally carried to Europe. Here, both the adults and young began to attack potato crops as a substitute for their normal food, rapidly stripping the plants of their leaves.

Many other leaf-eating species of beetle exist, such as the flea beetle, which attacks cabbages, turnips and sugar beets; and the asparagus beetle, which feeds on the young shoots of asparagus plants.

Weevils are a large group of beetles whose front part of the head is drawn out into a beak. They include a wide range of species that can cause severe damage to peas, beans, fruit and root crops, often by feeding on the flowers or seeds of the plants. One major weevil

ABOVE A larva of the Colorado beetle of North America. Like the adult, it feeds voraciously on leaves and causes extensive damage to potato plants.
BELOW The crawling water beetle (A) has relatively unspecialized legs. The carnivorous diving beetle (B) has long, hairy back legs for swimming and diving; small, hooked front legs for capturing prey, and unspecialized middle legs to steer through water. The whirligig beetle (C) has two pairs of small, paddle-like legs for skimming the water surface, and arm-like front legs for capturing prey.

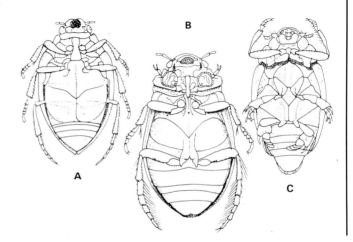

ABOVE The longhorn beetle is one of the most harmful species of wood-boring beetles. The female beetle chews notches around the branches of oak trees and lays her eggs in cracks in the bark, sealing them in with hardened secretions. When the larvae hatch, they live inside the trunk, using their powerful jaws to dig winding tunnels that reduce the wood to sawdust. The larvae take from three to four years to reach maturity. Then they metamorphose into adults and fly away. They reach between 1.9 and 2.4 in. in length excluding their antennae, which can measure approximately 4 in.

INSECTS CLASSIFICATION: 12

Beetles and weevils

Some 350,000 species of beetles (including weevils) constitute the order Coleoptera. They are divided into four suborders, reflecting the level of evolution reached by the various families. The suborder Archostemata is an ancient group consisting of two small families, though most of the species in them are fossils.

Suborder Adephaga contains about 30,000 species arranged in 10 families. These are mainly carnivorous beetles with large jaws and long antennae. The suborder has both land-dwelling and aquatic species, and they include the families Carabidae (ground beetles such as *Calosoma sycophanta* and *Carabus auronitens*; bombadier beetles; and tiger beetles such as *Cicindela concolor* of southern Turkey, *Cicindela hybrida* of Italy, and *Cicindela campestris*); Gyrinidae (whirligig beetles); and Dytiscidae (carnivorous diving beetles such as the great diving beetle, *Dytiscus marginalis*).

The suborder Myxophaga is a small group of tiny beetles that feed on algae and have aquatic larvae. Recently separated from the fourth and final family, Polyphaga, it has 22 species grouped into four families.

The largest of the beetle groups is the suborder Polyphaga whose approximately 248,000 species are divided into 150 families. These beetles have a wide geographical range, occupying almost every imaginable habitat except the open sea. Notable groups and species of beetles that are contained in this suborder include crop pests such as wireworms (family Elateridae); the Colorado beetle, *Leptinotarsa decemlineata*, of the USA, weevils (family Curculionidae) including the boll weevil, *Anthonomus grandis*, that attacks flowering cotton plants, bark beetles (family Scolytidae) such as the elm bark beetle, *Scolytus scolytus*; wood-boring beetles of the family Cerambycidae such, as the longhorn beetle, *Cerambyx cerdo*, and the deathwatch beetle, *Xestobium rufovillosum*, of the family Anobiidae; ladybugs (family Coccinellidae); dung beetles (family Geotrupidae); scarab beetles (family Scarabaeidae) including the green scarab beetle, *Kheper aegyptiorum*; stag beetles (family Lucanidae); and tenebrionid or darkling beetles (family Tenebrionidae).

pest is the boll weevil, which lays its eggs inside the buds or fruit of the cotton plants. When the larvae hatch out they eat away at the inside of the seed pods (or bolls), preventing the cotton fiber from forming between the seeds, and destroying the value of the crop. Similarly, the apple blossom weevil lays its eggs in the flowers of apple trees, preventing the fruit from developing properly.

Forest pests

The most important beetle pests of forest trees are the bark beetles, whose larvae dig deep tunnels beneath the bark of the trunk and branches. Such activity not only affects the trees' health directly but also encourages the onset of serious viral, bacterial or fungal infections. The damage the beetles do is never very obvious from the outside, but it is extensive inside the tree. The world economy loses many millions of dollars a year as a result of the activity of wood-boring beetles. The elm bark beetle is probably the best-known species, having virtually wiped out all British elms owing to a deadly fungus carried by the adults that causes Dutch elm disease.

Many other trees are victims of wood-boring beetles. Members of the beetle family Cerambycidae—fiery-red beetles with black markings—attack peach, cherry and apple trees. While the adults nibble the blossoms, their larvae live in the wood. There are also blackish brown wood-boring beetles that attack oaks, ashes, lime trees, and willows among others.

Household pests

Some species of beetles cause damage inside people's homes. Perhaps the most serious of these are the death-watch beetles and the woodworm beetles whose larvae bore their way through wooden joists, floorboards and furniture, causing them to crumble. Beetles also attack a variety of other items, including furs, carpets, leather, cooked and dried meats, stored grain or flour products, and natural-history specimen collections.

In spite of the damage done by beetles, only a tiny percentage of beetles are pests. The majority perform useful environmental tasks, such as pollinating flowers and breaking down dead plant and animal material. A few such species are of particular importance to humans. Ladybugs, for example, are ferocious predators of aphids (greenflies) and scale insects, and when present in large enough numbers, they are able to save crops

ABOVE **A dark-colored tenebrionid beetle that often lives in old cellars and on stony ground. Members of the large family live in a range of different habitats. Some prefer domestic habitats where they can attack** human food supplies, and others have adapted to life in the desert. Most are nocturnal and cannot fly. One species, the stink beetle, raises its abdomen and emits an unpleasant odor when it wants to repel predators.

from destruction by these parasites. In some cases, beetles have been sent far away from their native country to overcome pest problems. In North America, the population of gypsy moths has been controlled by the introduction of a European carabid beetle that preys on the moths' caterpillars. Similarly, dung beetles from Africa and South America are being used in Australia to help remove vast quantities of dung produced by cattle.

Beetle characteristics

Beetles occur in a wide range of shapes and colors. Their bodies are usually protected by a tough, hard exoskeleton that encloses them like armor and protects them from predators. In addition, their exoskeletons prevent them from drying out in hot weather and enable them to burrow through the ground without getting crushed.

Except for underground and cave-dwelling species, beetles have compound eyes of varying degrees of sophistication, enabling most species to see in color. Their antennae also vary in shape and size, but usually consist of 11 segments: they may be long and slender, or resemble miniature clubs, combs or spades. Alternatively, the antennae can be complex structures consisting of several plates. Whatever their

ABOVE Ladybugs are well known for their characteristic black spots on a vivid red or yellow body. The bright markings advertise their unpleasant taste, and their smooth, rounded shape protects **them from predators such as spiders. Both adults and larvae are formidable predators, and they are frequently used as a natural way to curb crop-destroying pests such as greenfly and scale insects.**

shape, they all carry many sensory structures and function as organs of touch and smell.

Almost all beetles have straightforward biting mouthparts composed of an upper lip or labrum, a pair of upper jaws, a secondary pair of lower jaws and a lower lip or labium. Their lower jaws and lower lips bear sensory palps for tasting and selecting food, while their upper jaws process the food. Some species of plant-eating beetles have upper jaws that bite and chew the food, while in predatory beetles they are sharp and pointed for capturing prey.

A three-part thorax

A beetle's thorax consists of three segments, each bearing one pair of legs, the size of which depends on their function. For example, dung beetles have broad, toothed legs that enable them to dig, while true water beetles have curved and paddle-like legs for swimming.

The first segment of the thorax is wingless and exposed; each of the remaining two segments bears a pair of wings (one of the few exceptions is the female glowworm, which has no wings at all). It is the first pair of wings that gives the beetle its strength. As beetles evolved, these wings slowly became toughened while remaining movable. Known as wing cases or elytra, they form a shield that covers the soft, upper part of the beetle's abdomen and encloses its flight wings. These elytra meet down the middle of the insect's back when it is not flying, but the beetle holds them forward and out of the way of its beating hind wings during flight. The second pair of thin, membranous flight wings are also folded across its body when not in use. Apart from these major characteristics, the internal structure of the beetle is similar to that of all other insects.

Development of the larvae

Beetles undergo complete metamorphosis from egg to adult with an intervening resting pupal stage. The eggs hatch into various types of wingless larvae that may be aquatic or land-dwelling. Some larvae have tough body coverings and long legs, enabling them to swim and run well. Others are soft-bodied, legless creatures that are capable of locomotion by moving their body segments. The wings develop internally during the growth of the larva, and before developing into winged adults the larvae go through a dormant pupal stage that usually takes place inside a protective pupal case. Pupae are not able to move about, although some are able to make defensive beating movements. In order to protect themselves from would-be predators, the pupae are usually hidden from view in the ground or under bark, but some (such as the ladybug pupae) hang freely from plants.

Tiger beetles

The tiger beetles belong to the suborder Adephaga. There are over 1500 species of tiger beetles, and they occur throughout the tropics, although some live in mild climates.

Although tiger beetles have a simple body structure, they are all highly effective predators. Their bodies are usually between 0.4 and 0.8 in. long, slightly concave, with three pairs of long, slender legs. The structure of their legs and the arrangement of their joints are perfectly suited for running. They have

Giant water bugs

The family Belostomidae contains the giant water bugs or toe biters, and consists of about 100 species that are widespread in North America, southern Africa and Asia—a few species live in eastern Europe. True to their name, giant water bugs are often huge, some species being nearly 4 in. long. They are some of the most ferocious of all insects and readily attack prey much larger than themselves. Giant water bugs antagonize not only other water insects but also frogs, salamanders and fish—in some cases, they have even attacked water snakes and birds that paused to drink at the water's edge. Like other bugs, they liquefy the internal organs of their prey before sucking up the contents through their beaks.

Apart from being strong swimmers, giant water bugs are proficient fliers. If the hunting in a particular pond is poor, they fly away in search of a more suitable habitat. During flight, they breathe like other insects, through stigmata on their thoraxes. Underwater, however, they use two retractable respiratory tubes at the rear ends of their abdomens.

Reproduction

Giant water bugs have an unusual method of reproduction. After mating occurs, the female climbs onto the back of the male and deposits over 100 eggs onto his wings, bonding the eggs to the surface of the wings with secretions that do not dissolve in water.

The added burden of the secretions and eggs prevents the male from opening his wings to fly, forcing him to remain in the pond until the eggs hatch a week later. The newly hatched larvae disperse into the water immediately or remain attached to the male's back for a little longer. After the larvae disperse, the female cleans the remains of the egg shells from the back of the male so that he is able to receive the next brood.

Aquatic bugs

The 150 species of the family Nepidae are aquatic bugs. Commonly known as the water scorpions, they are active hunters, usually lying in ambush for their prey. They have distinctive, raptorial (snatching) front legs that divide into two segments; the bugs stretch and contract the segments like the blade of a penknife as it opens and closes. The abdomen of the water scorpions terminates in two segments of varying

ABOVE The female of the giant water bug, *Belostoma foveolam*, cements her eggs onto the back of the male with adhesive secretions that do not dissolve in water. The male is unable to fly because of his cargo and carries the eggs until they are ready to hatch. He then floats at the surface of the water and dips his body as each egg hatches, so that the young can slide into the water.

length that lie against one another to form a breathing tube, supplying the insects with air during their regular visits to the surface.

Nepan species are carnivores, and lie motionless for hours waiting for a victim to pass within reach of their grasping claws. They prey on insects, tadpoles and small fish, impaling them on their beaks and paralyzing them immediately with their saliva. While lying in wait, they breathe through a long, respiratory tube that occurs at the end of their abdomen. Occasionally, the bugs rise toward the surface, letting the tip of their respiratory tube emerge above the water, so that they can inhale air.

The water scorpion, *Ranatra linearis*, commonly known as the water stick insect, has a long, thin body that grows to 1.6 in. in length. Like the water scorpions of the genus *Nepa*, the water stick insect has a long, slender breathing tube at the end of its abdomen. It inhabits the same habitat as Nepan water

ABOVE The water stick insect, *Ranatra linearis*, has a long thin body and a breathing siphon that is nearly as long as the rest of its body. Its coloring provides good camouflage in ponds and ditches. Resembling vegetation, it spends its time hidden among the waterweeds waiting for prey, but every so often it approaches the surface to take in air.
FAR RIGHT When traveling through the water, the water boatman *Notonecta glanca* swims on its back with powerful strokes of its hind legs.

scorpions, but prefers to live among water weeds, using its stalk-like camouflage for protection. The water stick insect hunts insects, tadpoles and small fish.

Water boatmen

Water boatmen of the family Notonectidae are among the strangest of all the water insects. They use an extraordinary form of backstroke to swim, plowing through the water on their backs with powerful strokes of their hind legs. The convex shape of the water boatman's back acts like the keel of a ship to enhance its passage through the water. Its classification name comes from the Greek *noto* ("back") and *necto* ("swimming").

Since they swim upside-down, water boatmen have a dark underside and a light-colored dorsal or upperpart to camouflage them against the surrounding water. In this way, they are difficult to see both from above and below, because the surface of the water forms a dark background from above and a light background from below. A layer of water-repellent hairs covers their bodies, trapping a layer of air bubbles around them. The trapped oxygen reflects the rays of light and gives the insects their silvery sheen. As they break the surface of the water, the water boatmen turn over onto their legs and "skate" across the surface in an action that resembles the pond skaters—they press their legs against the water surface, but the water-resistant hairs on their legs prevent them from breaking the surface film.

Water boatmen also feed on crustaceans, tadpoles and fry (young fish). They hunt the aquatic larvae of mosquitoes, including the *Anopheles* mosquito that carries the disease malaria. The voracity and aggressiveness of water boatmen make them completely asocial, unlike the pond skaters, which live in groups. When food is scarce, adult water boatmen hunt the young of their own species, even their own offspring. If their habitat becomes unsuitable, they move off in search of another pond.

Lesser water boatmen

Commonly known as the lesser water boatmen, the members of the family Corixidae resemble water

strong, bulky heads that contain two prominent eyes and a pair of long, curved jaws.

The tiger beetles' large eyes are adapted for hunting, while the inside edges of their jaws have sharp, powerful teeth that they use for capturing prey. Although all tiger beetle species have a similar structure, they occur in a wide variety of body colors. Their exoskeletons are always strikingly colorful—especially the wing cases, which can be silky or metallic in appearance. The wing cases of many species are decorated with colorful camouflage patterns.

Various habitats

Tiger beetles can be divided into at least three distinct categories according to their natural habitats: those that live in woods and fields; those that live in sand; and tree-dwelling species.

Despite the fact that tiger beetles have conquered such a wide variety of environments, all of them have similar predatory habits. They thrive in warm environments, and only become active in the middle of the day when they run around searching for food in the form of small beetles, grubs, caterpillars, ants, spiders and other creatures. As they move about, the beetles break into short, swift bursts of flight, skimming the ground to get a better view of their

ABOVE The green tiger beetle is an active predator and good flier. It has large, prominent eyes for hunting, long, running legs and large jaws.
BELOW The tiger beetle larva is predatory like the adult but hunts in a different way. It lives in a self-made tunnel in the ground. When hunting, it sits at the entrance with its head blocking the opening. It uses two spines that project from its back to grip the sides. When a prey is within reach, the larva makes a sudden grab for it with its large jaws and drags it into its tunnel.

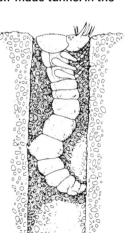
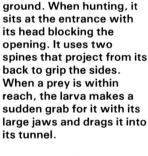
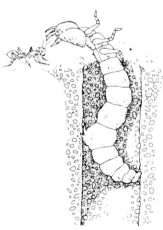

ABOVE Infestation of roses by rose aphids seriously damages or kills the plant. The effect of feeding can cause deformations of the host plant, ranging from deep pit marks in the stem or curled edges on the leaves to large growths. Damage from rose aphids is a major problem in the commercial growing of rose crops. The problem is worsened by the fact that the honeydew feces the rose aphid expels attract many other insects. Some species of ants tend the rose aphids, driving away predators and carrying the rose aphids to the most nutritious part of the plant.

There does not seem to be any kind of hierarchical order between one member of the group and another, nor does there seem to be any justifiable need for them to help one another in the search for food. The real behavioral significance of these swarms lies in the concentration of food sources. Once the food supply begins to dwindle the beetles move on in search of new reserves.

The tiger beetle *Cicindela concolor*, purplish red in color and glowing red and gold in the sunlight, lives along the unpolluted beaches of southern Turkey and occurs in dense swarms during the height of summer. These beetles wander back and forth along the beach, searching for small creatures among the clumps of seaweed left behind by the tide. The tiger beetle *Cicindela hybrida* inhabits the sand and shingle beds of mountain rivers in Italy, and has similar feeding habits. It is dark green in color with yellowish white specks. When the rivers are in flood, these beetles gather in large numbers to feed on the plant-eating insects that collect in the decaying matter left behind when the floods recede.

The wood and field-dwelling species such as *Cicindela campestris* are far less gregarious. The majority are solitary, although some live in small groups within a large hunting ground. Many species have well-camouflaged green bodies with white markings, and they lead a wandering existence, constantly searching for small insects and grubs.

Tree-dwelling species live in moist, tropical environments. They are small creatures with strong claws that enable them to run swiftly up and down tree trunks and branches in search of greenflies and other plant-eating insects. They keep down the numbers of these creatures and play an important role in the preservation of forests.

Deep-digging larvae

Tiger beetles usually lay their eggs on the ground. As soon as the larvae hatch, they dig deep, vertical or slanting tunnels where the ground is softest; sometimes, the tunnels are over 3 ft. deep. The larvae spend their entire preadult lives inside their tunnels, only occasionally poking their heads out above ground level to survey their surroundings. Their heads have huge, upward-pointing jaws and numerous simple eyes positioned for all-around vision. Tiger beetle larvae take from two to four years to mature.

hunting area. Few insects can compare with tiger beetles when it comes to speed of reaction. Once they have spotted a victim it has little chance of escape. The beetles stand still for a moment focusing upon the prey, with all their muscles poised ready to spring. Then they pounce suddenly with unparalleled ferocity, snapping repeatedly at the prey with their powerful jaws. The beetles then take shelter amid the vegetation and eat their food.

A gregarious life-style

Many species of tiger beetles, particularly those that live in sand, gather in large swarms that sometimes consist of many hundreds of individuals.

NATURE'S TANKS

Hidden predators

A tiger beetle larva rests inside the top of its tunnel gripping the tunnel wall with two hooks that project from its upper abdomen. It plugs the tunnel entrance with its head and surveys the ground for potential prey. When prey, such as a small insect, approaches the concealed larva tunnel, the tiger beetle larva makes a sudden grab for it. Once it has caught its victim, the larva drags it down and eats it in the safety of the tunnel. Some species of tiger beetle larva shelter in the flattened, hollow stems of grass or reeds, instead of digging tunnels.

Metamorphosis chamber

Shortly before it reaches full maturity, a tiger beetle larva digs a small chamber off the side of its main tunnel. Inside the chamber, it undergoes its final metamorphosis, developing first into a pupa and later into an adult.

Ground beetles

Over 22,000 species of ground beetles form the largest group within the suborder Adephaga. Ground beetles are particularly widespread in temperate regions but are uncommon in equatorial regions. They are one of the best-known groups of beetles, since many of the species are attractively patterned and colored. Apart from a few exceptions, the different species of ground beetles are similar in shape, but range in length from about 0.1 in. to between 3 and 4 in.—sometimes longer.

Most ground beetles are successful carnivores that live on land. Since the species *Calosoma sycophanta* is such a good runner and is so ferocious a predator of grubs, it has been introduced to American crop fields to combat the population explosion of destructive tussock moth caterpillars. Only a few species of ground beetles, such as *Zabrus tenebrioides*, are herbivores that feed mainly on grass seeds.

Adornment and color

All species of ground beetles have strong outer body coverings, and most are patterned with glistening metallic colors. Night-hunting species are the exception —they usually have black or dark-colored bodies that blend in with the darkness. Apart from their splendid

TOP **Many species of ground beetle are extremely attractive. Light reflects off the surface of their bodies, giving the wing cases a metallic-green appearance. Their bodies are frequently decorated with ridges, depressions or reliefs.**

ABOVE **One species of predatory ground beetle is used to control the spread of the tussock moth, whose caterpillar is a pest of leaf crops. Ground beetles easily catch the caterpillars, even though their prey is almost the same size as themselves.**

colors, many species possess special adornments, such as sturdy ridges, deeply depressed spots and irregular or chain-like reliefs.

Through evolution, ground beetles' bodies have adapted to their predatory life-styles. Their robust heads have large eyes and long, thread-like antennae for detecting prey, while their long legs are highly suited to running. For pulverizing prey, ground beetles have large, strong jaws that are often sharp and serrated.

ABOVE The ground beetle family is the largest in the suborder Adephaga, consisting of over 20,000 species. They are nocturnal predators with well-developed eyes, powerful mouthparts and long legs that are excellent for running. During the day, they hide under logs and stones. At night they hunt for food, preying on earthworms, snails and other insects. Both larvae and adults have similar life-styles and habits.

Ground beetle larvae are usually long and black. They have well-developed legs and jaws, since they have similar feeding habits to their parents. In some cases, the larvae are more aggressive than the adults.

Some species of ground beetles have extreme structural modifications to cope with their highly specialized diets. Snail-eating species, for example, possess elongated heads and first thorax segments to enable easy penetration of snail shells.

Extraordinary life-styles

Numerous species of beetles have specialized physiological characteristics suited to unusual ways of life. Some, such as *Carabus clathratus*, are amphibious, either moving about below the water's surface in search of worms and small snails, or hunting among stones and mud at the edge of running water. Several species live underground or in caves: being eyeless, they have overcome the adverse conditions of their environments by evolving long sensory bristles along the lengths of their bodies. One species of ground beetle lives in burrows on sandy beaches.

Chemical defense

When they are picked up or disturbed, many ground beetles secrete large quantities of poisonous chemicals—called quinones—through the mouth and the joints of the body. The blistering effect that quinones have on the skin is usually sufficient to deter ants, toads and other attackers.

The red-fronted, silky-winged bombardier beetles, such as *Brachinus* species, have highly specialized means of chemical self-defense. When it is intimidated, a bombardier beetle releases strong quinones from special glands in its abdomen, ejecting them from its body by powerful muscular pressure. The secretion explodes noisily on contact with the air, forming a boiling hot spray and a puff of foul-smelling smoke. Several species of bombardier beetles can repeat their discharges many times in quick succession and swivel their abdomens to take aim at would-be attackers.

Certain *Eleodes* species of beetles are less mobile than the bombadier beetles. To compensate, they lower their heads and raise their abdomens to spray quinones directly in their enemies' faces.

Some species of mice have learned how to avoid painful quinone burns and enjoy a meal of beetle flesh. A mouse snatches up a beetle and plunges its abdomen into the sand where the quinones are discharged harmlessly. Once a beetle is rendered harmless in this way, a mouse eats it from the head downward.

Carnivorous diving beetles

About 4000 species of carnivorous diving beetles are distributed throughout the world's warm temperate zones; all species live in still or slow-running freshwater. Carnivorous diving beetles vary in length between about 0.1 in. and almost 2 in., but all are similar in behavior and external appearance. Their streamlined bodies are concave and oval-shaped with smooth, shiny surfaces perfectly adapted for moving through water or air.

Although they are water dwellers, carnivorous diving beetles are competent fliers. Thus, when conditions such as drought, pollution or a food shortage threaten their existence, they fly away from their homes in search of better environments.

Locomotion

Carnivorous water beetles dislike dry land. If they are unlucky enough to fall onto the ground, they move clumsily, dragging themselves slowly along. Underwater, however, they swim gracefully, propelling themselves along with rhythmic movements of their

small, powerful back legs. The edges of the back legs are fringed with hairs to increase the surface area that pushes against the water. Many species use their front legs for prey capture and their middle pair for both steering and propulsion.

Portable air

Although they are well adapted to aquatic life, carnivorous diving beetles do not have gills and therefore cannot absorb oxygen directly from water. Instead, they make repeated visits to the water's surface for air, breaking through the surface tension with difficulty and exposing the rear parts of their abdomens. The beetles store air under their wing cases, drawing air into their bodies through abdominal respiratory holes. After replenishing their air supplies, carnivorous water beetles dive back beneath the water's surface. They have to swim with powerful strokes since the air stored under their wing cases makes them buoyant. Once underwater, carnivorous water beetles cling to water plants to prevent themselves from floating back to the surface.

Flesh eaters

Carnivorous water beetles usually hunt prey slightly smaller than themselves. Thus, small beetles of about

ABOVE A larva of the carnivorous diving beetle catches its prey with its arched, pointed jaws and injects it with a digestive fluid to liquefy its tissues. The larva then sucks up the juices through its hollow jaws.

BELOW When the diving beetle larva has matured, it leaves the water. Using its head and legs, it builds a pupal chamber in the mud nearby. Once inside, it pupates to complete its metamorphosis into an adult.

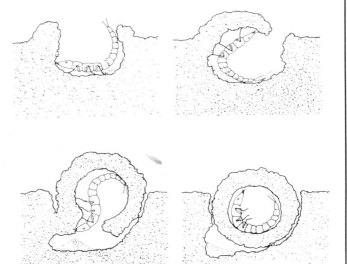

ABOVE **The great diving beetle lives in still or slow-moving water. It stores air in holes in its abdomen and as bubbles under its wing cases. Buoyant from the air, it clings to plants while looking for food.**
BELOW **Some female diving beetles have an abdominal** organ for piercing a hole in underwater plant stems where they lay their eggs (A). Others place their eggs between the stem and leaf (B). A larva breathes through holes in the tip of its abdomen (C). It sucks in the tissues of liquefied prey through its hollow jaw (D).

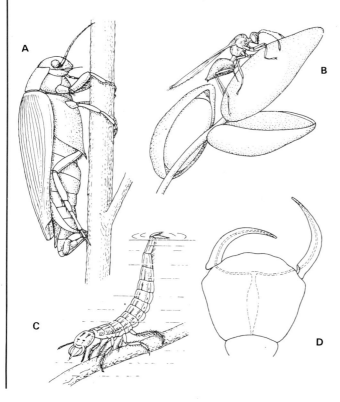

0.1 in. in length eat microscopic animals, larger beetles feed on insects, larvae and aquatic worms, while the largest eat small fish, tadpoles and newts. Although carnivorous diving beetles are predators, they do not miss a chance to feed on the corpses of fishes, amphibians, or any land mammals that fall into the water.

Reproduction and development

Mating is often preceded by an elaborate courtship, during which the male swims persistently around his chosen mate and strokes her gently with his antennae. Male carnivorous diving beetles are distinguished from females by their large front legs, which have a row of suckers along the underside. As soon as a female consents to mate, her suitor climbs onto her back and clings to her grooved wing cases with his suckers—which secrete a sticky fluid.

Ovulation

In some species of carnivorous diving beetles, the female's abdomen has a specialized egg-laying tube, or ovipositor, that is shaped like a small, serrated knife. During egg-laying, the female's ovipositor makes several deep, slanting incisions in the leaves and stems of underwater plants and passes eggs directly into the hole. Species that lack this specialized egg-laying organ gather up their eggs individually after ovulation and place them between the stem and leaf of an underwater plant. Because of their shape and color, they are camouflaged to resemble tiny buds.

The larvae of the carnivorous diving beetles have long, tapering bodies that are transparent. They inhabit the same surroundings as the adults, but prefer shallower water close to the edge. Although they lack specialized swimming limbs, the larvae are excellent swimmers and propel themselves with snake-like movements of their abdomens. Like adults, they breathe air and make frequent trips to the surface to store up oxygen in the respiratory holes at the tip of their abdomens.

PAGES 2466-2467 **The great diving beetle's streamlined, concave body is perfectly adapted for moving through water. Its back legs are fringed with hairs to** increase the surface area that pushes against the water, its middle legs are used for steering and propulsion and its front legs to capture prey.

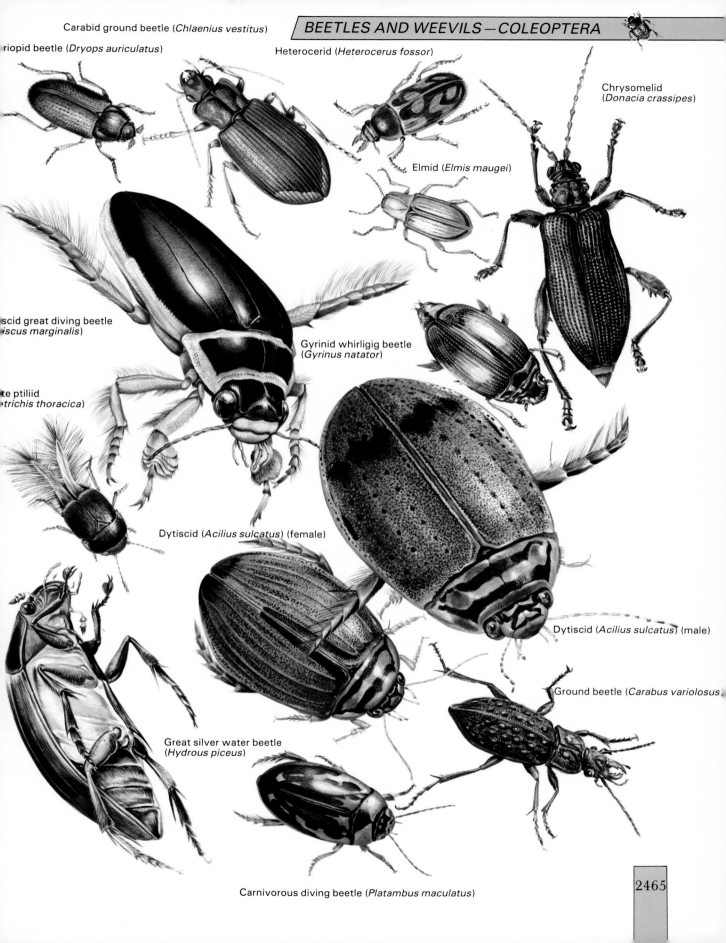

Carabid ground beetle (*Chlaenius vestitus*)

riopid beetle (*Dryops auriculatus*)

Heterocerid (*Heterocerus fossor*)

Chrysomelid
(*Donacia crassipes*)

Elmid (*Elmis maugei*)

scid great diving beetle
iscus marginalis)

Gyrinid whirligig beetle
(*Gyrinus natator*)

te ptiliid
trichis thoracica)

Dytiscid (*Acilius sulcatus*) (female)

Dytiscid (*Acilius sulcatus*) (male)

Ground beetle (*Carabus variolosus*

Great silver water beetle
(*Hydrous piceus*)

2465

Carnivorous diving beetle (*Platambus maculatus*)

Relentless predators

The larvae are relentless predators and attack any water creature that is comparable in size to themselves—adult insects and larvae, crustaceans, amphibians such as salamanders, newts, young frogs and even fishes. They have formidable mouthparts, consisting of arched, sharp jaws that project from the front of their heads.

A unique feature of a carnivorous diving beetle larva is that its mouth is closed at the front; a hollow channel runs through each jaw and opens at the sides. As soon as the mandibles of the larva grasp the victim, the larva pierces the skin of the prey with its jaws and paralyzes it with a poisonous liquid. At the same time, the larva injects digestive juices that liquefy the tissues of the victim, turning them into a mushy liquid. It then sucks out the victim's liquefied tissue through its mandibular channels until nothing remains of the victim except an empty husk.

Metamorphosis

When the dytiscid larvae are ready to metamorphose, they emerge from the water and select a site on the muddy bank to build a chamber in which they will complete their transition into adulthood. Using their heads and legs, the larvae mold a small, rounded cell to protect them as they pass through the pupal stage.

The pupal stage of their development is brief, but it is undoubtedly the most critical phase of the beetles' life cycle. Because it is immobile and enclosed within a case, the pupa remains in danger of drying out or of being flooded unexpectedly during the course of its metamorphosis. When the adult carnivorous diving beetle first emerges, it remains inside the mud chamber for a few days until its exoskeleton hardens. Then it comes out into the open and runs straight back into the water.

The whirligig beetles

The 400 species of the family Gyrinidae are shiny black or dark bronze in color. Commonly known as whirligig beetles, they differ from other aquatic members of the order Adephaga. Fossil remains of the whirligigs' ancestors date from the Jurassic epoch, 180 million years ago.

The whirligig beetles are believed to be the direct ancestors of the carnivorous diving beetles. Both types of beetle are the most specialized of all the aquatic insects. There is no competition between these two closely related families because adult carnivorous diving beetles live at the bottom of the water, while whirligig beetles occur at the surface of the water.

The bodies of the whirligig beetles have adapted for life at the surface of the water. They have a

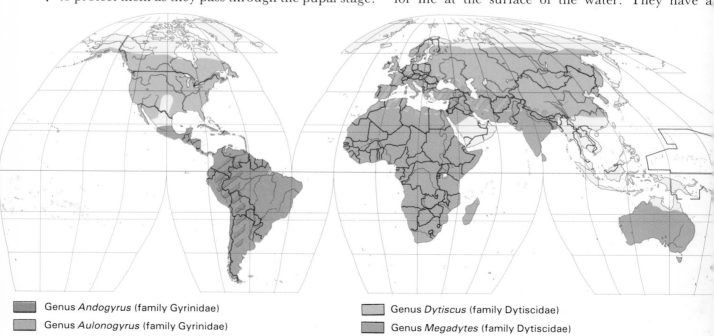

Genus *Andogyrus* (family Gyrinidae)

Genus *Aulonogyrus* (family Gyrinidae)

Genus *Dytiscus* (family Dytiscidae)

Genus *Megadytes* (family Dytiscidae)

flattened underpart to create a wide surface area, and their shiny or hairy upperpart repels water and remains completely waterproof. The whirligig beetles propel themselves forward through the surface film of the water by moving only their middle and rear pairs of legs. Although the upper segments of these legs are reduced, the joints are flattened and fringed with hairs, making them effective oars. A whirligig beetle does not use its slender front legs for swimming. The upper and lower sections of the leg oppose one another and are used as arms for grabbing prey.

Whirligig beetles are efficient swimmers. As they swim, the whirligigs hold their antennae in the surface film of the water. The antennae detect changes in the curvature of the surface film, allowing them to avoid colliding with each other as they weave sudden zigzag patterns in dense groups.

The whirligigs' characteristic movements resemble tiny speed boats as they scoot about, but they have a serious function—they form a highly developed method for investigating the surrounding territory for food. They capture their prey, which consists of small water insects, as they come to the surface. They also catch any type of land-dwelling or flying insect that happens to fall into the water.

ABOVE Whirligig beetles often live in small colonies on the surface of slow-moving water. They are small, dark beetles that skim the surface in an erratic, zigzag manner as they search for insect prey.
BELOW Whirligig beetles have a waterproof body covering, and they live half submerged in the surface film. Their middle and back legs are short and paddle-like for swimming. They use their front legs for capturing prey.
LEFT The map shows the world distribution of certain genera of water-dwelling beetles.

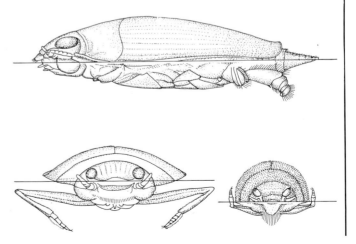

2469

ABOVE **Whirligig beetles have eyes that are adapted to their floating life-style. Each eye is divided into two parts. With the upper half, the beetles can see above the water; with the lower half, they look beneath it.**

BELOW **Using its head and legs, the mature whirligig larva builds itself a pupal chamber out of a ball of mud (A). Once safe from predators inside the chamber, it pupates before transforming into an adult (B).**

A

B

Whirligig beetles have extremely sharp eyes and locate their prey by sight. The eyes have a marked, dividing ridge across the middle that segments them into two parts. One part of the eye faces upward and the other faces downward, so that the beetle has a good view of its surroundings both above and below the water line.

Whirligig beetles skim about on the surface of ponds and slow-moving streams, detecting the movements of other insects—especially prey—with their sensitive antennae. If a threatening creature crosses their hunting grounds, the whirligig beetles hurl themselves at it with force. They even attack weaker members of their own species. Using their front legs as pincers, they seize the intruder and quickly tear it apart with their mandibles.

Although whirligig beetles have become highly adapted to life on the surface of the water, they are capable of moving about equally quickly underwater if they need to. When danger threatens, they defend themselves by quickly swimming under the surface and clinging to the stem of an underwater plant until it is safe to come back up to the surface.

Whirligig beetles submerge themselves to lay their eggs. Normally, they mate on the surface of the water, although occasionally they do so by the waterside. After they have mated, the female quickly swims toward the bottom, ready to lay her eggs. Sometimes she arranges them in long chains on underwater plants or stones. Otherwise, she piles them up on dead wood or semidecomposed vegetation. While the female is laying her eggs, she secretes a gelatinous substance that hardens as soon as it comes into contact with the water. The secretion forms a protective covering over the eggs and keeps them in place.

Unusual characteristics

Unlike the larvae of diving beetles, whirligig beetle larvae do not need to surface continually in order to take in air. They possess both gills and a windpipe. Their gills take the form of prominent growths on either side of their bodies. Gills are a common feature in many primitive insects, but they are most unusual among beetles.

Whirligig beetle larvae are carnivorous, as are the adults. Like the adults, they also digest their prey outside their own bodies, first liquefying it and then draining it into their mouths through channels in their jaws.

Another interesting characteristic of the whirligig beetle larvae is their behavior immediately before and during the pupal stage. When they have become fully developed larvae, they leave the water and drag themselves slowly up onto the banks to build a cocoon. Among some species, all the larvae move onto land on the same day.

Creating a pupal chamber

Once on land, the larvae set to work zealously to prepare a secure place to pupate. First, using their mandibles, they collect grains of sand and sediment and fragments of vegetation, shells, wood, leaves and seeds. Then, the larvae mold the mixture into a large ball and load it onto their backs. Carrying their load, the larvae then set off in search of a suitable place to undergo metamorphosis, a search that can take them a considerable distance from the water.

Usually whirligig beetle larvae settle on a piece of earth or climb up the stalk of a nearby water plant. Once they feel safe, they carefully put their supply of building materials down and skillfully set about building a round chamber, which they attach firmly to its support. Inside this refuge, they undergo the transformation into adulthood.

Nature's cleaners

Throughout the many classes of creature that comprise the animal kingdom, saprophagous and necrophagous species occur. Saprophagous species are those that feed on decaying matter, and necrophagous species are those that eat carrion. For a long time, most of them were unjustly persecuted by humans. Such was the case, for example, with hyenas, vultures and jackals.

Now, however, saprophagous and necrophagous species are being seen in a new light. It has become apparent that they play a vital role in rapidly and effectively recycling material that would otherwise rot and become a source of many kinds of dangerous infectious diseases.

Since beetles comprise an enormous and successful group—almost a third of all insects—it is not surprising that they include some of nature's scavengers. The majority of carrion beetles, for example, fulfill the extremely important function of demolishing organic matter, a task that they carry out unobtrusively and meticulously.

ABOVE The carrion beetle *Silva laevigata* preys on a snail. Like all members of the family, it also feeds on decomposing organic substances such as dead animals.

BELOW Two species in the carrion beetle family feed and reproduce in the carcass of a dead mole. Sexton beetles later bury the carcass; common carrion beetles do not.

A giant suborder

The largest division of beetles, the suborder Polyphaga, contains 150 families. One of the least known of them contains the carrion beetles. Carrion beetles (including burying or sexton beetles) are members of the Silphidae family. Small to medium in size, they are mostly black or dark brown in color. Their wing cases are often marked with conspicuous longitudinal ribs, and they have a textured surface that gives them a matte appearance.

For the most part, carrion beetles are inactive during the day. They hide underneath stones, slip into cracks that they dig out between the bark and trunks of dead or ailing trees, or lie among the roots of plants. In the evening, carrion beetles emerge and wander about in search of food.

A carrion beetle's most highly developed sense is that of smell. Using sensitive receptors on their thick, clubbed antennae, they can detect and locate sources of food from some distance away. Among other things, they eat rotting vegetation, withered fungi, excrement, manure heaps and corpses.

INSECTS
CLASSIFICATION: 13

Beetles (2)

The suborder Polyphaga contains 150 families of beetles. These include the Silphidae, which contains the carrion beetles such as *Oeceoptoma thoracicum* of central Europe, the temperate genus *Silpha*, the common sexton beetle, *Necrophorus vespillo*, and the black burying beetle, *Necrophorus humator*; the Staphylinidae (rove beetles), which contains carnivorous species such as *Paederus ruficollis* and *Ocypus olens*, the devil's coach-horse, *Staphylinus olens*, *Omalium riparium* that eats decaying vegetation, and termite- and ant-eating rove beetles of the tropical genus *Zyras*; the Lampyridae and Elateridae with some 2000 tropical and temperate glowworms (for example, the common European glowworm, *Lampis noctiluca*, and *Pteroptyx malaccae* of Thailand) and fireflies (such as the genus *Phrixothrix* from South America); the Dryopidae (long-toed water beetles, such as *Esolus angustatus* and *Elmis maugetii*); the Coccinellidae (ladybugs), which include the two-spotted ladybug, *Adalia bipunctata*, of Europe and Siberia, the four-spotted ladybug, *Chilocorus bipustulatus*, that attacks cochineal insects, the seven-spotted ladybug, *Coccinella septempunctata*, common in Britain, and the tiny mildew-eating species, *Thea vigintiduopunctata*; the Meloidae (oil and blister beetles) contains the oil beetle, *Mylabris variabilis*, common around the Mediterranean Sea, and the blister beetle, *Lytta vesicatoria*; the Tenebrionidae (darkling beetles) includes the blue helops, *Helops coerulens*, the churchyard beetle, *Blaps mucronata*, the sand-dwelling darkling beetle, *Phaleria cadaverina*, of European beaches, and the mealworm beetle, *Tenebrio molitor*.

Edible egg sites

Carrion beetles lay their eggs in the same environments that comprise their source of food, depositing them in short tunnels or roughly made round cells. The larvae usually grow extremely quickly, becoming fully developed in a few weeks or a month. They complete their metamorphosis in the ground without the aid of any kind of special pupal case.

One of the most common members of the carrion beetle family is the unmistakable species *Oeceoptoma thoracicum* with its striking terra cotta thorax and delicately beaded, black wing cases. It is prevalent in the wooded parts of central Europe, where it dwells on the plains and on woody mountain slopes. It is irresistibly drawn to any fermenting substance, and often scavenges among the piles of litter that people leave behind after their picnics.

The numerous species of the genus *Silpha* almost always inhabit the temperate zones. Their diet consists mainly of decaying vegetable matter, and they sometimes gather in great numbers, circling slowly around clumps of dying vegetation or semidecomposed fungi. Although they are mild and inoffensive creatures, they are capable of defending themselves most effectively. As soon as danger strikes, they regurgitate a few drops of foul-smelling, caustic liquid that deters any enemy from attacking.

Liquefied snails

A few species of carrion beetle deviate from the norm in terms of their diet. For example, the genus *Blitophaga* is vegetarian, and its members sometimes destroy sugar-beet crops. The genus *Ablattaria* is predatory, and its members feed exclusively on land-dwelling gastropods, especially snails.

Members of the genus *Ablattaria* are highly adapted to their specialized feeding habits. Consequently, they differ profoundly from other beetles in terms of both their behavior and their physical structure. For example, they have extremely long heads that enable them to reach inside the shell of a snail and attack their prey. Also, they digest their food outside their bodies—spraying the prey with a powerful secretion that dissolves its body tissues.

Predatory members of the family Silphidae and some types of Carabidae are extremely similar in shape, even though the two families have followed different evolutionary paths. They have all had to adapt the same type of mechanisms for feeding on the same kinds of food.

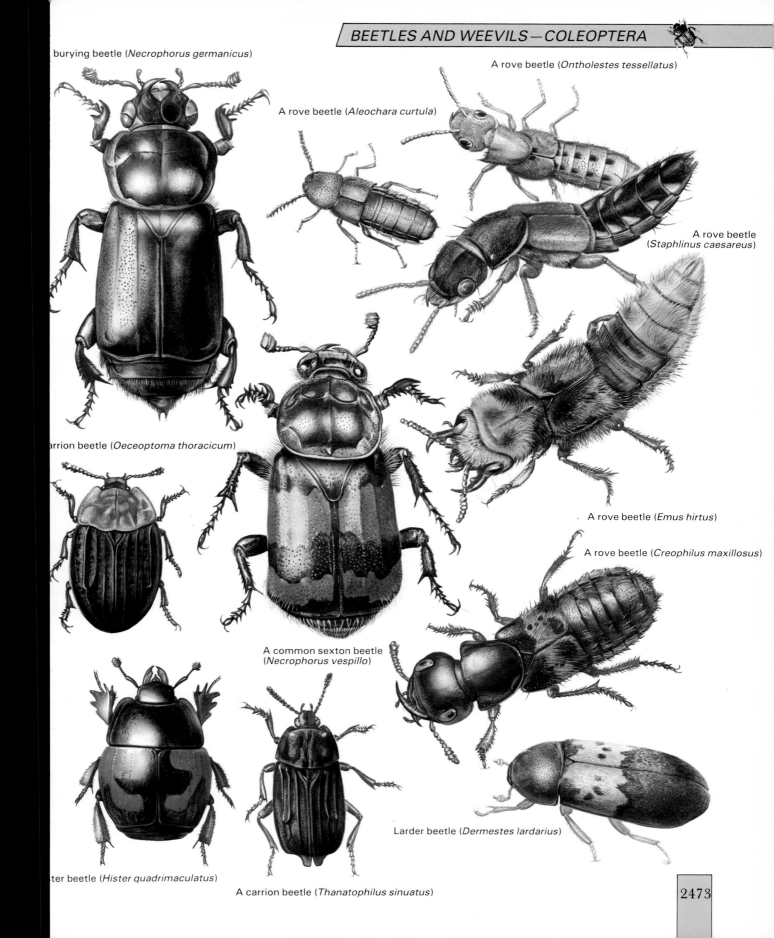

burying beetle (*Necrophorus germanicus*)

A rove beetle (*Ontholestes tessellatus*)

A rove beetle (*Aleochara curtula*)

A rove beetle (*Staphlinus caesareus*)

arrion beetle (*Oeceoptoma thoracicum*)

A rove beetle (*Emus hirtus*)

A rove beetle (*Creophilus maxillosus*)

A common sexton beetle (*Necrophorus vespillo*)

Larder beetle (*Dermestes lardarius*)

ter beetle (*Hister quadrimaculatus*)

A carrion beetle (*Thanatophilus sinuatus*)

2473

BURYING OR SEXTON BEETLES
— FEEDING IN A MORTUARY CHAMBER —

The term burying or sexton beetles applies to several large species of beetle in the family Silphidae. They grow to a length of about one inch, and are unusual in appearance, coloring and behavior. Easily recognizable species include Necrophorus humator or the black burying beetle and N. germanicus with their uniform black coloring, and N. vespillo and N. vestigator with their orange-yellow and black-banded wing cases. Unlike other members of the group, their bodies are not flat and they have club-shaped antennae with many nerve endings and powerful receptors that detect smells, enabling the beetles to locate the dead bodies of their prey. Experiments have shown that burying beetles can detect their prey from over half a mile away.

Burying beetles eat directly from fresh carcasses using their powerful jaws. If the carcass has already decomposed, they feed on the fly larvae that feed on the dead animal. They prefer small mammals such as field mice, rats, hamsters, moles and birds. Occasionally they eat small reptiles and amphibians.

Working in pairs

Burying beetles work in pairs consisting of a male and female. Once they have taken possession of a corpse, they defend it vigorously from all other creatures, including their own kind. When dealing with larger creatures, such as rabbits or large birds, burying beetles accept help from other couples—even members of different species.

Burying beetles' legs bear special digging structures enabling them to dig a large "mortuary" chamber underneath their prey. They let the body of the victim slide slowly into the chamber, and then cover it completely with the earth they have dug up. The beetles then drag the corpse into another underground chamber, where, using their jaws, they strip it of fur or feathers, dismember it, work it into a mass and roll it up into a foul-smelling ball of putrefied tissue.

Feeding from mother's jaws

The females dig another long tunnel in the walls of the chamber and lay

their eggs. They then make a hole in the body of the carrion where they feed and wait for their eggs to hatch. The larvae hatch in about five days, and as each larva emerges it makes its way to the source of food, following the direction of sounds produced by the female. The larvae put their jaws in the pit she has made in the carrion, but do not eat. Instead they wait for the female to come to them, and raise their heads to take liquid from her jaws. She feeds each in turn with the fluids exuding from the corpse—a unique situation for beetles, who usually abandon their young.

The mother continues to take care of the larvae until they transform into pupae. The adult burying beetles, no longer required by their young, leave the chamber and fly away. When the pupae emerge as adults, they go off in search of a new source of food.

FAR LEFT Black burying beetles cut the string that holds up a dead mouse with their sharp mandibles so that they can feed on the mouse and later bury it.
LEFT AND ABOVE Burying beetles prefer small prey, such as field mice, rats and birds. Once they have taken possession of a corpse they defend it vigorously from all other creatures. **ABOVE LEFT The female sexton beetle lays her eggs in a chamber near the carcass. When the larvae hatch, they move toward the food source where** the mother feeds them in a pit that she has made in the carcass. **BELOW A sexton beetle buries its prey in stages. It rolls the prey into a tight ball and digs it into the ground until the prey gradually disappears into an underground chamber.**

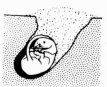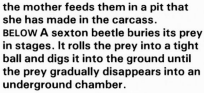

ABOVE The devil's coach-horse beetle adopts a defensive stance. Whenever it is confronted with danger or feels threatened, the beetle raises its abdomen, makes sudden movements backward and forward and then opens its jaws wide to scare off potential predators. It hides under stones during the day and hunts for prey, such as slugs, at night.

Rove beetles

Along the banks of many rivers, a tiny but conspicuous insect moves about incessantly among the stones. Its appearance is unmistakable. It is dark blue in color, with a red prothorax. Its abdomen is unusually mobile, capable of standing up vertically or bending back toward the top of its head. Known as *Paederus ruficollis*, it is an extremely common insect and typical of the family Staphylinidae, or the rove beetles.

The common feature that links members of the family Staphylinidae is one that is rarely encountered among beetles. All rove beetles have short, rectangular wing cases that cover only the first few segments of their abdomens. However, their long, membranous second pair of wings fits perfectly into the short crack between the two wing cases.

In other respects, the rove beetles have an extremely simple structure. Their bodies are usually spindle-shaped, with three pairs of limbs on either side. Their posterior limbs are fairly long, and the rove beetles use them for walking and running. Their rounded heads are equipped with poorly developed eyes and medium-length, necklace-like antennae.

Abdominal thrust

Some rove beetles have their own unique form of defensive behavior. When danger strikes, or even when they are merely disturbed in their activities, they point their mobile abdomens upward and make quick, darting movements backward and forward assuming an aggressive stance. In addition, many species secrete a powerful irritant liquid at the same time. The liquid, which is produced by special glands that are situated all along their bodies, can also harm humans. It causes serious lesions, or inflammations, if it comes into contact with the eyes or any other mucous membrane.

A number of rove beetles share the nests of ants, both as larvae and as adults. The arrangement is mutually beneficial. Some species of rove beetle larvae give off a chemical that stimulates brood-rearing behavior in the ants. The ants, in turn, feed the rove beetle larvae with regurgitated droplets of digested prey juice. Some mature rove beetles offer ants an abdominal secretion that curbs their aggressive

behavior. Other species are predatory, preying especially on sick and dead ants.

Some species of rove beetle—for example *Ocypus olens*, Staphylinus caesareus and *Emus hirtus*—commonly inhabit wooded areas. These three species are among the largest in the family and sometimes grow up to 1.2 in. in length. *Ocypus olens* is completely black in color and emits a strong, musky smell. *Staphylinus caesareus* is an attractive species with short, red wing cases. *Emus hirtus* is a strange creature with a conspicuous covering of golden hair.

The smaller beetles of the genus *Paederus* have a waterproof secretion that completely covers their bodies, making it easier for them to search for food underwater. They are able to endure long periods at a time underwater without having to surface for air.

In addition to the species of rove beetle that are carnivorous, many others feed on decaying vegetation. One example is *Omalium riparium*, which dwells among the piles of seaweed that are left behind on the shore by the tide. Other species of rove beetle eat either dung or carrion.

Termite hunters

Rove beetles of the genus *Zyras* inhabit tropical areas and live on a diet of ants and termites. Although they differ little in outward appearance from other members of the rove beetle family, their highly specialized feeding habits are unique.

A *Zyras* rove beetle begins its "hunt" by searching the outside of a termite mound for the entrance holes of tunnels. Once it has found a suitable hole, the beetle pushes its long abdomen inside, wriggles it about and discharges strong-smelling chemicals. The abdominal movements, combined with the spreading chemical odor, have a hypnotic effect on worker termites, who follow the rove beetle out of their nest. Out in the open, the beetle suddenly turns on the termites, decapitates them with its powerful mandibles and quickly devours them.

Ant-eating rove beetles

Certain ant-eating species of the genus *Zyras* live deep inside ant hills, where they feed mainly on the eggs and nymphs of their hosts. Through evolution, they have learned to mimic with great accuracy the external appearance of ants. However, imitative behavior alone would not be enough to protect rove

TOP Rove beetles run about tirelessly on the sandy or pebbly banks or on the bed of mountain streams. Their bodies are covered with a waterproof secretion that enables them to swim underwater in search of food.

ABOVE Some species of rove beetle, such as *Staphylinus caesareus*, habitually congregate on carrion and dung, where they feed on other insects that are attracted to the decomposing substances. Many rove beetles prey on nearby dead or sick ants.

beetles from the hostility of ants. In addition, they have developed an effective system of chemical self-defense: conspicuous glands on their abdomens produce noxious secretions that repel most attacks from ants.

Commensal rove beetles

Commensalism occurs when two animal species that live together derive mutual benefit from each other's activities. Several species of rove beetles occupy the nests of ants of the genus *Formica*, having a close commensal relationship with them. Members of the species *Dinarda dentata*, for example, usually inhabit the deep underground tunnels of ant hills, which they keep clean by feeding on leftover food, dead ants and even ant excrement. *Dinarda dentata* rove beetles are tiny creatures with sunken, reddish brown bodies.

Rove beetles of the species *Lomechusa strumosa* are large creatures that live inside ant hills. From numerous glandular openings on their bodies, they secrete a drug-like fluid that attracts ants. Ants accommodate the beetles in their nests, since they become addicted to the fluid. Every time an ant brushes its antennae against a "drug-peddling" rove beetle, it receives a large quantity of fluid in return for a dose of regurgitated food. Apart from being extremely appetizing, the fluid is highly intoxicating, acting quickly—and sometimes irreversibly—upon the nerve centers of the recipients. As if drunk, or drugged, the ants lose their social instincts completely and even forget to take care of their young.

Double exploitation

A tiny species of the same genus of rove beetles supplies intoxicating secretions to ant colonies, but lives at the expense of two different species of ants. During winter, the adult beetles live among colonies of *Myrmica* ants, exploiting them to the full by eating their provisions and, when these are exhausted, devouring their young. In early spring, they leave their winter homes and fly away to a colony of ants of the genus *Formica*. The new ant community is just as receptive as the old, and before long, it too is filled with drug-crazed insects—slaves to the rove beetle drug. As well as supplying the beetles with food on demand, the ants protect the beetles' eggs and rear their larvae.

Fortunately for the world's ant population, "drug-peddling" rove beetles are vulnerable to ant attacks at one stage of their lives. The most critical part of the

beetles' life cycle is metamorphosis, when they lie on the ground—completely immobile and defenseless. Ants take advantage of this weakness to consume huge numbers of the parasites, thereby eliminating the possibility of a beetle population large enough to destroy the world's ants.

Glowworms

Glowworms and fireflies are beetles of the families Lampyridae and Elateridae; members of both families possess the unusual ability to emit bright light—hence their popular name of glowworms. Nocturnal in their behavior, they inhabit the tropical regions of the world and, to a lesser extent, the temperate zones. All species have shapeless bodies with soft, dull-brown exteriors. In many Lampyridae species, the females are wingless.

An organ in the tail end of a glowworm's abdomen emits a cold light by means of a chemical reaction. It is similar to a car headlamp in structure: a piece of transparent, chitinous skin forms the lamp's "lens," while light is reflected from a layer of cells filled with microscopic crystals. The glow itself is generated between the crystals and the "lens," in a mass of cells that contains a dense network of tiny tracheae. Within the cell mass, in the presence of oxygen and the enzyme luciferase, a chemical called luciferin emits a bright light. Glowworms of the family Lampyridae produce a greenish yellow light, while the Elateridae have two types of light: they flash a green light when resting and an orange light during flight.

Nocturnal mating signals

Glowworms' lamps play an important role in their mating behavior. Adults of all species have an average life span of 30 days, during which time they eat only intermittently. They devote their short lives to finding partners with which to mate, most species being active during the hot, humid evenings of early summer.

Male and female glowworms of the family Elateridae are identical in appearance—unlike the Lampyridae

RIGHT The female common English glowworm, *Lampyris noctiluca*, is gray-brown in color with orange markings on the tips of her abdominal segments. The last three segments of her body are yellowish on the underside and strongly luminescent. Females differ little in shape from the larvae.

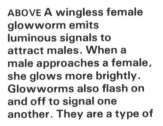

ABOVE **A wingless female glowworm emits luminous signals to attract males. When a male approaches a female, she glows more brightly. Glowworms also flash on and off to signal one another. They are a type of** beetle, and most of them are nocturnal.

ABOVE RIGHT **Female glowworms lay their eggs on grass. The pale yellow eggs are about 0.04 in. in diameter and are usually laid singly or in pairs.**

both sexes are equipped with well-developed wings. At night, they collect in swarms, hover close to the ground and produce flashes of light by which the sexes recognize and locate one another. The frequency and length of flashes varies between species to avoid the risk of futile encounters between members of different species.

Sexual differences

Marked sexual differences exist between male and female glowworms of the family Lampyridae. The common glowworm was once widespread in Europe, but today—due to the indiscriminate use of insecticides—its numbers are greatly reduced. Males of the species possess well-developed wings with which they fly clumsily throughout the night in search of mates. The females, however, resemble larvae without wings or wing cases. During the mating season, female

common glowworms climb to the top of blades of grass or small bushes and send out complex light signals at regular intervals.

Colony of lights

During their mating season, males of the Thai species *Pteroptyx malaccae* gather in dense swarms made up of thousands of individuals. Each male takes possession of a leaf (or leaf segment) among the branches of trees growing along riverbanks. The glowworms defend their chosen domains against all potential intruders, since they have deeply rooted territorial instincts.

After sunset, the male glowworms emit flashes of light to attract females for mating. At first, the light emissions are not synchronized with each other, but after a while each glowworm adjusts to the emission frequency of those around it. As a result, the whole colony flashes on and off like a Christmas tree. The females of the species choose their partners completely at random, but reject males that are unable to twinkle in unison with their fellows, since they are unsuitable for reproductive purposes.

Eggs and larvae

After fertilization, female glowworms dig holes in the ground, one beside the other, and lay small clusters of eggs. A few species deposit their eggs in water or inside termite nests.

Glowworm larvae feed on snails—the favorite food of many species of beetles. They descend on their victims with great speed and snap at them repeatedly with their sharp mandibles. The larvae kill their prey by injecting them with a powerful secretion from poison ducts in their mandibles. Prey is usually digested outside the body: a glowworm larva sprays the body tissues of its prey with protein-splitting saliva, reducing it to a pulp suitable for absorption through the mouth.

Other glowing insects

Several other species of light-producing insects are commonly called glowworms, although their lights do not seem to play a part in courtship rituals. They include the larvae of some beetles and gnats, as well as the railroad worm—a beetle of the South American firefly genus *Phrixothrix*, which flashes in red and green like a railroad signal.

Long-toed water beetles

The family Dryopidae, or long-toed water beetles, consists of a small number of species of robust, shiny, black, water-dwelling beetles measuring no more than about 0.1 in. in length. Widely distributed throughout the world, they live underneath the stones in streams and crawl along the streambeds. They have become highly specialized in order to lead a strictly underwater life-style but have no swimming apparatus whatsoever. It would be a hindrance and serve little purpose because the surrounding environment is never still. Instead they survive by resorting to complex and advanced methods of anchoring themselves to rocks or stones. Long-toed water beetles have simple but robust limbs, each ending in a pair of long, sharp claws that enables them to cling to the streambed. The slightest error can cost them their lives, since once they lose their grip they are at the mercy of the current. They are most vulnerable when they have to supply themselves with air in order to breathe.

Breathing through an air bubble

A few species, such as *Esolus angustatus*, that live in alpine and foothill streams, reach the surface by climbing slowly up the rocks. Once there, they stick an air bubble to their abdomens, which have a thick covering of waterproof hairs.

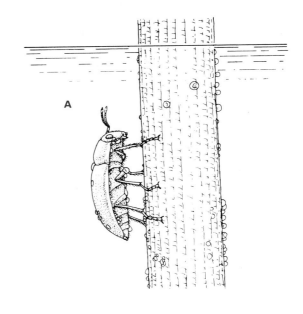

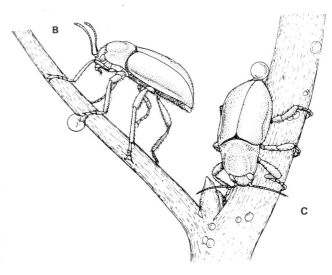

ABOVE The long-toed water beetles are strictly aquatic creatures and have evolved a system of breathing underwater. The species *Elmis maugetii* climbs up the stem of an underwater plant (A) in order to collect bubbles of oxygenized air from the surface of the plant. It first dislodges the bubble with its jaws, then takes the bubble with its foot (B) and places it on its abdomen. The body absorbs the oxygen during an exchange of gases; in due course, it releases waste gas in a bubble of carbon dioxide (C).

LEFT *Thea virgintiduo-punctata* is unique among the ladybug beetles. Unlike other species, which usually eat aphids, it feeds solely on mildew.

Both adults and larvae are frequent visitors to plants—particularly roses—where they can be seen feeding on the parasitic fungi that attack the leaves.

high up in the mountains. But despite the great variety of habitats they have managed to conquer, ladybugs are all alike in structure and size. Their bodies are hemispherical in shape and flat underneath. They have six legs that scarcely extend beyond the edges of their brightly colored wing cases, while their heads, which are small and equipped with a pair of tiny antennae, are almost entirely hidden underneath their thoraxes.

The coloration of ladybugs is generally red, yellow or black with spots or stripes in any one of these colors. The number of spots and stripes varies according to the species. However, a few ladybug species, such as *Coccidula rifa*, have brown bodies and lack conspicuous markings and are not usually recognized as ladybugs.

Defense mechanisms

The colorful ladybug species have a strong and unpleasant smell, and they taste bad to predators. Their bright colors serve as a warning to predators not to eat them. When threatened, many ladybugs retract their legs and antennae under their protective bodies, attach themselves firmly to the surface on which they are standing, and wait for the danger to pass. Some ladybug larvae have hollow spines, which, when ruptured, release sticky yellow blood (hemolymph) that contains foul-tasting chemicals. Some adult ladybug species produce the same substance from their "knee joints." The substance gums up the mouthparts and the antennae of an attacker.

Ladybugs are ferocious predators, and both the adults and the larvae feed on aphids or greenflies. Aphids feed by digging their long beaks into plants and sucking the sap. They are completely defenseless and have no chance of escaping from the ladybugs, which rapidly destroy dense colonies of them. Having decimated a swarm of these parasites, the ladybugs fly off in search of a new supply of food.

Carnivorous larvae

Ladybugs usually lay their orange-colored eggs on the undersides of leaves or in splits in the stems of

Other species of dryopid water beetles that inhabit lower altitudes have adopted another method for providing themselves with air. They feed on algae or vegetable remains, and as they wander around in search of food they pierce the air vessels of underwater plants with their mandibles. Using their legs and repeated blows of their bodies, they tear the air bubble away from the stem, capturing it as it escapes. The volume of air involved is small, and if the beetles had to breathe it directly, they would have to toil ceaselessly. Instead, the air bubble that clings to the underneath of their abdomens functions like a complex gill and the exchange of gases takes place on its surface, enabling the insects to stay underwater for long periods at a time.

Despite their adaptations to an underwater life, Dryopidae have well-developed wings and they will fly from one stream to another, covering quite a distance, when adverse conditions affect their immediate surroundings.

Ladybugs

The family Coccinellidae contains numerous species of small, brightly colored beetles, known as ladybugs. They occur throughout the world, from the Equator to the poles, and are found on the plains and

plants. Females lay several batches of 3-50 eggs, totaling 100-200 eggs. Because ladybugs feed on aphids, they choose places where these are abundant in which to lay their eggs, so that when the larvae hatch, they have a food source nearby. The eggs hatch in five to eight days into soft-bodied larvae that are covered, particularly on their backs, with colorful markings and protuberances. These protuberances take the form of sharp points or complex structures full of bristles and spines that ladybug larvae use for camouflage and self-defense. The larvae are active, grow quickly and feed voraciously. The larval stage lasts about three weeks, during which time thousands of aphids are eaten.

Economically important

Recent experiments have shown that during its active period as a larva and an adult, a ladybug is capable of consuming over 8000 aphids. These tiny beetles are of considerable economic importance in that they keep the numbers of plant pests within limits that are acceptable to the balance of nature. If the aphids were allowed to spread unchecked, they would destroy large expanses of woodland.

Equally important in terms of agriculture and forestry are the varieties of ladybug that feed on

ABOVE Two-spotted ladybugs are usually red, although their coloring varies considerably. Some have four spots; others have stripes formed by spots that have joined together. Females appear to select their mates on the basis of their color. In a largely red population, they prefer the black forms, while in a black population, they respond to the rarer red varieties. When confronted with adverse conditions, ladybugs move away as a group.

members of the family Coccidae, or scale insects. One scale insect species that they attack is the cochineal insect, a highly specialized bug that has adapted to a strictly parasitic life-style.

Two, four, seven and ten spots

The two-spot ladybug, *Adalia bipunctata*, distributed throughout Europe and Siberia, is small and has a single black spot on each red wing case. Black specimens with four red spots are common, or they may be yellow with black spots, the underside and legs being black. The four-spotted ladybug, *Chilocorus bipustulatus*, has a black body with vague red markings on its wing cases.

The seven-spotted ladybug, or *Coccinella septempunctata*, is one of the most common ladybug species in Britain. Measuring 0.2-0.3 in. in length, its wing case is orange-red in color. It has a black spot on the line

ABOVE The seven-spotted ladybug is a common garden species in Britain. When danger threatens, it spreads its wing cases and flies off. Its brightly colored spots are not simply an attractive decoration: they warn predators that the insect is distasteful. If it is attacked, the seven-spotted ladybug secretes a sticky substance that gums up the antennae and mouthparts of its predator.
FAR RIGHT A group of adult ladybugs of the species *Hippodamia convergens* hibernate throughout the winter on a single leaf. Ladybugs often congregate in houses and usually go unnoticed until they emerge in spring.

dividing its wing case, with three others further back on each side. It lives on any kind of vegetation infested by aphids. The seven-spotted ladybug produces one or more new generations a year, depending on the climate and environmental conditions.

The ten-spot ladybug is reddish or yellow, usually with five black spots on each wing case, but it may also be black in color. It has a brown underside and yellowish legs. The eyed ladybug, *Anatis ocellata*, is the largest British ladybug species. Measuring just over 0.4 in. in length, it has black spots on a red background, each spot being surrounded by a ring of yellow. It lives among pine foliage.

The two-spot and seven-spot ladybugs have interesting migratory habits, as do a number of other species.

When their immediate surroundings are affected by unfavorable conditions, such as adverse weather or lack of food, they make a long journey to another area.

Causing damage and spreading disease

Not all ladybugs are predatory; some eat pollen and play an important part in the process of pollination. Rare plant-eating species also occur. They eat the buds of a wide range of plants and are particularly harmful to vegetable crops.

The tiny ladybug species *Thea vigintiduopunctata* has a different type of diet altogether. An unmistakable creature with a striking pattern of black spots against a golden-yellow background, its diet, both at the larval and adult stages, consists of mildew, particularly the type that infests roses. However, its activity can cause problems: although it is useful on account of the large quantities of mildew it destroys, it can also unwittingly cause damage by transferring mildew spores to healthy plants, thereby laying the foundations for future infestations.

A long hibernation period

During the active periods of their lives, ladybugs are solitary creatures, but in temperate and cold climates they become gregarious. As soon as the weather starts to turn cold, ladybugs look for a hiding place, safe from enemies and harsh weather conditions. Here, they spend the long period of hibernation, during which time they are completely inactive.

Many types of beetles spend the winter isolated in their own specially built cells, or hidden away in some suitable shelter. Ladybugs usually take refuge among rocks, underneath the bark of trees, in cracks in walls and in sheltered corners of balconies. They may collect in large clusters consisting of hundreds of individuals of various species and live together, remaining completely inactive from October to February. Then, at the first signs of spring, the earliest species emerge and begin life again. The rest of the community gradually disbands as time goes on, depending on the special dietary needs of the species.

Fighting pests the biological way

Agriculturalists increasingly rely on chemicals to combat infestation of cash crops by pest insects, such as scales and aphids. Overuse of pesticides can cause serious ecological damage to the Earth's ecosystem. A

ABOVE The seven-spotted ladybug is extremely useful to gardeners and fruit growers because it devours huge quantities of pest species. The female lays her eggs among colonies of aphids so that the larvae (shown here) will have instant access to a good supply of food when they hatch. Seven-spotted ladybugs produce one or two generations each year depending on the climatic conditions.

the same time, biological methods of fighting pests have been neglected: the exploitation of the natural rivalry that exists between different orders of insects could be used more widely to keep down the number of pest insects.

During the 19th century, for example, the white mulberry scale, *Diapsis pentagona*, became widespread throughout Italy, threatening to destroy the mulberry plantations of local growers. In one of the earliest campaigns of pest control, the entomologist Antonio Berlese combated the infestation by introducing a small species of wasp into Italy, which, in its original habitat, was a parasite of *Diapsis pentagona*.

Predatory ladybugs

Similarly, predatory ladybugs feed on aphids and scale insects and, in large enough numbers, can save a crop from destruction. The cottony cushion beetle, *Icerya purchasi*, a member of the scale insect family, became a major pest of citrus fruits when it was accidentally transported from Australia to California in the mid-19th century. With no natural predators to keep it in check, the prolific cottony cushion beetle multiplied and, within a few years, threatened to wipe out the citrus fruit industry in the region.

Every effort was made to combat the blight using the range of pesticides that were available at the time.

But despite the efforts of agriculturalists, the scale insect continued to flourish because of a thick, waxy, protective secretion that covered its entire body. Adapted as a defense against the weather, the waterproof qualities of its body secretions allowed the cottony cushion beetle to withstand even the most powerful chemicals.

Natural insecticide

The situation became critical when the insect spread beyond the original center of infestation. After years of entomological research, it was discovered that the cottony cushion beetle originated in Australia. Surprisingly, despite the destructive efforts of the cottony cushion beetle, citrus fruit plantations in Australia continued to flourish, largely as a result of the predatory efforts of the tiny ladybug *Rodolia cardinalis*, a highly specialized hunter that kept the numbers of scale insects within satisfactory limits.

The introduction of the ladybug into California proved successful. It adapted well to its new habitat, finding not only a suitable environment but also a rich hunting ground. Conversely, it became necessary to ensure that the scale insect itself did not become extinct because this would have endangered the survival of the ladybug, which relied on it for food. Instead, the two species were maintained in perfectly balanced numbers. The tiny ladybug now occurs throughout the world, and is especially common in areas with large plantations of citrus trees.

Certain species of scale insects spread unopposed when the insect that is imported to restrict the pest finds the conditions in its new home unfavorable for reproduction. For example, the San Jose scale, *Quadraspidotus perniciosus*, has spread unopposed through North America, inflicting incalculable damage on fruit trees.

Oil beetles

The family Medoidae includes the oil beetles and the blister beetles. Oil beetles are so called because they exude an oily fluid from the joints of their legs. The blister beetles receive their name because their bodies contain the substance cantharidin, which causes blistering of the skin and a burning sensation. Both mainly occur in warm, dry climates throughout tropical regions, although a small number of species can be found in temperate zones.

The oil beetles and blister beetles are generally medium to large in size, growing to 1.2 in. in length. Unlike the brightly colored, cylindrical bodies of the blister beetles (their soft exoskeleton is usually a somber shade of black, purple or blue), the oil beetles are dull in color. Occasionally, species of oil beetles have a more vivid, golden-green or bronze coloration, with a strong metallic sheen.

Necklace antennae

Members of the family Meloidae have large, prominent heads, equipped with a pair of coarse antennae (the rounded segments of which resemble a necklace). Their legs are long and robust, with strong claws at the tips that enable them to walk across the ground and climb among vegetation with great ease.

Oil beetles and blister beetles have specialized defensive and reproductive behavior. The blister beetles are particularly vulnerable to predators because of their bright colors. When a bird, reptile or another insect attacks, they compress their abdomen and raise their blood pressure so much that they rupture their cuticle and emit a quantity of their own blood through joints at the base of their legs or neck. As soon as they relax their abdomen, the blood clots quickly. Oil beetles and blister beetles use "reflex bleeding" as a defense mechanism because their blood provides an extremely effective repellent, with a particularly unpleasant smell.

The oily, caustic effect of their blood comes from a highly toxic substance in their bodies called cantharidin, or Spanish fly. Renowned as an aphrodisiac because of its burning effect, cantharidin was once used medically. Physicians since ancient times have used cantharidin in bloodletting, in cases of respiratory infection and internally for kidneys (because of its diuretic effects). However, wrong and excessive use of the substance is dangerous and can prove fatal. Because of the poisonous nature of the oil-beetles and blister beetles, livestock breeders use pesticides to destroy them, not only because they cause illness if they are swallowed along with grass but also because they affect the taste of the milk yield.

Reproduction

The members of the oil-beetle genus *Meloe* have a unique and unusual life cycle that involves a succession of different larval forms. During the breeding season,

ABOVE **A ladybug of the genus *Chilocorus* crawls up a plant stem. Extremely valuable to gardeners, it preys on scale insects— small Homoptera that are less than 0.1 in. long. The scale insects constitute a major pest because they destroy plants** by piercing them with their sharp mouthpieces and sucking out their juices. BELOW **The ladybug, *Rodolia cardinalis*, preys on the larvae and females of the coccid scale insect family, which are citrus tree parasites that can destroy the trees.**

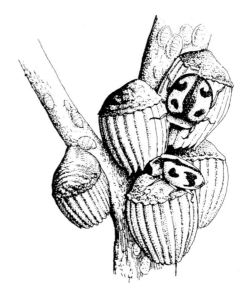

the male approaches the female and clasps her with his stout antennae. After fertilization, the abdomen of the female becomes swollen with thousands of eggs and protrudes beyond the rear end of her functionless wing cases.

Eventually, the female lays 4000 eggs in small groups, distributing them among cracks and holes in the ground. The eggs hatch after three to six weeks, and thousands of tiny, writhing black larvae emerge to swarm up the stems of surrounding plants. Because of their long, narrow bodies, oil beetle larvae are often mistaken for lice.

Hitching a ride

The larvae are very active and scramble up plants to sit in the flowers until a pollen or nectar-eating insect, such as a solitary bee, lands on the plant. When an insect settles on the flower, the larvae grip its bristles with their jaws and are carried away. Oil beetles that attach themselves to solitary bees are eventually carried to the bees' nest. They then abandon their hosts and search the bees' cell, feeding on honey, pollen and bees' eggs.

The remainder of the first larval stage of the oil beetle is spent in the cell, feeding on the nectar and pollen intended for the growing bee. The louse-like larvae experience a second larval stage of growth within a few days, undergoing a radical transformation in form.

Unfortunately, the larvae show little discrimination between hosts and grasp any hairy insect that lands on their flower. As a result, they inadvertently attach themselves to butterflies, beetles, wasps, bees and bumblebees and perish quickly. Because of this arbitrary selection process, only a few oil beetle larvae reach adulthood, limiting the extent to which the family thrives.

Immobile larvae

The second period of larval growth is a feeding stage, and the larvae differ from the previous stage in both diet and appearance. The larvae become soft, almost immobile creatures with short legs. Their spiracles occur high on their backs clear of the honey on which they are floating.

The larvae feed on honey, rapidly consuming the store that their hosts put together so laboriously. When the supply runs out, the larvae undergo further transformations and molt their skin several times, first into legless forms, then later into "pseudo-pupae." During the latter stage of growth, they develop minute legs but are unable to feed. Two months later, they pass through the pupal stage into adulthood.

Although oil beetles can be harmful to humans when they infest the hives of domesticated bees, both they and blister beetles can be beneficial, acting as parasites upon numerous varieties of harmful insects, particularly grasshoppers.

Hunting grasshoppers

The species of oil beetle *Mylabris variabilis*, which occurs in southern Europe, is an ingenious hunter. It has distinctive, ocher-colored wing cases, marked with three transverse, blackish brown bands. The female of the species has an excellent sense of smell that enables it to detect the egg cocoons of grasshoppers, even when they are buried deep in the ground. They dig small holes near the grasshoppers' eggs, which they then fill up with their own eggs so that their larvae will have an abundant supply of food when they hatch.

As soon as the larvae of these oil beetles hatch, they work their way inside the egg cocoons and devour the contents. Because of the particular feeding habits of the larvae, *Mylabris variabilis* was introduced into Sardinia after World War II to combat the grasshopper *Dociostaurus maroccanus*. During its periodic migrations, the grasshopper species caused severe damage to the already impoverished agricultural economy of the island. The effect of the introduction of *Mylabris* made itself felt within a few years, and now the numbers of the two species are perfectly balanced.

Blister beetles

During the breeding season of the *Lytta vesicatoria*, a brightly colored blister beetle that has a beautiful green body with a delicate, gold-bronze sheen, the fertilized female lays her eggs close to the nests of bumblebees or other types of Hymenoptera that dig

RIGHT With its highly developed sense of smell, an oil beetle can detect the egg cocoons of grasshoppers even if they are buried deep underground. When a female oil beetle finds an egg cocoon, she digs a hole close by and lays her eggs. When they hatch, the larvae have an abundant source of fresh food.

ABOVE A darkling beetle uses its long legs to scuttle along quickly so it can escape from potential predators. When disturbed, it emits a strong-smelling secretion that deters attackers. Darkling beetles are mainly active at dusk and during the night, and they are usually black or dark-colored.

shelters underground. The larvae are parasites and, immediately after hatching, their instinct leads them inside the host's den where they grow to adulthood.

Lovers of the dark

The family Tenebrionidae, or darkling beetles, are mainly active at dusk or throughout the night. They are usually black or bluish in color and, although some appear shiny, the majority are rather dull-looking. In rare cases, they have decorative whitish or ocher markings. The family of darkling beetles is extremely large, and it is impossible to give a general description of the family as a whole, because there are such marked differences in shape, size and habits between one species and another.

In most cases, darkling beetles are omnivorous, although they prefer plant matter. There are even some small, highly specialized tropical species that live in the nests of ants and termites, and eat alongside them. *Helops coeruleus*, commonly called the blue helops, is an unmistakable beetle with a long body and bluish and purple, longitudinally furrowed wing cases that have a faintly metallic sheen. The blue helops feeds on parasitic wood fungi and molds, but, when necessary, will eat various kinds of organic remains.

Members of the darkling beetle genus *Cossyphus* are unusual in that they have a camouflaged appearance. They could easily be mistaken for small, dried leaves because they have a rather flat prothorax, and their wing cases are brownish yellow. Furthermore, when danger strikes, they drop to the ground and lie quite still, so that they resemble small bits of vegetation.

Beetles of the genus *Blaps* are among the best-known darkling beetles, mainly because they are thought to be a danger to health and hygiene. Fat, sturdy-looking creatures with opaque, black teguments (coverings), they are widespread in fields and among the ruins of buildings as well as in damp kitchens and storehouses, where they move about extremely slowly on their long legs, searching for food. The churchyard beetles, *Blaps mucronata*, carry numerous types of parasitic worms that live at the expense of man and domesticated animals.

Sand dwellers

The sand-dwelling darkling beetles are completely different in appearance from those of the genus *Blaps* and are much faster moving. They spend their entire lives on sandy beaches or sand dunes; the tiny species *Phaleria cadaverina* is common on some European beaches, and can even be seen running on the hot sand in the middle of the day.

There are a variety of wing sizes within the darkling beetle family. Some of the species have large wings and are good or average fliers, capable of covering long distances even from one continent to another in some cases. But there are also species with very small wings and, in some extreme examples, the wing cases are actually fused together. Members of these last two species are confined to life on the ground.

It is said that every pool and oasis in the Sahara Desert, every spot where there is even a trace of water, houses its own peculiar species of darkling beetle. In order to survive in such hostile environments, these beetles spend much of the day buried deep in the sand, and only become active at night when they surface and go in search of food.

Some of the most distinctive of darkling beetles that live in arid or desert surroundings are the numerous members of the genus *Pimelia*. Their bodies are globular in shape, and their wing cases are marked by prominent ribs and raised dots. Many of the species camouflage themselves with a thick covering of sand grains held together by a sticky secretion. Members of the genus *Akis* are intensely black, and when walking upright on their long legs, they could be mistaken for large spiders.

Not all darkling beetles interfere directly in human activities, but those that do are particularly harmful. The darkling-beetle species *Tenebrio molitor* is found almost everywhere. It feeds on flour and wheat, polluting it with its excrement and foul-smelling secretions. However, humans exploit its prolific breeding for commercial purposes by selling its larvae (known as mealworms) as food for aviary birds and as fishing bait.

The Scarabaeoidea

Over 30,000 species of beetles are contained in four families within the superfamily Scarabaeoidea. Scarabaeoidea beetles inhabit all regions of the world, except the most inhospitable deserts and the polar regions. The Scarabaeoidae is an interesting superfamily, since its various species demonstrate a wide range of shapes, sizes and behavior.

Although the Hercules and sacred scarab beetles both belong to the family Scarabaeidae (of the superfamily Scarabaeoidea), they differ greatly in external appearance. A male Hercules beetle is a gigantic fierce-looking creature—sometimes over 7 in. in length. It has two large horns, which project from its head and back, and long pincer-shaped mouthparts. Hercules beetles inhabit the trees of the equatorial forests of the Amazon where they feed on sap and vegetable juices. The sacred scarab beetle, on the other hand, is a small dung-feeding, digging species of beetle without horns.

A detailed examination of their bodies, however, reveals striking similarities between the two species. The antennae, in particular, are similar in structure, differing greatly from those of any other type of beetle. Each antenna is comprised of several small sections strung together in a chain that ends in a club-shaped tip made up of thin, leaf-like plates—similar to a book. The size of these plates depends on the species. In some beetles, such as the cockchafer, the plates are spread out into a fan, which is always extended forward. In stag beetles, however, there is little movement of the plates. The size of the antennae indicates the sex of a Scarabaeidae beetle—males usually have larger antennal plates than females. In some male cockchafers the antennal plates may be half as long as the entire antenna. The antennal plates of females are small and resemble tiny buttons attached to the end of the antennae.

TOP **The desert beetle of the genus** *Pimelia* **has a rounded body, and its wing cases are marked by prominent ribs and raised dots. It has adapted to arid environments. Many species camouflage themselves with a thick** covering of sand grains, held together by a sticky secretion.

ABOVE **The desert-dwelling darkling beetle,** *Akis bacarozzo*, **is intensely black in color and, with its long legs, resembles a spider when it moves.**

C-shaped larvae

The larvae of Scarabaeidae beetles have a wide range of specialized feeding habits—they may feed on dung, plant roots or rotting wood. The larvae are permanently curled into a C-shape and are soft, whitish and extremely sturdy. Although they have three pairs of well-developed legs, they move as little as possible. Some Scarabaeidae larvae have swollen

2491

abdomens in which they store their feces throughout their larval existence. They only abandon their feces immediately before they pass into the pupal stage. Metamorphosis takes place in dead wood, or within strong, specially prepared chambers dug into the ground.

Distinct feeding habits

The Scarabaeoidea are divided into two distinct types of beetle, according to their feeding habits. Dung-feeding species frequently have somber coloration, such as black (although some are metallic in appearance). Species of chafers and stag beetles inhabit flowers and, to a lesser extent, trees. They usually have striking, multicolored coloration, except for many of the stag beetles, which are dark in color.

Dung beetles

Dung beetles are fascinating creatures of immense ecological importance. They fall into two families: Scarabaeidae (including the scarabs and species of the genus *Aphodius*); and Geotrupidae (which include the dor beetles). Many species of dung beetle show parental care involving the burial of dung stores to provide food for larvae. The species concerned include the sacred scarab, the minotaur beetle (*Typhoeus typhoeus*), the dor beetles (genus *Geotrupes*), *Copris*, and the giant *Heliocopris dominus*. Members of the South American genus *Phaenus* have strikingly decorative heads and thoraxes. Unlike the other genera, these tropical beetles have stunning multicolored bodies with a metallic sheen.

The genus *Aphodius*

The genus *Aphodius* contains more species of dung beetle than any other genus of the Scarabaeidae family. Its members inhabit most parts of the world. Dung beetles vary in length from about 0.1 in. to a maximum of 0.4 in. Since they are all structurally alike, the different species are difficult to identify. Their bodies, which are cylindrical and rather squat, are usually black or brown with large yellowish or reddish spots on the wing cases. The front legs are adapted for digging, while the back ones are very short. The tiny antennae have small clubbed tips equipped with the plate-like structures typical of dung beetles.

Although their antennae are small, *Aphodius* beetles can detect the smell of dung from quite a distance away. They fly swiftly toward dung, keeping close to

TOP AND ABOVE The mealworm beetle (top) is frequently regarded as a pest because it invades and ruins stocks of meal and cereals. However, it is also useful because it is easy to rear and the larvae (above) can be sold as fishing bait and food for captive birds.

The widely distributed species of darkling beetle, *Tenebrio molitor*, dislikes the light and hides away in dark corners.
FAR RIGHT The map shows the geographical distribution of certain kinds of flower-eating beetles of the family Scarabaeidae.

the ground. After alighting upon it, they dig a number of short, winding tunnels toward the center of the dung, where they lay their eggs. Thus, when the larvae hatch, they have an unlimited supply of food and sufficient moisture for their survival. The female usually remains in the dung after laying her eggs and stays with her young. The males, however, die shortly after mating.

Species of the genus *Aphodius* do not have highly restricted feeding habits. Many species live in the dung of a wide range of mammals, and some (such as *Aphodius subterraneus*) have even adapted to eating rotting vegetation. A very few species (such as *Aphodius rufipes*) spend part of their lives in the burrows of dor beetles, where they feed on the dung provided by the dor beetle for its own larvae.

Grape-cutter beetles

Some species of dung beetles have feeding habits and reproductive behavior that differ profoundly from those of their closest relatives. One of the most classic and well-studied cases is that of the grape-cutter beetle, *Lethrus apterus*—a black species that grows up to an inch in length. It inhabits all parts of southeast Europe from Bulgaria to the Ukraine.

Male grape-cutter beetles are easily recognized by their enormous heads with long tusks that point downward from the jaws. During the mating period, they engage in furious battles to win the favors of a female. A mating couple of grape-cutter beetles dig a vertical tunnel in a spot where the soil is crumbly. When the tunnel is about 1 ft. 6 in. deep, they excavate several oval brood chambers—measuring 2-2.4 in. long—that are linked to the main tunnel by short passages. When the first stage of building is complete, the female enters each of the brood chambers and makes further tunnels measuring 2.7-3 in. long in the back walls. In each of these, she lays one egg.

When the eggs have been laid, the male and female return to the open air. Using their strong, serrated jaws, they cut fresh leaves and shoots (particularly grape shoots) which they carry into the brood chambers. Here, they break up the plant material and work it into a soft paste that ferments slowly. When the larvae hatch out, they move quickly toward the plant paste—a food source. They bury themselves in it and remain there until they are fully grown—a process that takes about two months. The larvae usually build acorn-shaped cocoons in which to pupate.

Unusual dung beetles

Carrion beetles display strange behavior: they live either in the nests of predatory birds, where they feed

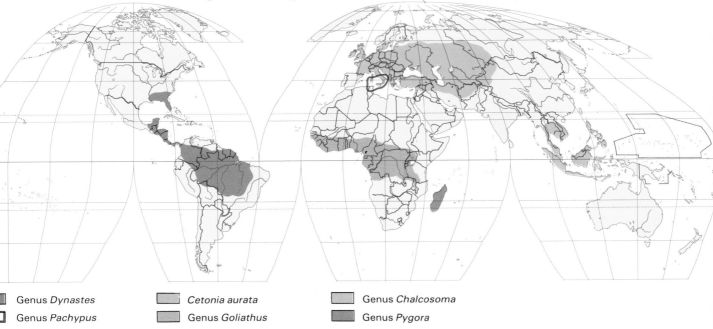

■ Genus *Dynastes*	▨ *Cetonia aurata*	▨ Genus *Chalcosoma*
◨ Genus *Pachypus*	▨ Genus *Goliathus*	▨ Genus *Pygora*

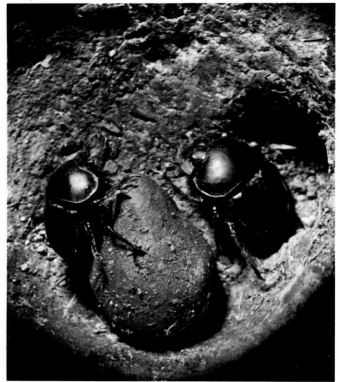

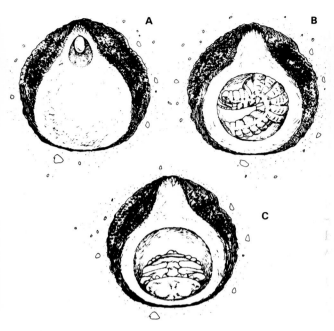

ABOVE In her underground retreat, a female sacred scarab beetle shapes a ball of dung into a pear-shaped brood chamber. She makes a small hollow in the top of the dung into which she lays a single egg.
ABOVE RIGHT The scarab beetle egg is well protected inside its dung brood chamber (A). When the larva hatches, the dung provides food and moisture, and the larva eats away at the walls of its chamber, rotating as it does so (B). Eventually the larva pupates (C), before emerging as an adult beetle.
FAR RIGHT The map shows the geographical distribution of several kinds of dung beetles.

on droppings and the remains of food, or else in corpses that have reached the last stages of decomposition.

Scarabaeinus termitophilus, a highly specialized Brazilian species, has undergone considerable structural and behavioral changes connected with the parasitic life-style it leads inside the nests of termites.

The taxonomic position of the mysterious Mediterranean genus *Pachypus* is somewhat uncertain—many experts place it somewhere between dung beetles and the flower-dwelling varieties. Many aspects of the biology of these species are obscure. The genus is characterized by extreme differences between the sexes in both appearance and life-style. The males have squat, sturdy bodies and long, bristly legs; they are competent fliers that usually live among flowers or vegetation. The females, on the other hand, have neither wings nor wing cases and spend their entire lives in deep tunnels dug into chalky ground. They only come to the surface during the reproductive period, when they allow the tips of their abdomens to protrude from their tunnels and emit powerful sexual hormones to attract males. Nothing is known about the biology of the larvae of this species.

Plant-dwelling Scarabaeidae

While dung beetles have strange and interesting habits but rather dull coloring, the plant-dwelling Scarabaeidae show rather uninteresting behavior but many are strikingly colored. The adults live among vegetation where they feed on pollen, petals, leaves or sweet-tasting fluids, sometimes causing considerable damage to crops. The larvae usually live in soil and feed on vegetable remains or roots, although some species live in dead wood or ants' nests.

Rose chafers

Most chafers are colorful beetles with brilliant metallic sheens—due to the way their body surfaces reflect light. Unlike other members of the family Scarabaeidae, their wing cases do not cover most of their bodies; thus they can stretch out their flying wings simply by lifting their wing cases very slightly.

The rose chafer (*Cetoniia aurata*), is a common European species of about 0.8 in. in length. In summer, it rests inside flowers, showing a particular preference for roses. The coloring of rose chafers varies greatly from one subspecies to another. The most typical color scheme is metallic green with small whitish markings on the wing cases, but many individuals have a two-tone color scheme consisting of reddish thoraxes and green or bluish wing cases. Others are fiery red, blue or even black all over. The adults feed on pollen, nectar and fruits, while the larvae feed on organic matter in the soil or on decaying wood. The larvae of the related species *Potosia cuprea* are more specialized—they grow and develop inside the nests of wood ants, feeding on the wooden walls of the nest.

The bee beetle, *Trichius fasciatus*, measures less than 0.4 in. in length and lives on thistles and wild bramble growing on hills and mountain slopes. Its wing cases are decorated with alternate yellow and black bands, which mimic the coloring of wasps and bees, thus deterring would-be predators.

Tropical beauties

The closer that beetles of the rose chafer family live to the tropics and the Equator, the more striking are their colors and sizes. Some equatorial species grow to gigantic proportions. The magnificently colored beetles of the genus *Rhomborrhina*, for example, have enamel-like green, blue and red-gold body coverings. They are widespread over Southeast Asia, the Philippines and the southern islands of Japan. The even larger beetles of the Central African species *Stephanorrhina guttata* are equally impressive. Their wing cases are emerald green with clearly visible white spots, while their thoraxes have coppery red outlines. The giant members of the species *Eudicella grallii* and *Chelorrhina savagei* have striking red and black colorings and hard, prominent Y-shaped swellings on their heads.

Members of the species *Dicranocephalus bourgoini*, of southern China and Taiwan, are characterized by their chamois-colored velvety bodies and long, antler-like protuberances on each side of their heads.

Some of the largest-known insects belong to the rose chafer subfamily *Cetoniinae*, including the huge Goliath beetles of equatorial Africa, which can be as large as a man's fist. Despite their huge size, Goliath beetles have a delicate appearance, due to their coverings of tiny, pastel-colored scales. They spend most of their time flying in the tops of forest trees, rarely coming to the ground. Female Goliath beetles lay their eggs in rotting wood, which provides nourishment for the larvae.

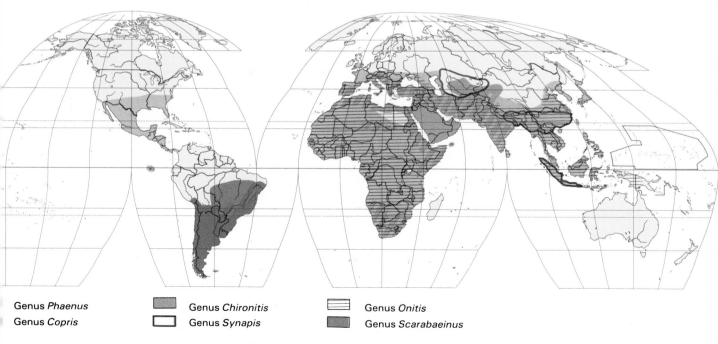

Genus *Phaenus*
Genus *Copris*
Genus *Chironitis*
Genus *Synapis*
Genus *Onitis*
Genus *Scarabaeinus*

DUNG BEETLES
—————— ROLLING DUNG BALLS ——————

Dung beetles feed on feces and have a particular preference for the dung of herbivorous mammals. They make an important contribution toward the disposal of enormous quantities of waste matter as well as playing a vital role in fertilizing and aerating the soil.

The sacred scarab beetle, a species of dung beetle, measures about an inch long and occurs around the Mediterranean.

Scarab beetles pair off and mate without undertaking any courtship rituals, and rival males do not fight over a female. When a male and female have found a suitable place to mate, they dig deep vertical tunnels that serve as underground dens using their powerful front legs, equipped with

a row of strong notches along the outside edge. When they have finished digging their dens, the partners separate and fly off to inspect the immediate surroundings. As soon as they spot a pile of dung, they pounce upon it. Using their front legs, which function like serrated knives, they cut out a chunk of dung and mold it into a ball measuring 1.2-1.6 in. in diameter. They roll it back to their tunnel by walking backward and pushing it with their back legs. The dung beetles require great patience and determination, as they invariably encounter obstacles along the way, such as stones or piles of fallen vegetation, which they must overcome.

Laying her eggs in the dung

The beetles deposit a dung ball in each tunnel and the male disappears. Before laying her eggs, the female molds each ball of dung into a pear-shaped structure with a tightly packed base and a loosely packed top. She then makes a small hollow inside the upper part of the dung, connecting it to the outside by a narrow ventilation shaft. She lays a single egg in each hollow, and it remains dormant until the following spring. When the larva hatches, it feeds on the dung by chewing away at the walls of its protective chamber and rotating inside it. If a hole appears in the brood chamber, the larva reseals it with its own feces. The eggs are well protected

in their underground dung balls, and their survival rate is high.

Working in pairs

In the minotaur beetle, Typhoeus typhoeus, *the male and female work even more closely together. Occurring throughout most of Europe, the minotaur beetle has long, pointed horns that extend forward from its thorax. The female minotaur seeks out a pile of dung (preferably rabbit, though sheep, deer or cow dung is also used) and then digs a vertical tunnel, to a depth of 5 ft., close by. Toward the bottom of the tunnel she digs several chambers off to the side. Meanwhile, the male assists her by carrying the loosened soil to the surface—an arduous task that sometimes takes several weeks to complete. When completed, the beetles fill the underground tunnels up with dung. Unlike the sacred scarab beetle, the minotaur does not lay its eggs in the dung mass, but in the soil a short distance away.*

Members of the genus Geotrupes *are dumpy, convex beetles, commonly known as dor beetles. The common species* G. vernalis *and* G. stercorarius *vary in color, but are usually greenish black or bluish black with a faint metallic luster. They dig their tunnels directly underneath cattle dung, but each of them does so according to a different pattern, helping entomologists distinguish between the species.*

FAR LEFT With a large, upwardly curved horn on its head and a humped thorax, the Spanish crescent-horned beetle is an unusual-looking dung beetle. The size of the horn varies but is larger in males, and probably plays a role in courtship display for attracting females.
ABOVE The dor beetle, *Geotrupes vernalis*, feeds on the dung of herbivores and digs a brood chamber at the bottom of a funnel-shaped tunnel that may be 8 in. deep.
BELOW The African dung beetle, *Kheper aegyptiorum*, is one of many species in the family Scarabaeidae that roll dung. The female cuts out a rounded portion of dung much larger than herself from a dung pile (A) and shapes it into a neat sphere; by standing on her front legs and pushing with her back ones (B), she rolls the dung to a suitable site for burying. The beetle buries the dung ball by excavating the soil from underneath it (C); when it is low enough she then covers it up. Once the dung has been buried, she molds it into a pear shape and lays a single egg inside it (D).

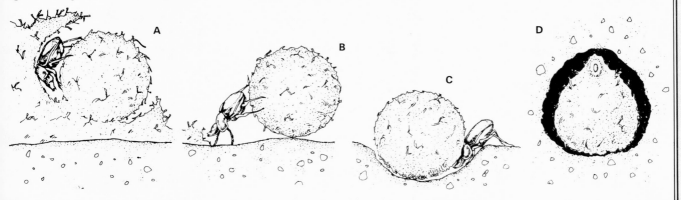

Cockchafers

Cockchafers belong to the family Scarabaeidae, and they include the metallic green *Cetonia* and the duller-colored May beetles and June beetles. When flying, they hold their hardened forewings away from their bodies, and their transparent, membranous hind wings provide power for flight. Their coloring is often dull, but the sexes can be distinguished by their antennae.

The best-known species is the common cockchafer, *Melolontha melolontha*. Males of the species—unlike the females—have extraordinarily large fans on their antennae. The adults are active in May, feeding on the leaves of deciduous trees and often damaging them severely. Females lay 60-80 eggs deep in the ground in clutches of about 15 eggs each. After about six weeks, the larvae hatch and live in the ground, feeding on roots. Depending on the environmental conditions, they take from three to five years to reach adulthood. During cold weather or times of drought, cockchafer larvae burrow deeper into the ground for protection. They usually pupate toward the end of June, and the adult beetles emerge about two months later. They stay in the ground and hibernate throughout the winter in cocoons until the following May.

Garden chafers

Garden chafers are predominantly tropical beetles, and all have characteristically convex bodies. There are numerous species of garden chafer, many of which are harmful to agricultural crops. The pest species *Anomala vitis* and *A. ausonia* are green garden chafers with vivid, coppery sheens. They are common throughout central northern Europe, where they feed on fruit

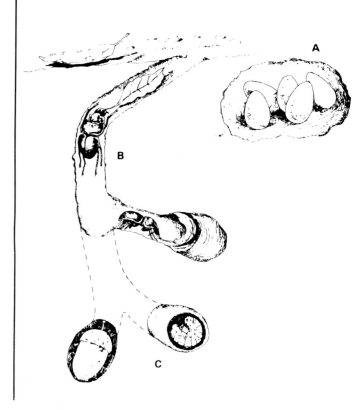

ABOVE LEFT The rhinoceros beetle is quite harmless. The adults feed on sap that exudes from tree trunks, or on leaves or buds, while the larvae live on a diet of rotting vegetation.
LEFT The reproductive behavior of the scarab beetles varies between species, but usually involves the excavation of an underground nest in which the eggs are laid. The nest of the dung beetle, *Copris lunaris*, contains a number of oval-shaped dung balls, each containing a single egg (A). The grape-cutter beetle digs a number of brood chambers leading off from the bottom of a single vertical tunnel. The beetle brings cut leaves (B) down to the brood chambers where it chews the leaf into a pulp and leaves it to ferment as a source of food for the larva. When the larva is ready to pupate, it builds itself a protective acorn-shaped cocoon (C).

trees and vines—the larvae eat the roots while the adults nibble at the buds.

Garden chafers of the Brazilian species *Rutela lineola* often cause severe damage to coffee plantations. It is readily distinguished by its shiny black body with numerous small, deep-yellow specks. *Phyllopertha horticola* is an example of a British pest species of garden chafer. Its larvae usually infest poor-quality grassland on light soil. They feed on the roots of turf, leaving it spongy. There may be up to a million larvae per acre in badly infested land. The adults often emerge from their pupae simultaneously in a synchronized group.

The beauty of some of the garden chafers is exemplified by the species *Mimela aurata*, of central Europe. Their sexual differences are unique among the species. The males have purple wing cases, red-tinged greenish thoraxes and bodies covered in fine wrinkles. The females are green all over their bodies.

Rhinoceros beetles

Rhinoceros beetles are the largest family within the artificial grouping of the plant-inhabiting Scarabaeoidea. They are strange-looking beetles that commonly inhabit hot, humid, tropical and equatorial regions. Some species are enormous and monstrous-looking. Male rhinoceros beetles are very distinct from

ABOVE Unlike most members of the rose chafer family that have metallic colorings, a few species —such as *Trichius zonatus* seen here—have patterned bodies. The black and yellow stripes of this beetle imitate the colorings of wasps and form a protection against predators.

the females since their heads and thoraxes are adorned with impressive horns of different shapes and sizes. The females are often smaller than the males.

Despite their belligerent appearance, rhinoceros beetles are harmless. They cannot bite, and their robust, decorative horns are incapable of causing injury. The diet of the adults also contrasts with their appearance: most feed on the sap that exudes from tree trunks, although some eat leaves or buds. The larvae grow and develop on a diet of rotting vegetation.

The rhinoceros beetle, *Oryctes nasicornis*, inhabits almost all regions of Europe, seeking out warm spots among the vegetation of coastal areas. The species is chestnut brown in color, with reddish brown hairs on its underside. The males have large, backward-pointing horns on their heads, and their thoraxes have raised ridges with three short projections. The females are the same color as the males, but they have few traces of ornamentation. Their most visible projection is a growth that protrudes from the front of their heads.

ABOVE The common cockchafer feeds on the leaves of deciduous trees, particularly fruit trees. It has brown wing cases and a black head, and can be recognized by its large reddish brown antennal fans that are especially long in the males.

Among the largest beetles in the world are the species of rhinoceros beetles that live in the luxuriant forests around the tropics and the Equator. The massive Hercules beetle, *Dynastes hercules*, for example, grows up to 8 in. in length. The males and females differ so markedly in appearance that, for a long time, the two sexes were thought to belong to separate species. The male is smooth and shiny, with convex wing cases that are a beautiful olive-green color with large black spots. It has a huge, sword-shaped horn, measuring 2.7 to 4 in. long, growing from its thorax and extending forward in a large arc over its head. The front of its head also extends into a horn that curves upward and has several sturdy notches. In contrast, the female resembles a large cockchafer, with beaded wing cases covered in a thick layer of reddish hairs.

Smaller rhinoceros beetles

Tropical forests are home to many species of slightly smaller, but equally striking species of rhinoceros beetle. The males of the Central American species *Megasoma elaphas*, for example, measure about 5 in. in length and have three short horns on the thorax and a long, hooked horn extending from the front of the head. Males of the unmistakable species *Golofa porteri* of Colombia are about 3 in. long with two long, slender, pointed horns—one rising vertically from the top of the head with two rows of sharp teeth on its inner edge, and the other extending from the center of the thorax.

Several species of rhinoceros beetle live in the river forests of Southeast Asia. One is *Chalcosoma atlas*, which is a beautiful dark-green color with a metallic sheen. The male has a single stout, branching and forward-pointing horn on the front of its head. Two thin, curved, tapering horns frame the main horn and extend forward from the front corners of the beetle's thorax. Members of the strange species *Allomyrina dichotomous* have horns on their heads that divide into two points.

In several primitive species of rhinoceros beetle there are no discernible differences in appearance between the sexes. In the species *Pentodon bidens* and *P. algerinus*, for example, both males and females are black and globular. They inhabit many regions in central southern Europe, and both larvae and adults are capable of causing considerable damage to a wide variety of crops. Another rare and primitive species is

Calicnemis latreillei. It inhabits sandy beaches in the Mediterranean Sea and the Atlantic Ocean, and dwells underneath piles of seaweed left behind by the tide.

Stag beetles

The stag beetles are an important family of beetles contained in the large superfamily Scarabaeoidea. There are more than 1200 species, and most inhabit tropical regions. Like other members of the superfamily, their antennae have club-shaped tips that are made up of several plate-like structures. Unlike their relatives, however, stag beetles have characteristic elbow-like joints in their antennae.

Male and female stag beetles differ structurally. In most cases, the males have monstrously enlarged jaws—the same length as their bodies or even longer. Some are visibly arched; others are simply elongated. They have a series of strange enlargements along their inside edges that vaguely resemble the antlers of a deer. Some experts say that the "antlers" are a decoration, designed to attract females. Others maintain that the stag beetles use them to seize the female and hold onto her during mating, or as weapons when they compete against other males.

Female stag beetles are fairly similar to the males in appearance. Their jaws are equally sturdy and prominent. But they are much shorter than those of

ABOVE *Polyphylla fullo* is the largest of all European cockchafers, measuring about 1.2 in. long. It has a distinctive, marbled, black and white coloring, and the antennae of the male are exceptionally broad, leaf-shaped structures. It lives in sandy areas, where the adults feed on pine trees and the larvae feed on the roots of grasses and other small plants.

the males and do not possess antler-like enlargements. Instead, they are serrated along the inside edge.

From their appearance, stag beetles could easily be mistaken for fierce predators, especially with their large chewing mouthparts. However, they are harmless creatures and do not bite except in self-defense. Most stag beetles feed on the sap that exudes from natural cracks in tree trunks, and do not use their jaws even to pierce the trunks.

Stag beetles lay their eggs in small chinks in the bark of dead or dying trees, particularly broad-leaved trees with wide trunks. The whitish larvae take several years to develop—up to five or six years in some species. They live inside winding tunnels that they chew out of wood, thereby providing themselves with effective protection and an inexhaustible supply of food. Once a larva reaches maturity, it makes its way to the outer part of its tree trunk and builds an oval-shaped chamber, inside which it pupates before emerging as an adult in midsummer.

Most stag beetles become active at dusk, when they fly slowly and noisily from tree to tree. Since night-flying stag beetles are black-brown in color, they blend in with the surrounding darkness. However, a few Australian species belonging to the genus *Lamprina* are active during the day, when they feed on flowers. Depending on the available light, the bodies of these beetles appear to be a vivid, metallic color with a green luster and a reddish gold or coppery tinge.

The common stag beetle

The common stag beetle, *Lucanus cervus*, inhabits most parts of Europe, living in woods of broad-leaved trees. The females are usually about 1.5 in. long, while the males can reach a length of 2.7 in. Common stag beetles emerge at dusk and climb tree branches with extraordinary agility, using their powerful jaws and long legs that terminate in strong claws.

During the mating season, male stag beetles fight strenuous duels according to a precise ritual. Two opponents come face to face astride a branch and study one another like expert fighters. Then they push each other roughly and strike out with their horns. The winner is the one who manages to dislodge his opponent. The struggle hardly ever ends in injury or death—usually one of the contenders concede defeat. The victor becomes undisputed master of the surrounding territory and is entitled to mate with all the females in the vicinity. During mating, a male grips the female firmly by the thorax, using his powerful jaws. When males are attacked or disturbed by an intruder, they react in an aggressive manner. They raise their heads and stretch out their front legs, then rock backward and forward rhythmically, with their monstrous jaws wide open.

Strange species

Species of stag beetle become progressively more unusual and more numerous toward the tropics and the Equator. For example, the beautiful, majestic and extremely delicate species *Chiasognathus granti* inhabits the forests of the Andes. It measures 1.5-2 in. in length and has a chestnut-ocher coloring with a slight metallic sheen. The males have unusual jaws divided into straight, sharp lower pincers and long curving upper pincers with dense rows of tiny teeth along the inside edges. The gigantic species *Allotopus rosenbergi* of Borneo grows up to 4 in. long. It has a massive, hemispherical body and relatively small jaws. Its coloring is olive-green with a soft, shiny lacquered appearance.

The monstrous species *Eurytrachelus titan* is found throughout the Malay Archipelago. It grows up to 3 in. in length, and has an enormously enlarged thorax and sharp, serrated and extremely robust jaws. The giraffe stag beetle, *Cladognathus giraffa*, from the island of Flores, off the Canadian coast, has long, straight jaws that contain an impressive row of teeth along their inside edges.

A strange species of blind, wingless stag beetle, *Vinsoniella caeca*, inhabits the island of Mauritius. It has adapted to a life beneath the bark of trees.

Since the earliest recorded times, stag beetles have been associated with superstition. The ancient

INSECTS CLASSIFICATION: 14

Beetles (3)

Four families of the suborder Polyphaga constitute the superfamily Scarabaeoidea. The largest of these, the family Scarabaeidae, contains more than 20,000 species and is grouped into several subfamilies: the Aphodiinae are mostly dung beetles and include the important genus *Aphodius* with more than 1000 species (such as *Aphodius subterraneus* and *Aphodius rufipes*); the Scarabaeinae (scarab beetles) has some 4500 mostly tropical species, including the sacred scarab, *Scarabaeus sacer*, the dung beetle, *Copris lunaris*, and the Brazilian species *Scarabaeinus termitophilus*; the Melolonthinae (cockchafers such as the European cockchafer, *Polyphylla fullo*) contains more than 10,000 species worldwide; the Rutelinae (garden chafers); the Cetoniinae (rose chafers, including the genera *Trichius* and *Rhomborrhina*, as well as the largest beetle species—the goliath beetles of equatorial Africa); and the Dynastinae (rhinoceros beetles) containing such giants as *Dynastes hercules* of South America that grows up to 6.7 in. long. The three other families are the Geotrupidae with about 300 species, of which 100 belong to the genus *Geotrupes* (such as the dor beetle, *Geotrupes vernalis*) that live in Europe, Asia and North America; the Trogidae (hide beetles and carrion beetles including those of the genus *Trox*); and the Lucanidae (stag beetles) with over 1200 species, including the Andean *Chiasognathus grantii*, the 3-in.-long *Allotopus rosenbergi* of Borneo, and the giraffe stag beetle, *Cladognathus giraffa*, from Flores, an island in the Indonesian archipelago.

Romans revered them, believing that the strange ornamental horns on their heads had healing properties and brought good luck. At the same time, the barbarians of central Europe blamed stag beetles for outbreaks of fire, believing that they carried away pieces of burning ember with their jaws. Today, the most primitive human tribes still use the heads of stag beetles as ornaments, and in some places their bodies are ground into a fine powder and used as miracle cures.

ABOVE The lesser stag beetle is an oblong, flat beetle. It has a wide head, but its jaws are not as enlarged as those of the common stag beetle. The lesser variety occurs in deciduous woods, where the larvae live in rotting tree stumps or fallen branches.

Leaf beetles

There are more than 30,000 species of leaf beetles in the suborder Polyphaga. The majority are brightly colored with a metallic sheen. Some are globe-shaped or hemispherical; others have flat or elongated bodies. Leaf beetles have small heads that are usually partly covered by the front edge of the thorax. They have a pair of segmented antennae, compound eyes and strong, chewing mouthparts. Their legs are short but strong, and the so-called flea beetles, such as *Chaetocnema tibialis*, have back legs that are adapted into jumping organs.

Leaf beetles can cause immense damage to the plants on which they feed—despite the fact that the largest species rarely exceed 0.4 in. in length. In many cases, both adults and larvae feed on more than one species of plant, and in some years they appear in swarms that are large enough to destroy vast areas of crops and badly damage forests.

A number of species, such as the bloody-nose beetle, display interesting defensive behavior. They can put any enemy to flight, even one much larger than themselves, by secreting a few drops of "blood" from their joints. The blood is foul-smelling and has a burning effect.

Development

Female leaf beetles usually lay their eggs in clutches and build a covering to protect them. Females of the genera *Clytra, Labidostomis* and *Cryptocephalus*, for example, lay their eggs on the surface of plants and cover them with a carefully arranged structure made out of small scales of feces. The shape of the structure varies according to the species. The tortoise beetles of the genus *Cassida* cover their eggs with a thick protective layer of spongy secretion that hardens to a horny consistency on contact with the air. Remarkably, the females of a number of *Chrysomela* and *Chrysocloa* species incubate their eggs inside their bodies and wait until they are ready to hatch before they lay them.

Leaf beetle larvae are usually small and soft, and move about slowly on their six short legs. In most cases their bodies have no protective covering, and they live in the open air where they are defenseless against their many enemies. Some species manage to overcome their vulnerability by building themselves a protective shell. The most primitive method is the one adopted by the asparagus beetle larva, which covers its back completely with its own feces.

Larvae of the tortoise beetle adopt a more complex method of protection. Each time a larva molts, it holds its old skin against its back, attaching it to the forward-pointing fork at the end of its abdomen. Gradually, the larva acquires a strong, protective shield, which it then coats with its feces. The tortoise beetle larva can move its abdominal fork, and this enables it to swing its shield in different directions to face oncoming attackers.

Some types of larvae protect themselves with tube-like shelters that they mold together from feces, earth, clay and pieces of vegetation. The larvae drag their shelters around like mobile homes, only letting the front part of their bodies emerge. Larvae of the genus *Donacia* are unusual, since they live underwater and obtain oxygen from the air vessels of the aquatic plants on which they feed.

When environmental conditions are favorable, leaf beetles exist in huge numbers. Economically, they can be extremely harmful to agriculture and forestry. Hundreds of species cause varying degrees of damage, and the most common and devastating is the Colorado beetle.

Colorado beetles

The dreaded Colorado beetle, *Leptinotarsa decemlineata* is responsible for widespread crop damage. The beautiful yellow-and-black striped beetle is indigenous to North America, where it originally fed on several wild plants of the potato family. The species gradually acquired a taste for common potatoes when the vegetables were introduced into North American farms, and it is now a serious threat to potato farmers.

Both larvae and adult Colorado beetles feed on the leaves and buds of the potato plant, quickly stripping it of all its foliage so that it cannot produce tubers. The Colorado beetle was accidentally brought over to Europe toward the end of the 19th century. It began its activities in France and England, and gradually spread all over the continent. It has since managed to cross the Alps and is spreading eastward. Despite numerous preventive measures, every year sees new and serious epidemics.

Other crop pests include the asparagus beetle; the tortoise beetle, which feeds on sugar beets; and the red beetle, *Lilioceris merdigera*, which feeds on garlic and onion crops. Some genera, such as *Haltica, Psylliode* and *Phyllotreta*, feed on a wide variety of crops, while others feed on trees. *Melasoma populi*, for example, is a globe-shaped beetle with red wing cases and a bluish black prothorax, which damages poplar groves. Beetles of the genus *Pachybrachis* feed on oak trees. The larvae of the insignificant-looking species *Galerucella luteola* gnaw away at elm leaves to such an extent that they leave nothing but the veins, which come to resemble pieces of lace.

Longhorn beetles

The family Cerambycidae contains 25,000 species of longhorn beetles. They are elegant in shape and varied in color. They live in woodlands, some species living in rotting wood, others in healthy trees. Longhorn beetles feed on the sap of trees, pollen, nectar and wood. Some species feed solely on leaves, although this is rare. They are excellent fliers and commonly occur in forests and woods with plenty of clearings. Adult longhorn beetles do not interfere with human activities, but they may cause serious damage to trees.

A leaf beetle (*Liloceris lilii*)

A click beetle (*Elater sanguineus*)

A click beetle (*Corymbites cupreus*)

fungus feeder
riplax aenea)

A garden chafer
(*Phyllopertha orticola*)

-feeding beetle
cheira octoguttata)

A plant-feeding beetle
(*Olocrysa fastuosa*)

orn beetle (*Oberea oculata*)

A weevil (*Lixus iridis*)

An elm bark beetle (*Scolytus scolytus*)
showing brood galleries under bark

2505

One major characteristic that helps to distinguish longhorns from other types of beetle is their long, many-jointed antennae that are often the same length as their bodies, sometimes even longer. Their antennae are important organs, their basic function being to perceive smells. In many species, the antennae can be used to distinguish the sexes—male longhorn beetles have longer antennae than the females, with a larger number of segments.

Longhorn beetles' heads bear a large pair of compound eyes and chewing mouthparts with strong serrated and notched jaws. They have long bodies, with a strong outer covering, supported by three pairs of long, rather slender legs, each ending in a pair of large, sharp claws.

Destructive larvae

During the reproductive season, which sometimes sees fierce fights between males in order to win a mate, the females of many longhorn beetle species make several cracks in the bark of trees by striking at it with their jaws. They attack both the trunks and branches of a wide variety of trees. (Some species are restricted to a particular food plant, while others can live on a wide range of plants.) The female longhorn

ABOVE The Colorado beetle, *Leptinotarsa decemlineata*, is longitudinally striped black and yellow and its thorax is spotted black and yellow. The specific name *decemlineata* means ten-striped, as there are five black stripes on each wing cover. A dreaded potato pest, it feeds on the leaves as adult and larva. They damage the haulm, or aboveground part of the plant, which may be completely stripped of its leaves, so that the tubers cannot develop.

INSECTS
CLASSIFICATION: 15

Beetles (4)

There are over 30,000 species of leaf beetles in the suborder Polyphaga, and all belong to the family Chrysomelidae. They include the flea beetles (such as *Chaetocnema tibialis*), and many pest species such as the Colorado beetle, *Leptinotarsa decemlineata*, widespread throughout Europe and North America; tortoise beetles of the genus *Cassida*; the asparagus beetle, *Crioceris duodecimpunctata*; the red beetle, *Lilioceris merdigera*; the red poplar leaf beetle, *Chrysomela populi*; and the black leaf beetle, *Chrysomela sanguinolenta*.

The family Cerambycidae has 25,000 species of longhorn beetles, and includes the musk beetle, *Aromia moschata*, of Europe and Japan; the species *Rosalia alpina* and *Megopsis scabricornis* of central Europe; the tanner beetle, *Prionus coriarius*; the timberman, *Acanthocinus aedilis*; the British spotted longhorn, *Strangalia maculata*; and the 5-in.-long *Macrodontia cervicornis* that occurs in South America.

Weevils

The weevils make up the largest division of the beetles, with some 50,000 species in the family Curculionidae. They are especially notorious for the damage they do to plants and crops. Among the pest species are *Curculio elephas* that eats acorns and chestnuts; *Lixus junci*, the enemy of sugar beets; *Rhynchites auratus*; and the apple-blossom weevil, *Anthonomus pomorum*. The leaf-rolling weevils of the subfamily Attelabinae include the species *Byctiscus populi*, and the red oak roller, *Attelabius nitens*, of Europe.

beetle lays a single egg in each crack, covering it with a paste made of wood nibblings and saliva. The larvae hatch into soft, legless creatures with extremely powerful jaws that chew their way inside the trunk of the tree. During their development, the larvae dig long, winding tunnels into the tree, feeding on the wood fibers as they go. Many species of longhorn beetle take four years or more to reach maturity, and can grow to over 6 in. in length and 1.2 in. wide. Longhorn beetle larvae inflict a great deal of damage on trees during the course of their development. The trees often become prematurely weakened and fall down during storms or succumb to infection, since the agents that cause disease not only have an easy way in but a convenient network through which they can spread.

The diversity of the longhorns

The musk beetle, *Aromia moschata*, which occurs throughout Europe and Japan, measures up to 1.4 in. in length and has a metallic-looking body with a luster that varies between green, copper, blue and red in color. The larvae grow and develop inside willow trees, and the adults emit a strong smell of musk, derived from chemicals in the willow leaves on which they feed.

The rare and delicate species *Rosalia alpina*, from central Europe, has bluish gray wing cases with striking crossways black bands and large tufts of dark hair at each joint of its long antennae. A rare species, it

ABOVE LEFT The red poplar leaf beetle feeds on willows and poplar trees, both as larva and as adult.
ABOVE RIGHT *Chrysomela sanguinolenta* is a black leaf beetle identified by the red stripe on each side.
BELOW The flea beetle has powerful hind legs for jumping (A). A female tortoise beetle uses anal secretions to build a cocoon for her eggs (B). The egg-filled cocoon (C) hardens in the air to form a tough shell. Leaf beetles of the genus *Lamprosoma* cover their single egg with a layer of feces (D) and the larva hatches inside the safety of this cocoon (E).

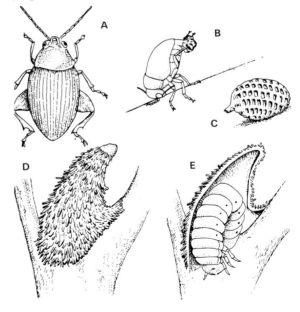

THE LEAF ROLLERS
——LAYING EGGS IN LEAF ROLLS——

Weevil species of the subfamily Attelabinae, commonly known as leaf rollers, have unusual reproductive habits. Female leaf rollers have a highly specialized method of providing their offspring with food and shelter. They lay their eggs on leaves, which they then roll up to provide a protective shelter. Different species have different ways of rolling up leaves, and some of these are more complex than others.

One of the best and most thoroughly studied examples is the species Byctiscus betulae. *Measuring 0.2-0.4 in. in length, it has a sparkling metallic body that changes in color from green through blue to a reddish color. It eats a wide variety of plants, and can sometimes be harmful to fruit*

trees and vines. Once the female has been fertilized, she cuts through the stalk of a leaf so that it hangs downward and eventually withers from lack of sap. She sits on the leaf and rolls it up lengthways, from stem to tip, a laborious task that sometimes takes several days, depending on the size of the leaf.

She lays her eggs in the folds of the resulting cigar-shaped structure, that she sticks together with anal secretions. She may lay up to six eggs at a time, but most female leaf rollers lay only one egg. When the larvae hatch, the tissues of the leaf provide them with an ample supply of food, and within a few weeks they are ready to transform themselves into pupae. The larvae

leave the rolled-up leaf and drop to the ground. They each dig a protective pupal chamber in which they over-winter before emerging as adults the following spring.

A more complicated method

Some species of leaf rollers undertake a more complicated method of rolling leaves. Instead of simply rolling the leaf lengthways, they make a number of incisions and then roll it up crossways, following an extremely precise procedure. The result is a short, fat roll that resembles a small barrel.

The red oak roller, Attelabius nitens, which occurs throughout Europe, provides a particularly good example of this method. A female red oak roller builds her nest by cutting through the leaf near its base, from either edge across to the midvein. Using her jaws, she makes a surface cut in the midvein, so that the part of the leaf below

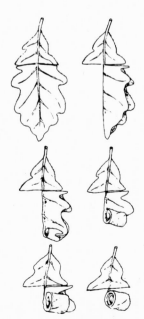

that point will wither. She then cuts through the secondary veins enabling her to fold the opposite sides of the leaf together. Starting from the tip and working upward, she folds the leaf up, tucking in the edges, and sticking the leaf together with her jaws as she rolls it. When the roll is finished, she may lay up to seven eggs.

Red oak rollers are an interesting and unusual species in that they fall victim to a parasitic species of weevil known as the cuckoo weevil. Unable to roll up leaves for itself, the cuckoo weevil seeks out the nests of the red oak roller and lays its own eggs there. Cuckoo weevils sometimes lay their eggs while the nest is still being built, or else they puncture a hole in the side of a completed nest and lay their eggs there.

FAR LEFT The weevil species *Apoderus coryli* lays from one to four eggs in a leaf roll that it makes by rolling the leaf crosswise from the tip, after cutting it almost completely in two near its base.
CENTER LEFT Red oak rollers cut leaves crosswise and roll them lengthwise to form a fat, barrel-shaped structure.
RIGHT The leaf rolling weevil *Byctiscus populi* cements her egg to the leaf when rolling it inward. The finished structure is only about 0.1 in. thick but offers enough food for the developing larva.
BELOW (left to right) Species such as *Byctiscus betulae* make cigar-shaped leaf rolls. The weevil punctures the leaf stalk, causing the leaf to wilt, and uses anal secretions to hold the roll together.

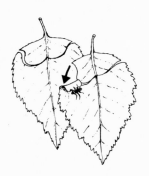 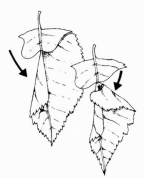 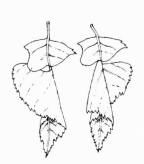 

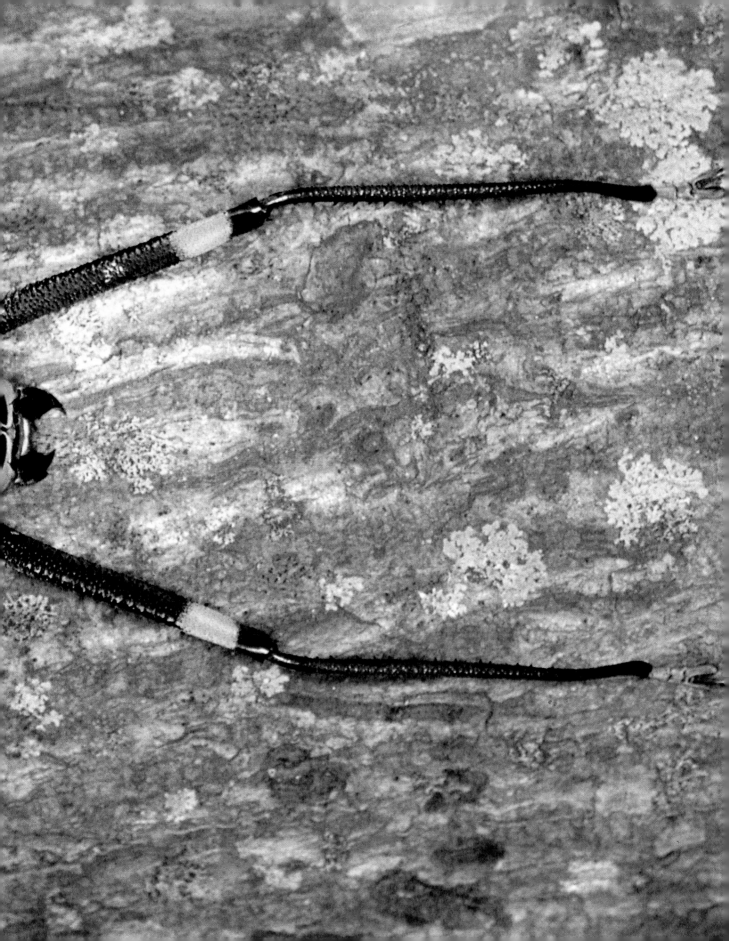

ABOVE Longhorn beetles are renowned for their enormously long, necklace-like antennae. The timberman, *Acanthocinus aedilis*, lives on old pine trees where it is well camouflaged by its brown coloring.

PAGES 2510-2511 The decorative harlequin beetle, *Acrocinus longimanus*, of Central and South America and the West Indies, displays its black, brown and red markings and long antennae that are longer than its entire body length.

is now protected by law in many places. Adult musk beetles may be seen between June and September on felled beech trees, and the larvae develop in the trunks of diseased beech trees.

Other species of longhorn beetle feed on a variety of trees. For example, the tanner beetle, *Prionus coriarius*, lays its eggs in the decaying trunks of a variety of broad-leaved trees, as well as in those of conifers. Squat-bodied, dark chestnut-brown in color and with notched antennae, tanner beetles can usually be seen at the edges of woods between July and September. They swarm at night but hide during the day, and produce a chirping sound by rubbing a ridge on the upper part of their legs against the edge of their wing cases.

The longhorn beetle species *Megopsis scabricornis* of central Europe is a dull ocher color and has robust lengthwise ridges on its wing cases. It attacks almost

any kind of broad-leaved tree. The adults spend the day concealed beneath the bark or inside larval passages, only flying after dusk.

Members of the genus *Purpuricenus* have red wing cases decorated with large black spots. They tend to grow and develop inside the branches of various kinds of fruit trees, particularly peach and apricot trees.

The male members of the longhorn beetle species *Acanthocinus griseus* and *A. aedilis* (the timberman beetle) have antennae that are over four times the length of their bodies. Their larvae attack the trunks of conifers, and they install themselves in sawmills and attack the wood there.

Other smaller kinds of longhorn beetle, such as *Oberea oculata*, found in Europe and Siberia, or members of the genera *Calamobius*, *Phytoecia* or *Agapanthia*, develop inside herbaceous plants and can damage cereal crops.

Wasp-like beetles

The larvae of some types of longhorn beetle are useful to the environment. They live in felled tree trunks and fallen branches, and speed up the process of decomposition. One of these is the British spotted longhorn, *Strangalia maculata*, which resembles a wasp on account of its yellow-and-black striped wing cases

(clearly an imitative color scheme). Further examples of mimicry are provided by many members of the genus *Leptura* and the tiny wasp beetles of the genus *Clytus* that have black wing cases decorated with hairy, whitish or yellow stripes. The wasp beetles even fly in quick, jerky movements characteristic of solitary wasps.

Some of the tropical species of longhorn beetles deserve a separate mention, simply because of their beautiful or strange appearance. One such beetle is *Macrodontia cervicornis*. Inhabiting South America, it grows up to 5 in. in length and has impressive jaws like those of stag beetles. Longhorn beetles of the genus *Batocera* which occur primarily in Asia, have variously colored bodies with a metallic luster.

The robust and colorful members of the genus *Sternotomis* live in the equatorial regions of Africa. The strange species *Acrocinus longimanus* inhabits the rain forests of South America. It has velvety wing cases, decorated with pink, black and greenish patterns. The front legs of the males are more than twice the length of their bodies, which measure 2.7 in. in length.

Weevils—beetles with long noses

There are approximately 50,000 species of weevils that belong to the family Curculionidae. Tiny beetles,

ABOVE Adults of the spotted longhorn species *Strangalia maculata* are always found on flowers, while their larvae grow and develop inside felled tree trunks and dead wood. The adults are elegant-looking beetles whose yellow and black wing cases imitate the coloration of wasps.

they measure no more than about 0.1 in. in length. They have rather dumpy bodies and move slowly and clumsily. They can be distinguished from all other insects by their snout-like heads, which vary in length and width. They have simple mouths located at the tip of their "snouts," with small but powerful jaws that they use to bore holes in vegetation, either for feeding purposes or in order to lay their eggs. A pair of jointed antennae with a characteristic "elbow" joint extends from the front of their heads.

Most species of weevils behave like plant-eating insects at all stages of their lives. Some are restricted to one specific host plant, and others are occasional parasites upon a wide range of plants and eat every part of them, including the leaves, flowers and seeds. The larvae of weevils feed on either the roots or the internal tissues of plants, causing serious damage to the living plant. When weevils collect in large numbers among crops or fruit trees they cause serious damage.

ABOVE The most characteristic feature of weevils is their long snout, or proboscis. The female *Curculio elephas* uses her snout to bore into chestnuts and acorns. She makes a deep hole in the fruit and lays an egg inside it. Then she seals **the opening with a wad of chewed pieces of food. The larvae develop inside the hole, and when the fruit falls to the ground, they escape and prepare their nymphal chamber. There they undergo the transformation into adulthood.**

The weevil, *Curculio elephas*, is a plant feeder, both as an adult and a larva. During its reproductive period, the female uses the terminal jaws on her snout to drill a hole into young, tender acorns or prickly chestnut shells that contain unripe seeds. The female then swivels around and extends a long, egg-laying ovipositor from inside her body and deposits a single egg in the hole she has made, insulating it with a plug made from bits of chewed foods. The action of the larva within the shell of the acorn or nut makes it susceptible to molds and plant fungi, so altering its taste and smell. In the case of chestnuts, infestation by weevil larvae means that they cannot be sold.

The egg remains deep inside the growing plant tissue until the nut or acorn falls from the tree in autumn. The larva then gnaws its way out and prepares a pupal cell for itself in the ground, where it will pupate into adulthood. Because of their effect on the stem, bud or fruit of the plant they inhabit, weevils are often regarded by humans as a blight.

Apple bud eaters

Members of the genus *Anthonomus* are serious pests, particularly the apple blossom weevil, a species that appears very early in the spring and eats away at the flower buds of apple trees or, occasionally, pear trees. Despite its reputation as a blight, the female apple blossom weevil is not prolific and only lays twenty eggs, depositing them in buds at the beginning of March. The larvae grow quickly and reach adulthood after two weeks. They then hibernate until conditions are suitable for reproduction in the following spring.

Sugar-beet pest

The weevil species *Lixus junci* is particularly harmful to sugar-beet crops. Shaped like a spindle, it has a thick covering of minute, yellow scales on its body. Females of this species lay their eggs in the ribs of sugar-beet leaves, boring a hole with their mandibles and then bunging the hole up immediately afterward with a plug made from bits of chewed food. After hatching, the larvae dig tunnels down through the leaves until they reach the root of the sugar-beet plant, where they remain until fully grown.

Members of the genus *Phyllobius* sometimes congregate in large numbers in fruit trees. They are minute insects, measuring 0.2-0.5 in. in length. They have vivid coloring with a silky sheen; usually their bodies have an emerald green or yellow-green tinge, depending on the angle at which light strikes their scales.

An egg in a stone

In many species of weevils, parental care reaches a level comparable with the gregarious order Hymenoptera. The female of the species *Rhynchites auratus* digs into the flesh of a plum until she reaches the stone. She then bores a shallow hole into the hard, outer covering of the kernel and injects a single egg, covering it with a thick blanket of chewed vegetation to protect it from the sticky substances that the host plant produces. When a larva hatches out, it pierces the wall of the stone, so that it can get inside and feed. Members of the family *Attelabinae* have unusual breeding behavior, rolling leaves up like a cradle and laying their eggs inside.